LIVING WITH OTHER CREATURES

LIVING WITH OTHER CREATURES

Green Exegesis and Theology

Richard Bauckham

BAYLOR UNIVERSITY PRESS

Cover Design by *the*BookDesigners
Cover Image: Cameos of biblical figures (ceramic), Israeli School / The Israel Museum, Jerusalem, Israel / The Bridgeman Art Library International

Unless otherwise stated, Scripture quotations are from the New Revised Standard Version (NRSV) of the Bible, copyright 1989, Division of Christian Education of the National Council of the Churches of Christ in the United States of America. Used by permission. All rights reserved.

Library of Congress Cataloging-in-Publication Data

Bauckham, Richard.
Living with other creatures : green exegesis and theology / Richard Bauckham.
270 p. cm.
Includes bibliographical references (p. 233) and index.
ISBN 978-1-60258-411-2 (pbk. : alk. paper)
1. Human ecology--Biblical teaching. 2. Human ecology--Religious aspects--Christianity. I. Title.
BS660.B39 2011
261.8›8--dc23
                                        2011039329

Printed in the United States of America on acid-free paper with a minimum of 30% pcw recycled content.

Contents

Abbreviations

AB	*Anchor Bible*
ACCS	Ancient Christian Commentary on Scripture
AGAJU	*Arbeiten zur Geschichte des antiken Judentums und des Urchristentums*
Ap. Mos.	*Apocalypse of Moses*
Apoc. Ab.	*Apocalypse of Abraham*
Apost. Const.	*Apostolic Constitutions*
AV	*Authorized Version*
b. B. Mets.	*Babylonian Talmud tractate Baba Metsia*
b. Qidd.	*Babylonian Talmud tractate Qiddušin*
2 Bar.	*2 Baruch*
Barn.	*Epistle of Barnabas*
BCE	*Before Common Era*
Ber.	*Berakot*
Bib	*Biblica*
BJRL	*Bulletin of the John Rylands University Library of Manchester*
BNTC	Black's New Testament Commentaries
C. Ap.	*Contra Apionem*
CBQ	*Catholic Biblical Quarterly*
CE	*Common Era*
1 Clem.	*1 Clement*
Clem. Hom.	*Clementine Homilies*
Deut. Rab.	*Midrash Rabbah on Deuteronomy*
EKKNT	Evangelisch-katholischer Kommentar zum Neuen Testament

2 Enoch	*2 Enoch (Slavonic Apocalypse of Enoch)*
m. 'Abod. Zar.	Mishnah tractate *'Abodah Zarah*
m. 'Erub.	Mishnah tractate *'Erubin*
EstBib	*Estudios bíblicos*
EstEcl	*Estudios eclesiásticos*
EvQ	*Evangelical Quarterly*
Exod. Rab.	*Midrash Rabbah on Exodus*
G. Bart.	*Gospel of Bartholomew*
Gen. Rab.	*Midrash Rabbah on Genesis*
Gitt.	Babylonian Talmud tractate *Gittin*
HTKNT	Herders theologischer Kommentar zum Neuen Testament
m. Ḥull.	Mishnah tractate *Ḥullin*
b. Ḥag.	Babylonian Talmud tractate *Ḥagigah*
ICC	International Critical Commentary
Jdt.	Judith
JHI	*Journal of the History of Ideas*
JJS	*Journal of Jewish Studies*
Jos. Asen.	*Joseph and Aseneth*
JR	*Journal of Religion*
JSJSup	Journal for the Study of Judaism in the Persian, Hellenistic, and Roman Periods: Supplement Series
JSNTSup	Journal for the Study of the New Testament: Supplement Series
JSPSu	Journal for the Study of the Pseudepigrapha: Supplement Series
Jub.	*Jubilees*
m. Ker.	*Mishnah tractate Keritot*
L.A.E.	*Life of Adam and Eve*
Lad. Jac.	*Ladder of Jacob*
LCL	Loeb Classical Library
Lev. Rab.	*Midrash Rabbah* on Leviticus
LXX	Septuagint (the Greek Old Testament)
MT	Masoretic Text (of the OT)
NICOT	New International Commentary on the Old Testament
NIGTC	New International Greek Testament Commentary
NRSV	New Revised Standard Version
NTS	*New Testament Studies*
OTL	Old Testament Library
Ps.-Phoc.	Pseudo-Phocylides
Pss. Sol.	*Psalms of Solomon*

Qu. Ezra	*Questions of Ezra*
REB	Revised English Bible
RHPR	*Revue d'histoire et de philosophie religieuses*
b. Sanh.	Babylonian Talmud tractate *Sanhedrin*
m. Sanh.	Mishnah tractate *Sanhedrin*
SBS	Stuttgarter Bibelstudien
SBT	Studies in Biblical Theology
SCHNT	Studia ad Corpus Hellenisticum Novi Testamenti
b. Shabb.	Babylonian Talmud tractate *Shabbat*
m. Shabb.	Mishnah tractate *Shabbat*
Sib. Or.	*Sibylline Oracles*
Sir.	Sirach/Ecclesiasticus
SNTSMS	Society for New Testament Studies Monograph Series
SVTP	Studia in Veteris Testamenti Pseudepigraphica
T. Ab.	*Testament of Abraham*
T. Adam	*Testament of Adam*
T. Benj.	*Testament of Benjamin*
T. Dan	*Testament of Dan*
T. Isaac	*Testament of Isaac*
T. Iss.	*Testament of Issachar*
T. Jud.	*Testament of Judah*
T. Levi	*Testament of Levi*
T. Naph.	*Testament of Naphtali*
T. Reub.	*Testament of Reuben*
T. Sim.	*Testament of Simeon*
t. Sot.	Tosefta tractate *Sotah*
T. Zeb.	*Testament of Zebulon*
TDNT	Theological Dictionary of the New Testament (ed G. Kittel and G. Friedrich; trans. G. W. Bromiley; 10 vols; Grand Rapids, 1964–1976)
Tg.	*Targum*
TLZ	*Theologische Literaturzeitung*
Tob.	Tobit
TSAJ	Texte und Studien zum antiken Judentum
WBC	Word Biblical Commentary
Wis.	Wisdom of Solomon
b. Yeb.	Babylonian Talmud tractate *Yebimot*
ZNW	*Zeitschrift für die neutestamentliche Wissenschaft und die Kunde der älteren Kirche*

Preface

When I look back, I realise that from an early age it has always seemed obvious to me that the meaning Christian faith finds in this world encompasses not only human life but also the non-human creation and that God the Creator delights in and cares for all his creatures. So it was no doubt natural that, as my awareness grew of the multiple ecological crises into which human abuse of the non-human creation has brought us, I should have wanted to think out a properly Christian approach to them, rooted in Scripture and integrated into the central themes of Christian theology.

Jürgen Moltmann and Francis of Assisi were both important influences on the way my thinking in this area developed in the 1980s and early 1990s. My earliest published article along these lines was appropriately entitled 'First Steps to a Theology of Nature' (*Evangelical Quarterly* 58 [1986] 229–244). I also became aware of the need to meet the challenge of Lynn White's famous historical claim that Genesis and the Christian tradition were the ideological roots of the ecological crisis and was able to draw on my training as a historian to show that the origins of the modern project to conquer nature have much more to do with the Renaissance than with the Bible or the pre-modern Christian tradition. (The historical account that appears as chapter 2 in this volume was first written long before its original publication in 2002.)

In 1994 I was invited to give one of a series of Stephenson Lectures in the University of Sheffield under the overall title of 'Creation, Ecology and the New Age Movement,' and chose to give a critical assessment of Matthew Fox's creation spirituality, which was then at the height of its popularity. Later I compared Fox's creation spirituality with that of Francis of Assisi in the essay that appears in this volume as chapter 9, where I argue that the latter is the more biblical and Christian of the two.

Alongside these aspects of 'green theology,' it became important to me to explore the ecological relevance of much more of the Bible than the few texts around which the discussion of emerging 'green theology' tended to focus (especially Genesis 1:26–29 and Romans 8:18–23). A truly Christian 'green theology' must surely relate its concerns to Jesus, the Gospels and Christology. And so in the 1980s I gave a seminar paper in Manchester entitled 'Christology and the Greening of Christianity' and lectures at Wycliffe College, Oxford, under the title 'How Green are the Gospels?' None of these were published but they have fed into my later writings on the theme (especially chapters 3, 5 and 6 in this volume). When Andrew Linzey invited me to contribute to a volume of essays on Christianity and animals, I wrote what remains the only extended treatment of Jesus and animals that anyone has published. It re-appears in this volume as chapter 4.

Another aspect of biblical theology that I became convinced was vital for developing an authentically Christian ecological outlook was the theme of creation's praise of God. I was able to develop this, first, when Celia Deane-Drummond (who had written her doctoral thesis on Moltmann's ecological theology under my supervision in Manchester) asked me to contribute an essay to the first issue of the journal Ecotheology that appeared under her editorship. Then, when my friend Mark Bredin (also a former doctoral student of mine, who wrote his thesis in St Andrews on the Book of Revelation) asked me to write an essay for an issue of *Biblical Theology Bulletin* he was editing, devoted to Revelation and ecology, I decided to look more closely at those heavenly priests of creation's praise, the four living creatures. These two essays are re-published in this volume as chapters 7 and 8.

As these examples illustrate, much of my work on 'green theology' developed in response to invitations to contribute to books and conferences. David Horrell and his colleagues in the research project 'Uses of the Bible in Environmental Ethics' at the University of Exeter invited me to give a seminar paper that became a chapter in their important collection, *Ecological Hermeneutics* (London: T. & T. Clark, 2010), and is republished here as chapter 3. The Faraday Institute for Science and Religion in Cambridge hosted an interdisciplinary colloquium in which I was privileged to participate; my paper on 'Jesus, God and nature in the Gospels' was published with the others in the volume *Creation in Crisis: Christian Perspectives on Sustainability* (ed. Robert S. White; London: SPCK 2009). I decided not to include it in this volume because it overlaps to a large extent with other essays that I have included. I was invited to speak to the conference of the Society for the Study of Christian Ethics in 2008, when their subject was the Sermon on the Mount, and wrote the paper that now appears as chapter 6 in this volume.

Chapter 10, which has not been previously published, originated when I was asked by my friend Poul Guttesen (who wrote his doctoral thesis on Moltmann's theology and the Book of Revelation under my supervision in St Andrews) to speak on the Bible and biodiversity in the Faroe Islands during the International Year of Biodiversity (2010). The invitation sent me back to the texts to discover their relevance to this issue that I had not previously considered in biblical detail.

At the invitation of Sarum College, Salisbury, I gave the Sarum Theological Lectures for 2006 in Salisbury Cathedral. (The lectures were entitled 'Beyond Stewardship – Rediscovering the Community of Creation.') This gave me the opportunity to do what I had long intended – to bring together my work on ecological interpretation of the Bible into an overall synthesis. Eventually I was able to expand and prepare these lectures for publication as my book *Bible and Ecology: Rediscovering the Community of Creation* (London: Darton, Longman & Todd; Waco: Baylor University Press, 2010).

I then decided it would also be useful to bring together a collection of my essays, representing the work I have done in this field over the course of some twenty-five years. The essays on biblical themes treat them in much more detail than was possible in Bible and Ecology, and I have also included the more historical and theological essays that have accompanied my biblical work. I have written chapter 1 to introduce this volume. It provides an overview of the major ecological themes of the Bible as a context within which the other essays that explore specific biblical themes in detail can be set.

Over the course of those twenty-five years I have been indebted to a great many people, far more than I can mention or even (I regret to say) remember. I am grateful to all those who have at every stage got me thinking and writing by inviting me to give lectures or contribute essays to journals or volumes. I am grateful to all those who have asked searching questions or offered insightful comments when I have given much of this material in lectures and seminar papers. I must also mention my students in St Andrews, because for several years I taught an undergraduate Honours module on 'The Bible and Contemporary Issues,' in which ecological issues played an important part, and I also taught a postgraduate version of that course in the distance learning programme 'Bible and Contemporary World.' Engaging with students on these matters was always rewarding and I am sure assisted my thinking in ways I cannot now clearly distinguish.

When I first started thinking about 'green theology' such a subject scarcely existed. Now it is a flourishing field of research and debate. More importantly, perhaps, in the same period Christians have been 're-entering creation' (to borrow a phrase from Edward Echlin) and waking up to their ecological responsibilities. These essays will be of no value unless they make some contribution to Christian worship, Christian spirituality and Christian practice. The praise of God the Creator and Renewer of his whole creation and an end to the war of aggressive conquest that modern humanity has waged against God's other creatures are their goal.

I am writing this soon after the earthquake and tsunami that devastated northern Japan in March 2011. This situation has made me very aware that a major topic – that of natural disasters – lacks any detailed treatment in either Bible and Ecology or this present volume. It is a serious lack that perhaps I shall be able to remedy in the future. But, remembering that a sense of close relationship with nature, both as a delight and as a threat, is deeply rooted in Japanese culture, I should like to dedicate this book to my friends in Japan: Hideo and Michiko Okayama, Masanobu and Kaoru Endo, Paul and Chiharu Yokota, Takanori and Miyako Kobayashi, and Norio Yamaguchi.

Richard Bauckham
Cambridge, 23 March 2011

1.

The Human Place in Creation – a Biblical Overview

George Monbiot, an influential British writer on environmental matters, recently wrote that 'we inhabit the brief historical interlude between ecological constraint and ecological catastrophe'.[1] He meant that for most of human history (including the periods in which the Bible was written) humans lived within considerable restraints imposed on human life by their natural environment. Humans made use of their environment, of course, in various essential ways, most importantly farming, but their power over most of nature was severely limited. All that changed in the modern period, when the great western project of scientific-technological domination of nature was dedicated to the unlimited extension of human power over nature and its subjection to human use and benefit. This project continues. Only quite recently have we realized the potential of biotechnology to make unprecedented changes to the living world around us and to human nature itself.

At the same time we have become more and more aware that this attempt to subjugate nature to human purposes has had unforeseen and unwanted effects of huge and disastrous proportions. Climate change is the most obvious and the most immediately dangerous. What we thought was a process of ever-increasing human control over nature, the abolition of ecological constraints, has in fact set processes in motion that we are powerless to control. The brief historical interlude between ecological constraint and ecological catastrophe is very nearly over.

---

[1] George Monbiot, *Heat: How to Stop the Planet Burning* (2nd edn; London: Penguin, 2007), p. xxi.

From a Christian point of view what is obviously at stake here is the proper relationship between humans and the rest of God's creation. If Christians are to behave responsibly at this critical moment in the planet's history, we must reflect long and hard on how God intends us humans to relate to the rest of his creation on this earth. To see the world, as Christians do, as God's creation, to know ourselves to be creatures of God, put here to live among other creatures of God, must make a difference to the huge issues of lifestyle that are becoming unavoidable for everyone who has any sense of what is happening to our world.

This is perhaps even more necessary because in the last few decades it is Christianity that has often been blamed for the ecological crisis in which we now find ourselves. The modern project of dominating nature originated in the context of western Christian culture, which, it is claimed, promoted the idea that humans are fundamentally different from the rest of nature, that the rest of nature was made by God for human use, and that it is not only the human right, but the God-given task of humans to exploit the rest of creation for human benefit. As a historical account there is some truth in that charge, but only a very partial truth (as Chapter 2 will make clear). But it does suggest that the appropriate place for us to start a consideration of what the Bible has to say about all this is the first chapter of Genesis.[2]

Human Authority in Creation (Genesis 1:26–8)

To understand our place within creation Christians have most often gone to a rather obvious place: the narrative of God's creation of all creatures in the first chapter of the Bible. On the sixth day of the week of creation,

> God said, 'Let us make humankind in our image, according to our likeness; and let them have dominion over the fish of the sea, and over the birds of the air, and over the cattle, and over all the wild animals of the earth, and over every creeping thing that creeps upon the earth.' So God created humankind in his image, in the image of God he created them; male and female he created them. God blessed them, and God

---

[2] The rest of this chapter summarizes the fuller treatment of these themes in my book, *Bible and Ecology: Rediscovering the Community of Creation* (London: Darton, Longman & Todd/Waco, Texas: Baylor University Press, 2010).

said to them, 'Be fruitful and multiply, and fill the earth and subdue it; and have dominion over the fish of the sea and over the birds of the air and over every living thing that moves upon the earth.'(Gen. 1:26–8)[3]

This authority in creation, given by God to humans, has traditionally been known as the human dominion over creation. By virtue of their creation in God's image, humans in some sense represent within creation God's rule over his creatures. Very often this has been taken to mean that the rest of creation has been made by God solely for human use. Very often in the modern period it has been taken to mandate the scientific-technological project of achieving unlimited domination of nature.

In reaction against that, Christians sensitive to the ecological problems of recent decades have insisted that this is not a mandate for exploitation, but an appointment to stewardship. In other words, the human role in relation to other creatures is one of care and service, exercised on behalf of God and with accountability to God. Creation has value not just for our use, but also for itself and for God, and humans are to care for creation as something that has inherent value. That understanding of the human dominion as stewardship has, I think, been enormously helpful to Christians thinking out what God's purpose for us is in the present crisis.

However, I think we need to go further. Christian focus on this one text in Genesis 1, even when it is understood in terms of stewardship, is problematic for two reasons:

1. The neglect of the rest of Scripture. We need to read this text in its proper context in the rest of Scripture. That means both attending to ways in which the rest of Scripture provides important indications of how we should understand the dominion, and also recognizing that there are other key themes in Scripture that illuminate our relationship to other creatures. We need to take account of these other themes alongside the idea of dominion. They cannot be simply reduced to the idea of dominion.
2. What has been deeply wrong with much modern Christian reading of Genesis 1:26–8 is that it has considered the human relationship to nature in a purely vertical manner: a hierarchy in which humans are simply placed over the rest of creation, with power and authority over it. But humans are also related horizontally to other creatures, in

---

[3] Biblical quotations in this chapter are from the NRSV.

the sense that we, like them, are creatures of God. To lift us out of creation and so out of our God-given embeddedness in creation has been the great ecological error of modernity, and so we urgently need to recover the biblical view of our solidarity with the rest of creation.

We shall begin with the context of Genesis 1:26–8 in the scriptural canon, though for our present purposes we shall limit this to the context within the first five books of the Bible, the Torah.

Human solidarity with the rest of creation

While the Genesis narratives significantly distinguish humans from the rest of creation, they also portray them as one creature among others. The *fundamental* relationship between humans and other creatures is their common creatureliness. In Genesis 2:7 God forms the first human from the earth, just as he does all other living creatures, flora and fauna. Adam's earthiness is emphasized by the wordplay between his name Adam and the Hebrew word for the ground, 'adamah. This earthiness of humans signifies a kinship with the earth itself and with other earthly creatures, plants and animals. Human life is embedded in the physical world with all that that implies of dependence on the natural systems of life.

While the seven-day creation account in Genesis 1 does not say that God made humans out of the ground, it makes a parallel point by dating the creation of humans to the sixth day of creation. The six days of creation are designed according to a scheme in which God first creates, on the first three days, the physical universe, and then, on the following three days, its inhabitants. On the first day God creates day and night, on the second the sea, on the third the dry land. The inhabitants of each sphere follow in the same order: on the fourth day, the heavenly bodies; on the fifth day, the sea creatures; and on the sixth day, the land creatures – all of the land creatures: animals, reptiles, insects, and humans. Humans do not get a day to themselves. They are, from the perspective of this scheme of creation, land creatures, though the rest of this account of their creation distinguishes them as special among the land creatures.

So it is a misreading of Genesis 1 itself to isolate the vertical dimension from the horizontal. According to Genesis, our creation in the image of God and the unique dominion given to us do not abolish our fundamental community with other creatures. The vertical does not cancel the horizontal.

Living in a theocentric creation

The seven-day creation narrative is often said, especially by those who hold it responsible for modern ecological destruction, to be anthropocentric. Humanity is the last and climactic creation of God. Surely this must mean that the rest has meaning and purpose only in relation to humanity. But, for one thing, to say that humans are the crown of creation is not the same as saying that the rest of creation exists solely for them. After each of God's acts of creation, the narrative tells us that God saw that it was good – good in itself, giving pleasure and satisfaction to God. God did not have to wait till he had created humans to see that the creation was good. God valued and values all the creatures he created. But also, secondly, the account is not anthropocentric, but *theocentric*. Its climax is not the creation of humans on the sixth day, but God's Sabbath rest, God's enjoyment of God's completed work on the seventh day (Gen. 2:2). Creation exists for God's glory.

Ruling fellow-creatures – hierarchy qualified by community

I have stressed the importance of the horizontal relationship of humans with other creatures, our common creatureliness. This horizontal relationship with fellow-creatures is vital to the proper understanding of the vertical relationship of authority over others. Since Genesis 1 presents this authority as a kind of kingly rule, it is relevant to recall the only kind of human rule over other humans that the Old Testament approves. The book of Deuteronomy allows Israel to have a king of sorts, but it interprets this kingship in a way designed to subvert all ordinary notions of rule (17:14–20). If Israel must have a king, then the king must be a brother. He is a brother set over his brothers and sisters, but still a brother, and forbidden any of the ways in which rulers exalt themselves over and entrench their power over their subjects. His rule becomes tyranny the moment he forgets that the horizontal relationship of brother/sisterhood is primary, kingship secondary. Similarly, the human rule over other creatures will be tyrannous unless it is placed in the context of our more fundamental community with other creatures.

Ruling within the order of creation – sharing the earth

Returning to the Genesis 1 account of the week of creation, we should note that it presents a picture of a carefully ordered creation. The order is already established before the creation of humans. The human dominion is not granted so that humans may violate that order and remake creation to their own design. It is taken for granted that the God-given order of the world should be respected by the human exercise of limited dominion within it. Moreover, the manner in which the account of the work of the sixth day ends is significant in a way rarely noticed. Having said to humanity that all kinds of vegetation are given them for food, God continues by *telling humanity* that he has given every kind of vegetation as food to all land animals: every animal, every bird, every creeping thing, every living thing (1:29–30). Why does God say this at this point, after the creation of humanity, and why does he say it to humans? Surely to stress that human use of the earth is not to compete with its use by other creatures. This is a massive restriction of the human dominion and chimes well with contemporary concerns. A similar point is made in Genesis 9, where God's covenant is made not only with Noah and his descendants but also with every living creature; it is for the sake of them all that God promises never again to destroy the earth in a universal deluge (Gen. 9:8–17). It is home for them all and they all have a stake in that covenant.

Preserving creation

One of the most obvious interpretations of the human dominion within the book of Genesis itself follows just a few chapters on from the creation account: the story of the flood (Gen. 6 – 8). In this story Noah is given by God the task of preserving other creatures – specifically preserving species – that would otherwise have perished. This is a form of caring responsibility for other creatures that has come spectacularly into its own again today.

Letting creation be

One further way in which the Torah provides interpretation of the Genesis dominion is the legislation for Israel's use of the land in the legal parts of the Pentateuch. How Israel is to use the land God gives her to live from is a key concern of the law of Moses. It involves Israel's use and enhancement of the land, but it also imposes strict limits, especially in the form of the Sabbatical institutions: the weekly Sabbath, the Sabbatical Year that recurs every seven years, and the Jubilee Year (the Sabbath of Sabbaths) that recurs every fifty years.

These are not just about good farming practice, but about keeping the economic drive in human life within its place and not letting it dominate the whole of life.

In Israel's land legislation, the human dominion is exercised as much in restraint as in active use. Particularly striking is the concern for wild animals. In the Sabbatical Year fields, vineyards and orchards are to be left to rest and lie fallow, 'so that the poor of your people may eat; and what they leave the wild animals may eat' (Exod. 23:11; similarly Lev. 25:7). Even within the cultivated part of the land, wild animals are expected to be able to live. This is a kind of symbol of respect for wilderness, reminding both ancient Israel and later readers of Scripture that dominion includes letting nature be itself. There is value that should be respected and preserved in the wild as well as in the humanly cultivated.

Summary

To summarize, when we read Genesis 1:26–8 in its biblical context, we see that the dominion, the God-given authority of humans within creation is:

a. An authority to be exercised by caring responsibility, not domination;
b. An authority to be exercised within a theocentric creation, not an anthropocentric one;
c. An authority to be exercised by humans as one creature among others;
d. A right to use other creatures for human life and flourishing, but only while respecting the order of creation and the right of other living beings also to life and flourishing;
e. An authority to be exercised in letting wild nature be as well in intervening in it, an authority to be exercised as much in restraint as in intervention.

Putting Us in Our Place (Job 38 – 39)

Perhaps the strongest biblical antidote to the hubris that in modern times has so often attended ideas of dominion or stewardship is God's answer to Job out of the whirlwind.

Chapters 38 – 39 of the book of Job are in fact the longest passage about the non-human creation in the Bible, a fact which should surely have guaranteed them a larger place than they have had in discussion of biblical views of creation. But they are also potent poetry. Bill McKibben has called them 'the first great piece of modern nature writing', and claimed that nothing quite comparable with their appreciation of wild nature is to be found subsequently until the writings of John Muir.[4] He may be right.

Most of the book of Job consists of a debate between Job and his friends about the moral order of the world. Surely the all-powerful, all-wise, perfectly righteous God will order the world so that people get what they deserve? This theme of God's ordering of the world is the obvious point of connexion with what God, when he finally intervenes in the debate, says in answer to Job. But God's speeches approach the matter from an entirely different angle. God invites Job into a vast panorama of the cosmos, taking Job on a sort of imaginative tour of his creation, all the time buffeting Job with questions. Virtually every sentence is a question. Just a few of them will give the flavour of the whole:

> Where were you when I laid the foundation of the earth? (38:4)
> Can you bind the chains of the Pleiades,
>   or loose the cords of Orion?
> Can you lead forth the Mazzaroth in their season,
>   or can you guide the Bear with its children? (38:31–2)
> Can you hunt the prey for the lion,
>   or satisfy the appetite of the young lions? (38:39–40)
> Is the wild ox willing to serve you?
>   Will it spend the night at your crib?
> Can you tie it in the furrow with ropes,
>   or will it harrow the valleys after you? (39:9–10)

These chapters need to be read slowly and imaginatively in order to receive their full impact.

The effect is to deconstruct and reorder Job's whole view of the world. God puts Job in his place. He draws Job's attention to creatures over which he plainly does not exercise dominion. The point is that Job has no bearing on the value or purpose of their existence for their own sake and for God's sake. Job is not the unique reference point for all God's purposes in his creation. The lesson is to teach Job his place

---

[4] Bill McKibben, *The Comforting Whirlwind: God, Job, and the Scale of Creation* (Grand Rapids: Eerdmans, 1994), pp. 57–8.

as one creature among others. The effect is rather like that of one of David Attenborough's great wildlife documentaries, which leave one stunned by the staggering diversity and complexity of creation. Even if we can now answer one or two of God's questions to Job (such as 39:1: 'Do you know when the mountain goats give birth?'), the answers only give way to countless new questions. We are still as ignorant as we are knowledgeable about the rest of creation on this planet, not to mention the rest of God's universe. That we are capable of managing the planet should be as absurd to us as it was to Job. What we are all too capable of is destroying much of it.

Humanity within the Community of Creation

In the introduction to this chapter I was critical of the way too much interpretation of Genesis 1:26–8 isolates it from the rest of Scripture and from the relevance other parts of Scripture may have to understanding the human relationship with other creatures. We have made a start in remedying that by looking at ways in which that text's context in the Torah helps us to understand what the human dominion means. We have also seen, from Job, that the Bible contains a powerful antidote to the hubris engendered by an arrogant and exaggerated view of ourselves as wielding some kind of godlike sovereignty over the rest of God's creation – as though it were our creation, not God's. God's answer to Job puts us in our place as a creature among other creatures and in a cosmos that has its own meaning and value independently of us.

In order to develop further the sense in which we need to complement the idea of dominion with a much stronger sense of co-creatureliness, I shall introduce two further biblical themes that deserve our attention alongside the Genesis dominion. These themes help us to put the Genesis dominion itself in its place as one of several ways in which the Bible understands humans to be related to the rest of creation. Crucially, these two themes develop what I have called the horizontal relationship of humans to other creatures as fellow-creatures. They help us to balance the vertical with the horizontal.

The first of them I call 'humanity within the community of creation'. The Bible fully recognizes the extent to which nature is a living whole to which human beings along with other creatures belong, sharing the earth with other creatures of God, participating, for good or ill, in the interconnectedness of the whole. In Genesis 9, as I have already mentioned, the covenant God makes after the flood is not

only with Noah and his descendants but also with every living creature: it is for the sake of them all that God promises there will never
again be a universal deluge. But the great creation psalm, Psalm 104,
is probably the most effective biblical portrayal of God's creation as a
community of creatures.

In some ways Psalm 104 resembles Job 38 – 39. Both begin with
poetic evocations of God's initial creation of the world, more like each
other than either is like Genesis 1, and both move smoothly from there
into a panoramic view of the parts and members of creation. Both
deny humans a place of supremacy or exceptionality. But Psalm 104
puts us in our place in the world in a much gentler way than God's
answer to Job. Here there is no sense that human hubris needs shat-
tering. Rather there is a sense that within the praise of God for his creation we fall naturally into the place he has given us alongside his
other creatures.

In Psalm 104 we see creation as a community of many living creatures, each with their place in the world given them by God their
Creator, each given by God the means of sustenance for their different
forms of life. It is a wonderfully diverse creation, and within this
diversity humans appear simply as one of the many kinds of living
creatures for whom God provides. What gives wholeness to this reading of the world is not human mastery of it or the value humans set
on it, not (in contemporary terms) globalization, but the value of all
created things for God. This is a theocentric, not an anthropocentric
world. God's own rejoicing in his works (v. 31) funds the psalmist's
own rejoicing (v. 34), as he praises God, not merely for human life and
creation's benefits for humans, but for God's glory seen in the whole
creation. In a different way from Job's, the psalmist is taken out of
himself, lifted out of the limited human preoccupations that dominate
most of our lives, by his contemplation of the rest of God's plenitude
of creatures.

Psalm 104 is one of several biblical passages that state that God provides for all living creatures (Ps. 147:9,15–16; Job 38:19–41; Matt. 6:26).
In these passages there is the implication that the resources of the earth
are sufficient for all, provided creatures live within created limits. This
theme of God's provision was taken up by Jesus in the Sermon on the
Mount, when he compared humanity with the birds and the wild flowers (Matt. 6:25–34). Here we find that Jesus has very much made his
own the psalmist's understanding of the world as a common home for
living creatures, in which God provides for all their needs. The consequence Jesus draws – from the psalmist's vision of the world to advice

on how his disciples should live – is that we need have no anxieties about day-to-day material needs, but should live by radical faith in the Father's provision for us. Because the generous and wise Creator takes care of all these things for us, we are free to give our attention instead to seeking God's kingdom and God's righteousness in the world.

Jesus holds up for us the example of the birds, for whom God provides, as he does for all his creatures. But Jesus adds a reflection not in the psalm: 'Look at the birds of the air; they neither sow nor reap nor gather into barns, and yet your heavenly Father feeds them' (Matt. 6:26). Interpretations of this verse have varied from supposing that Jesus contrasts the birds, who do not work, with people, who do – if God feeds even the idle birds, how much more will he provide for people who work hard for their living? – to, alternatively, supposing that Jesus compares the birds, who do not work, with his disciples, who do not work either. The point is probably neither of these. Rather it is that, because the birds do not have to labour to process their food from nature, but just eat it as they find it, their dependence on the Creator's provision is the more immediate and obvious. Humans, preoccupied with the daily toil of supplying their basic needs, may easily suppose that it is up to them to supply themselves with food. This is the root of the anxiety about basic needs that Jesus is showing to be unnecessary. The way humans get their food allows them to focus on their own efforts and to neglect the fact that, much more fundamentally, they are dependent, like the birds, on the resources of creation without which no one could sow, reap or gather into barns. The illusion is even easier in modern urban life. But the birds, in their more obvious dependence on the Creator, remind us that ultimately we are no less dependent on the Creator.

Of course, Jesus was speaking of basic needs. The presuppositions of his theology are very far from the wasteful excess and the constant manufacture of new needs and wants in contemporary consumer society. Jesus intended to liberate his disciples from that anxious insecurity about basic needs that drives people to feel that they never have enough. But in our society that instinctive human anxiety about having enough to survive has long been superseded by the drive to ever-increasing affluence and obsessive anxiety to maintain an ever-rising standard of living. It is this obsessive consumption that is depleting the resources of nature and depriving both other species and many humans of the means even to survive.

Belonging to the community of creation must for us mean living within limits, and the psalmist and Jesus assist us to do so, both by reminding us of our place within the community of God's creatures and by encouraging us to recognize God's caring provision for all his creatures. (This theme is explored more fully in Chapter 6.)

The Praise of God by All Creation

Arguably the most profound and life-changing way in which we can recover our place in the world as creatures alongside our fellow-creatures is through the biblical theme of the worship that all creation offers to God. There are many passages in the Psalms (e.g. Ps. 19:1–3; 97:6; 98:7–8; and especially 148) that depict all God's creatures worshipping him, and the theme is taken up in the New Testament too (Phil. 2:10; Rev. 5:13). According to the Bible, all creatures, animate and inanimate, worship God. This is not, as modern biblical interpreters have sometimes supposed, merely a poetic fancy or some kind of animism that endows all creatures with consciousness. The creation worships God just by being itself, as God made it, existing for God's glory. Only humans desist from worshipping God; other creatures, without having to think about it, do so all the time. A lily does not need to do anything specific in order to praise God; still less need it be conscious of anything. Simply by being and growing it praises God. It is distinctively human to bring praise to conscious expression in words, but the creatures remind us that this distinctively human form of praise is worthless unless, like them, we also live our whole lives to the glory of God.

It is indeed distinctively human to bring praise to conscious expression in words, but the Bible does not make of this the notion that the other creatures somehow need us to voice their praise for them. That idea, that we are called to act as priests to nature, mediating, as it were, between nature and God, is quite often found in recent Christian writing, but in my view it intrudes our inveterate sense of superiority exactly where the Bible will not allow it. Rather than supposing that other creatures need us to enable them to worship, we should think of the rest of creation assisting our worship. In Psalm 148, which is the fullest example of a psalm in which all creatures are called upon to praise their Creator, the praise begins with the angels and descends, through the heavenly bodies and the weather, to the creatures of earth, reaching humans only at the end of the whole movement. This order is not designed to make us inferior to all the other creatures, but it does give us the sense of a cosmos of creatures glorifying God already, before we ourselves join in. There is a whole universe of praise, a continuous anthem of glory, happening all around us if we choose to notice it. Attending to it can catch us up into the praise of the God who created all things and is reflected in all his creatures.

The key point is that, implicit in these depictions of the worship of creation, is the intrinsic value of all creatures, in the theocentric sense of the value given them by their Creator and offered back to him in praise. In this context, our place is beside our fellow-creatures as fellow-worshippers. In the praise in which we gratefully confess ourselves creatures of God there is no place for hierarchy. Creatureliness levels us all before the otherness of the Creator. It would be very good if we could restore to our Christian worship today something that was more common in the Christianity of the past: ways of consciously situating our own worship within the worship that all our fellow-creatures constantly give to God. Nothing could better restore our sense of creatureliness, and our recognition that the rest of creation is not mere material for us to use by making it into something more useful to us, but a creation that exists for the glory of God, as we are called to do. (The subject of creation's praise of God is treated more fully in Chapter 7.)

This idea of worshipping our Creator along with all the other creatures really has nothing in common with nature worship, of which some modern Christians seem to be pathologically afraid. It is true that in the biblical tradition nature has been de-divinized. It is not divine, but God's creation. But that does not make it nothing more than material for human use. Nature has been reduced to stuff that we can do with as we wish, not by the Bible, but by the modern age, with its rejection of God and its instrumentalizing of nature. The Bible has de-divinized nature, but it has not de-sacralized nature. Nature remains sacred in the sense that it belongs to God, exists for the glory of God, even reflects the glory of God, as humans also do. The respect, even the reverence, that other creatures inspire in us is just as it should be. It leads us not to worship creation (something that is scarcely a serious danger in the contemporary western world) but to worship with creation. According to chapter 5 of the book of Revelation, the goal of God's creative and redemptive work is achieved when every creature in heaven, on earth, under the earth and in the sea joins in a harmony of praise to God and the Lamb (5:13).

2.

Dominion Interpreted – a Historical Account

Introduction

In a hugely influential passage of Scripture, Genesis 1:28 speaks of a 'dominion' (the most usual English translation) over other living creatures given by God to humans at their creation. In Genesis itself, it is clear that humans, while given a special status and responsibility for other creatures, are themselves creatures alongside their fellow-creatures. Their 'dominion' is within the created order, not, like God's, transcendent above it. Distinguished from their fellow-creatures in some respects, they are also like them in many respects. A crucial issue that will be highlighted in our exploration here of the history of interpretation of this Genesis text is the extent to which interpreters have retained a sense of the horizontal relationship of humans with their fellow-creatures along with the vertical relationship of dominion that sets them in some sense above other creatures on earth. The loss of the horizontal relationship, in effect treating humans as gods in relation to the world, was, I shall argue, probably the most fateful development in Christian attitudes to the non-human creation. Only with this development did interpretation of Genesis 1:28 take its place in the ideology of aggressive domination of nature that has characterized the modern west.

The word 'dominion' easily enough suggests the charge of domination, i.e. of exploitative power by which humans have treated the rest of nature, animate and inanimate, as no more than a resource for human use and material for humans to fashion into whatever kind of world they might prefer to the existing one. Such an attitude has undoubtedly characterized the modern west, and has been essential to the course that the modern scientific and technological enterprise has taken, with vast implications in the economic sphere. It could well be seen as the ideological root of the ecological crisis of recent decades, and those who have tried to pin a major share of responsibility for our contemporary ecological problems on the western Christian tradition (with or without its Israelite and Jewish roots) have often focused especially on the notion of human dominion over nature given in Genesis 1. In this they have followed the lead of the celebrated article, 'The Historical Roots of Our Ecologic Crisis', by the medieval historian (a specialist in the history of medieval technology) Lynn White, Jr, first published in 1967 and reprinted a number of times since then,[1] hugely influential[2] and still so in spite of the many attempts to refute its central thesis.[3] It is a very brief article, bursting with confident and ill-substantiated generalizations that cry out for more detailed historical investigation. Yet the very simplicity of its provocative thesis has earned it a great deal of attention and has proved a useful stimulus to some of the more detailed historical study that needs to be done[4] if the thesis is to be accepted, rejected or qualified.

---

[1] Lynn White, 'The Historical Roots of Our Ecologic Crisis', *Science* 155 (1967): pp. 1203-7; reprinted in *Western Man and Environmental Ethics* (ed. Ian G. Barbour; Reading, Massachusetts/London/Ontario: Addison-Wesley, 1973), pp. 18–30; *The Care of Creation* (ed R.J. Berry; Leicester: Inter-Varsity Press, 2000), pp. 31–42.

[2] Although White has subsequently contributed little more to the debate, he is 'the most cited author in the field of the eco-theological discussion', according to H. Baranzke and H. Lamberty-Zielinski, 'Lynn White und das dominium terrae (Gen 1,28b): Ein Beitrag zu einer doppelten Wirkungsgeschichte', *BN* 76 (1995): p. 56. On the influence of White's article in solidifying the view of many environmentalists that the Judeo-Christian religious tradition is the enemy, see the interesting autobiographical comments by Max Oelschlaeger, *Caring for Creation: An Ecumenical Approach to the Environmental Crisis* (New Haven/London: Yale University Press, 1994): pp. 22–7. For White's own later contributions, see Roderick Frazier Nash, *The Rights of Nature: A History of Environmental Ethics* (Madison, Wisconsin: University of Wisconsin Press, 1989): p. 95.

[3] E.g. Bill McKibben, *The Comforting Whirlwind: God, Job, and the Scale of Creation* (Grand Rapids: Eerdmans, 1994): pp. 34–5. Donald Worster, *Nature's Economy: A History of Ecological Ideas* (2nd edn; Cambridge: CUP, 1994): pp. 27–31, still follows White, even though in his *The Wealth of Nature: Environmental History and Ecological Imagination* (New York/Oxford: OUP, 1993): pp. 207–19, he argued that White's thesis was mistaken in that the real roots of the ecological crisis lie not in the Christian tradition but in modernity.

[4] See especially Jeremy Cohen, *'Be Fertile and Increase, Fill the Earth and Master It': The Ancient and Medieval Career of a Biblical Text* (Ithaca/London: Cornell University Press, 1989); Cameron Wybrow, *The Bible, Baconianism, and Mastery over Nature: The*

White's central claim was that Christianity, as 'the most anthropocentric religion the world has seen', set human beings above nature (sharing, 'in great measure, God's transcendence of nature'),[5] de-divinized and de-sacralized nature,[6] and thus made nature into mere raw material for human exploitation ('no item in the physical creation had any purpose save to serve man's purposes'). By contrast with religious attitudes that either reverence nature as divine or place human beings within nature alongside other creatures, the Christian view has robbed nature of any value other than its usefulness to humanity. Christianity has understood human beings to have been set over the rest of creation by God and given the right and even the duty to subject the whole of nature to human use. This view, based on and appealing to the key biblical text of Genesis 1:26,28, was in White's view the ideological basis for the arrogant and aggressive domination of nature which has led to the ecological destruction of modern times.[7] Since the rise of western science and technology, through which this domination of nature has been attempted, dates from the eleventh century, a period in which the traditional Christian view of the world was largely unchallenged in western Europe, White can argue that the modern attempt at technological conquest of nature derives directly from this traditional Christian view.

The thesis – which Wybrow calls 'the mastery hypothesis'[8] – is not peculiar to White, whose original contribution was probably only his association of it with the late medieval beginnings of modern technological development, his own specialist area, whereas other versions of the thesis tend to see at least the ideological impetus for the modern scientific and technological project developing in the early modern period. Essentially the same thesis as White's had, before

---

Old Testament and its Modern Misreading (New York: Peter Lang, 1991). Also in part responding to White is Keith Thomas, *Man and the Natural World: Changing Attitudes in England 1500–1800* (2nd edn; London: Penguin, 1984), see pp. 22–5.

5 White, 'Historical Roots', p. 25.

6 The word 'nature' is problematic for a number of reasons, not least because, as generally used, it seems to presuppose that humans are not part of nature; see Richard Bauckham, 'First Steps to a Theology of Nature,' *EvQ* 58 (1986): pp. 229–31. But the word is almost impossible to avoid, and will be used in this chapter in its usual sense in this context, referring to the non-human creation (and often limited to this planet).

7 See also the even more trenchant statement of this case by Arnold Toynbee, 'The Religious Background of the Present Ecological Crisis,' in David and Eileen Spring, eds, *Ecology and Religion in History* (New York: Harper, 1974), pp. 137–49.

8 Wybrow, *Bible*, Introduction and *passim*.

White, been argued by Christian theologians and historians[9] who wished to claim that modern science and technology, regarded positively as the great achievements of the modern age, were the fruit of the Christian world-view. This apologetic approach was part and parcel of a broad Christian theological strategy of justifying modernity – even its secularity – as the product of Christianity. It is ironic that, with the ever-more apparent failures of modernity, the same strategy is now adopted by those who blame all the failures and evils of the modern period on Christianity, ignoring the anti-theological trend of modernity at the same time as they are themselves deeply indebted to it.

There have been many responses to White's thesis[10] and the present chapter is another. Insofar as White made a claim about the meaning of Genesis in its own terms, responses from the perspective of biblical exegesis can fairly be said to have refuted it over and again. But the historical claim about the indebtedness of the modern project of dominating

---

[9] Examples in Wybrow, *Bible*, Introduction, and Baranzke and Lamberty-Zielinski, 'Lynn White', pp. 50–2.

[10] See, e.g. René Dubos, 'Franciscan Conservation versus Benedictine Stewardship,' in *Western Man* (ed. Barbour), pp. 114–36; L.W. Moncrief, 'The Cultural Basis of Our Environmental Crisis,' in *Western Man* (ed. Barbour), pp. 31–42; James Barr, 'Man and Nature: The Ecological Controversy and the Old Testament', *BJRL* 55 (1972): pp. 9–32 (these three articles can also be found in *Ecology* [ed. Spring], pp. 114–36, 76–90, 48–75); William Leiss, *The Domination of Nature* (New York: George Braziller, 1972); John Macquarrie, 'Creation and Environment' in *Ecology* (ed. Spring), pp. 32–47; John Passmore, *Man's Responsibility for Nature: Ecological Problems and Western Traditions* (London: Duckworth, 1974); Udo Krolzik, *Umweltkrise – Folge des Christentums?* (Stuttgart/Berlin: Kreuz Verlag, 1979); Robin Attfield, 'Christian Attitudes to Nature', *JHI* 44 (1983): pp. 369–86; Richard H. Hiers, 'Ecology, Biblical Theology, and Methodology: Biblical Perspectives on the Environment', *Zygon* 19 (1984): pp. 43–59; Bernhard W. Anderson, 'Creation and Ecology', in *Creation in the Old Testament* (ed. Bernhard W. Anderson; London: SPCK/Philadelphia: Fortress, 1984), pp. 1–24; Jeremy Cohen, 'The Bible, Man, and Nature in the History of Western Thought: A Call for Reassessment', *JR* 65 (1985): pp. 155–72; Cameron Wybrow, 'The Old Testament and the Conquest of Nature: A Fresh Examination', *Epworth Review* 17 (1990): pp. 77–88; Wybrow, *Bible*; Cohen, 'Be Fertile'; Tim Cooper, *Green Christianity* (London: Hodder & Stoughton, 1990), pp. 33–8; Robin Attfield, *The Ethics of Environmental Concern* (2nd edn; Athens, Georgia/London: University of Georgia Press, 1991), chapters 2–3; Robert Murray, *The Cosmic Covenant* (London: Sheed & Ward, 1992), pp. 161–6; Stephen R.L. Clark, *How to Think about the Earth* (London: Mowbray, 1993), pp. 8–19; E. Whitney, 'Lynn White, Ecotheology and History', *Environmental Ethics* 15 (1993): pp. 151–69; Baranzke and Lamberty-Zielinski, 'Lynn White'; Theodore Hiebert, *The Yahwist's Landscape: Nature and Religion in Early Israel* (New York/Oxford: OUP, 1996).

nature to long-standing Christian views of the human relationship to nature is a more complex one and not so easily answered. Our focus in this chapter will be on the history of the various and changing Christian interpretations of the Genesis idea of human dominion over the world, in an effort to specify how and to what extent interpretation of this idea is implicated in the beginnings and development of the modern scientific-technological project of the domination of nature. I shall make clear from the start that the history of interpretation of Genesis 1:28 and associated biblical themes has been much influenced by non-biblical ideas about the human relationship to the rest of nature.

The history of Christian attitudes to the rest of nature and ideas about the human relationship to the non-human creation is a complex subject, on which much detailed research still needs to be done.[11] A focus on the idea of human dominion and interpretation of Genesis 1:28 cannot tell us everything, but the prominence Lynn White and his followers and critics have given to this aspect of the matter is not unjustified. It is, however, important to keep in view other aspects of Christian thought about creation that could be seen to qualify or moderate what is said about the human dominion as such. We shall therefore keep the latter idea at the centre of attention, but notice also the bearing that other aspects of Christian thought had on it. My argument owes a good deal to previous responses to White and other discussions of the matter, but attempts a further clarification of the historical development. I think that Jeremy Cohen's claim that, as a result of his study of Jewish and Christian interpretations of Genesis 1:28 in the patristic and medieval periods, Lynn White's thesis 'can now be laid to rest'[12] was a little premature. Not only does much remain to be said about those periods, but also the interpretation of Genesis 1:26,28 in the early modern period (not reached by Cohen's study)[13] is of crucial importance to

---

[11] Pioneering surveys are Clarence J. Glacken, *Traces on the Rhodian Shore: Nature and Culture in Western Thought from Ancient Times to the End of the Eighteenth Century* (Berkeley/Los Angeles: University of California Press, 1967) (an immensely learned and valuable resource); H. Paul Santmire, *The Travail of Nature: The Ambiguous Ecological Promise of Christian Theology* (Philadelphia: Fortress Press, 1985) (a study of the mainstream theological tradition, which employs a rather questionable interpretative schema).

[12] Cohen, *'Be Fertile'*, p. 5. Unfortunately for our purposes, this book, though initially stimulated by White's thesis, gives far more attention to the command in Genesis 1:28 to 'be fruitful and multiply' than it does to the idea of human dominion.

[13] He makes brief reference to the Protestant Reformers only: *'Be Fertile'*, pp. 306–9.

the debate.[14] Cameron Wybrow's important book[15] partly supplies this latter gap in the discussion, but is rather narrowly focused on the exegetical validity of the interpretations of Genesis that gained ground in the early modern period, while underestimating the extent to which medieval theology prepared the ground for, without determining, the early modern development.

My argument will be that White's historical thesis does contain an important element of truth, but that it fails as a whole because White neglected other elements in the traditional Christian attitude (or attitudes) which significantly balance and qualify the features on which he seized, and because White also neglected the new developments in the understanding of the human relationship to nature that occurred in the early modern period and to which the modern project of aggressive domination of nature can be far more directly linked than it can to the Christian tradition of pre-modern times.

The question of the origins of the contemporary ecological crisis is, of course, a much larger historical question. Answering that question would involve taking account of the modern ideology of progress (to which the ideas we shall discuss contributed only a small ingredient), modern individualism and materialism, industrialization and consumerization, the money economy and globalization – in short, a whole network of factors that characterize modernity.[16] Most of these factors can be understood only as the supersession of Christian ideals, values and practice by post-Christian and secular modes of thought, goals and forms of life. On this broad scale, the search for the origins of the contemporary ecological crisis in Christianity is certainly looking in entirely the wrong direction. But it remains significant that much Christian thought in the modern period went along with major aspects of these developments in modernity and itself gave them Christian justification. Our story, though only a small part of an account of the origins of modernity from an ecological perspective, will throw some light on what can be seen in retrospect at least to have been an ideological co-option of biblical and traditional themes to an alien end.

---

14 This is recognized by Gerhard Liedke, *Im Bauch des Fisches: Ökologische Theologie* (Stuttgart/Berlin: Kreuz Verlag, 1979), pp. 66–8; and (though with less reference to exegesis) Passmore, *Man's Responsibility*, pp. 18–23.

15 Wybrow, *Bible*; especially Part 3.

16 The best succinct account of the origins of the ecological crisis is Michael S. Northcott, *The Environment and Christian Ethics* (Cambridge: CUP, 1996), ch. 2; see also Attfield, *Ethics*, chapter 1.

The Dominant Theological Tradition

According to Genesis 1:28, God commanded humanity to 'subdue' the earth and to have 'dominion' over other living creatures. The interpretation of this notion of human dominion by Christian theologians and exegetes remained fairly consistent from the time of the Fathers, through the Middle Ages, until the early modern period in the West. It was an interpretation strongly influenced by Greek philosophical (mainly Stoic but also Aristotelian) ideas about human uniqueness and superiority over the rest of nature. Since pagan writers who expounded these ideas spoke explicitly of human dominion over the earth (e.g. Cicero, *Nat. d.* 2.60; *Hermetica* 3.3b) and exalted the special place of humanity in creation, it must have seemed natural to Christian thinkers with a Hellenistic education to read the Genesis account in such terms, especially as the principal philosophical alternative was argued by the Epicureans, whose general world-view seemed much more alien to the biblical Christian view. Indeed, all the ingredients of the Christian reading of Genesis in Aristotelian and Stoic terms are to be found already in the first-century Jewish philosopher Philo of Alexandria, who did so much to interpret Jewish monotheistic faith in Hellenistic philosophical terms and from whom some of the early Fathers learned how to do the same for their Christian faith. Philo not only propounded a Stoic interpretation of human dominion throughout his works,[17] but also in his *De Animalibus* he defended, explicitly and at length, the Stoic position against the Epicurean views of his apostate brother Alexander.[18] Similarly, the great third-century Alexandrian Christian theologian Origen explicitly supported the Stoic view against the Epicurean position maintained by his pagan opponent Celsus (*C. Cels.* 4.74).

In this way a series of ideas about the human relationship to the rest of creation, which were not of biblical but of Greek philosophical origin, came to be associated with the Genesis text and regarded, for most of Christian history, as the Christian view. In the first place, the rest of creation was held to have been made by God for humanity.

---

[17] Abraham Terian, *Philonis Alexandrini De Animalibus: The Armenian Text with an Introduction, Translation and Commentary* (Chico, California: Scholars Press, 1981), pp. 36–45. But Peder Borgen, 'Man's Sovereignty over Animals and Nature According to Philo of Alexandria', in *Texts and Contexts* (ed. Tord Fornberg and David Hellholm: FS L. Hartman; Oslo: Scandinavian University Press, 1995), pp. 369–89, stresses Philo's affinities with Jewish literature.

[18] See the translation and introduction in Terian, *Philonis Alexandrini De Animalibus.*

This highly anthropocentric view of the world derives not from the biblical tradition but from Aristotle (*Pol.* 1.8)[19] and the Stoics (e.g. Cicero, *Nat. d.* 2).[20] It was taken up enthusiastically by early Christian writers (e.g. Origen, *C. Cels.* 4.74-5; Lactantius, *Div. Inst.* 7.4-6; Nemesius, *De natura hominis* 10) and seems to have been thereafter unquestioned until the sixteenth century.[21] In the early modern period it was still dominant. It was, for example, unequivocally and influentially expressed by John Calvin (*Inst.* 2.6.1; *Comm.* Gen. 1:26).

Secondly, the sense in which the world was made for humanity was understood in strongly utilitarian terms.[22] All creatures exist for the sake of their usefulness to humanity.[23] In the face of the objection that many creatures do not seem at all obviously useful for human life, the Stoics were famous for their ingenious explanations of the usefulness of each of the animals: for example, that fleas are useful for preventing oversleeping and mice for preventing carelessness in leaving cheese about.[24] Similar attempts to explain all features of the natural world as deliberately designed by God to supply specific human needs can be found in many Christian writers, from the Fathers (e.g. Origen, *C. Cels.* 4.78; Lactantius, *Div. Inst.* 7.4) to the eighteenth century.[25] It seems to have been only in the seventeenth century that such explanations began to lose their power to convince.[26]

Thirdly, human dominion over the world was therefore understood as the right to make use of all creatures for human benefit. Compare the following statement by Cicero, writing in the Stoic tradition:

> The human race has dominion over all the products of the earth. We enjoy the treasures of plains and mountains; ours are the streams, ours the lakes; we cultivate the fruits and plant trees; we give fertility to the soil by works of irrigation; we restrain, straighten or divert our streams

---

[19] Cf. Glacken, *Traces*, pp. 47–48.

[20] Terian, *Philonis Alexandrini De Animalibus*, p. 51; Glacken, *Traces*, p. 57. See also Xenophon, *Mem.* 4.3.2–14, where this idea is attributed to Socrates and which influenced the Stoics. It was also adopted by Jewish writers from the first century onwards: Borgen, 'Man's Sovereignty,' p. 379.

[21] One sixteenth-century Christian writer who denied it was the English Protestant martyr John Bradford: Thomas, *Man*, p. 166.

[22] Cf. Glacken's comment on Xenophon: Glacken, *Traces*, p. 44.

[23] Stoic thinkers could also speak of the creation's aesthetic value for humanity: see Glacken, *Traces*, pp. 52, 57.

[24] Terian, *Philonis Alexandrini De Animalibus*, p. 51; cf. Glacken, *Traces*, pp. 57, 61.

[25] Thomas, *Man*, pp. 19–20.

[26] Thomas, *Man*, p. 166; cf. Passmore, *Man's Responsibility*, pp. 20–2.

– in short, with our hands we set about the fashioning of another nature, as it were, within the bounds and precincts of the one we have (*Nat. d.* 2.60)

with this by the fourth-century Christian theologian Didymus the Blind, commenting on Genesis 1:28:

> God has made [the gift of dominion to humanity] in order that land for growing and land for mining, rich in numerous, diverse materials, be under the rule of the human being. Actually, the human being receives bronze, iron, silver, gold, and many other metals from the ground; it is also rendered to him so that he can feed and clothe himself. So great is the dominion the human being has received over the land that he trans- forms it technologically – when he changes it into glass, pottery, and other similar things. This is in effect what it means for the human being to rule the whole earth.[27]

Both passages express the normal and natural ancient view that human beings have the right to use their environment to sustain and enhance their life, heightened by the typically Greco-Roman enthusi- asm for humanity's ingenuity in making something ordered and useful out of wild nature, by landscaping, farming, taming animals, mining, and the technological arts.

Fourthly, this understanding of human dominion was allied to a strongly hierarchical view of the world. Aristotle (*Pol.* 1.8) held that plants were created for the use of animals, animals for the use of humanity, along with the view, generally repudiated by Stoics and Christians, that some human beings are naturally intended to be sub- jected to others. The Stoics held that the irrational creation (including animals) exists for the sake of the rational, and human beings for the sake of the gods,[28] a view which the Christian writer Lactantius, for example, merely adapted to his belief in the Christian God: the world was made for living creatures, other living creatures for humanity, humanity (who alone can appreciate God's creation and worship the Creator) for the worship of God (*Div. Inst.* 7.4–6).[29] The hierarchical

---

[27] Quoted in Cohen, '*Be Fertile*', p. 227 (and see n. 18 on that page for further patris- tic references).

[28] Terian, *Philonis Alexandrini De Animalibus*, p. 51.

[29] For similar hierarchical thinking in the Fathers, see David Sutherland Wallace- Hadrill, *The Greek Patristic View of Nature* (Manchester: Manchester University Press/New York: Barnes & Noble, 1968), pp. 114–5.

nature of the medieval Christian world-view, along with the influence of Aristotle, appears in Thomas Aquinas, who regarded it as the natural order of things that the imperfect are for the use of the perfect. Hence plants make use of the earth, animals make use of plants, human beings make use of plants and animals: 'Therefore it is in keeping with the order of nature, that man should be master over animals.' This natural order corresponds to 'the order of Divine Providence which always governs inferior things by superior' (*Summa theologiae* 1.96.1; cf. 2.64.1). In this way, Thomas can link the natural hierarchy to the dominion over other creatures given to humanity by God, taking it for granted that this dominion is the right of the superior to make use of the inferior.

Fifthly, humanity was distinguished from the animals by an absolute difference in kind: only human beings are rational.[30] This was a controversial view in the ancient world,[31] since it is so easily challenged from observation of animal behaviour, but it was the Stoic view,[32] taken over by most Christian writers and associated by them with the idea of humanity's creation in the image of God (Gen. 1:26–7).[33] Human beings uniquely reflect or participate in the divine rationality, and this is what gives them their superiority to the animals by virtue of which they exercise their God-given dominion over the animals (Gen. 1:26).[34] This view did not, of course, mean that animals lacked any sort of consciousness or feeling. Hardly anyone seems to have thought that until the seventeenth-century philosopher René Descartes reduced animals to the status of mere machines.[35] But, in confining to human beings free will, moral responsibility, and the ability to understand and reason, and therefore also immortality and relationship with God, this view did put human beings on a quite different metaphysical level in the hierarchy

---

[30] This is not the general biblical view. Job 35:11 regards humans as more intelligent than animals and birds, but not as the only rational creatures. However, Jude 10 and 2 Pet. 2:12 do allude, for their particular polemical purpose, to the Stoic view that animals are irrational (and in the latter case, also to the Stoic view that the irrational animals have been created for the use of rational beings, i.e. humans).

[31] Cf. Terian, *Philonis Alexandrini De Animalibus*, pp. 49–50.

[32] Passmore, *Man's Responsibility*, p. 15.

[33] For Augustine's view, see Gillian Clark, 'The Fathers and the Animals: The Rule of Reason?', in *Animals on the Agenda* (ed. Andrew Linzey and Dorothy Yamamoto; London: SCM Press, 1998), pp. 67–79.

[34] Cohen, *'Be Fertile'*, pp. 226–59; David Cairns, *The Image of God in Man* (2nd edn; London: Collins, 1973), pp. 116–19. For the early modern period, see Thomas, *Man*, pp. 30–3.

[35] Descartes' view was anticipated by Gomez Pereira in 1554: Thomas, *Man*, p. 33.

of creation. They stand between the animals and the angels (who are purely immaterial intellects). Although theoretically the theological tradition's insistence on the goodness of the body as integral to human nature created by God and on the hope of the resurrection of the body should have ensured humanity's solidarity with the rest of the material creation, the emphasis on humanity's distinctiveness as akin to the angels and to God himself in immaterial rationality elevated humanity above nature. Human beings were encouraged to see themselves as a quite different kind of creature ruling over a creation inferior to them.

Finally, the Stoic view was that because irrational animals and rational human beings were radically unequal, there could be no question of justice or injustice in dealings between them.[36] Thomas Aquinas gave this Christian form in his insistence that we can have no duty to love irrational creatures, as we have to love God and our human neighbours (*Summa theologiae* 2.65.3). This is a consistent consequence of the view that animals exist only for our use, but for Christians it raised the problem of the Old Testament's apparent concern for animals, in its laws urging consideration for their needs (e.g. Deut. 25:4) and its commendation of kindness to animals (Prov. 12:10). However, Philo had already provided the answer to this difficulty: the value of kindness to animals is only as a way of learning to be kind to human beings (*Virt.* 81, 116, 125-60).[37] Thomas Aquinas (*Summa contra gentiles* 3.113) and other Christian theologians took the same view.[38] This dogma that animals could have no rights could lead good people to take callous views, such as the seventeenth-century Anglican divine Isaac Barrow's description of vivisection as 'a most innocent cruelty, and easily excusable ferocity'.[39]

Though all derived from Greek philosophical rather than biblical thought, this set of ideas dominated the Christian theological tradition up to the early modern period and is certainly not without its influence today. As we shall see, this interpretation of the human dominion over nature did provide the ground on which the theoretical foundations for the modern technological project of aggressive domination of nature would be erected by others. However, it did not in itself provide the ideological impetus to that project. In order to appreciate this point, we need to notice some important qualifications of the view we have outlined.

---

[36] Terian, *Philonis Alexandrini De Animalibus*, p. 52.
[37] Terian, *Philonis Alexandrini De Animalibus*, p. 45.
[38] Thomas, *Man*, p. 151.
[39] Quoted in Thomas, *Man*, p. 21.

In the first place, neither the theological tradition nor the exegetical tradition of commentaries on Genesis 1 was very interested in the human relationship with nature.[40] They were much more interested in interpreting the image of God in humanity in terms of humanity's relationship to God than in terms of humanity's relationship to the rest of creation.[41] Though this in itself is evidence of the theological tendency to detach human beings from the natural world, it hardly provides a theological impetus to the implementation of human dominion by conquest of nature. Secondly, the human dominion over nature was generally understood as a static fact (at any rate since the fall, which impaired it). The theologians convey no sense of a divine command which human beings are obligated to fulfil by extending their exploitation of nature.[42] They take it for granted that the text refers merely to the usual ways in which people were using nature in their time. Their interpretation of the dominion simply gives a rather conventional blessing to what their contemporaries were doing in their fields and their workshops with no need for special theological motivation. Thus, even though the rhetoric, as in the quotation from Didymus above, might try to match the apparently large scope of the biblical text, the concept of human dominion was in fact severely limited.

Thirdly, the fundamental notion was of a world created ready for and adapted to human use, not of a world open to radical reshaping for human purposes.[43] Cicero's remarkable idea (quoted above) of a human transformation of nature, such as to constitute the creation of a kind of second nature,[44] was to be taken up, as we shall see, in the Renaissance, but notably does not find echoes in the Christian tradition up to that time. Certainly, human ingenuity and inventiveness, as proof of our superiority over the animals, were a conventional theme inherited from classical sources. Nature provides scope for this inventiveness by not providing us with clothing and shelter directly, thus obliging us to find out how to make our own.[45] But the twelfth-century theologian Hugh of St Victor shows how this inventiveness was understood (*Didascalion* 1.9).[46] He specifies three kinds of work: the

---

[40] Cohen, *'Be Fertile'*, p. 268.

[41] Cohen, *'Be Fertile'*, pp. 309–10.

[42] Liedke, *Im Bauch*, p. 65.

[43] Passmore, *Man's Responsibility*, p. 17.

[44] On the theme, see Glacken, *Traces*, chapter 3.

[45] Glacken, *Traces*, pp. 54, 108; Lactantius, *Div. Inst.* 7.4.

[46] Liedke, *Im Bauch*, pp. 65–7, following Krolzik, *Umweltkrise*, 77ff. (I have not been able to see this work), sees in Hugh of St Victor's *Didascalion* a turning-point in the

creative work of God, who brings things into being out of nothing, the work of nature, which brings hidden potentialities into actuality, and the work of human artificers, who merely put together things disjoined or disjoin what is put together. They cannot do the work of God or of nature, but can only imitate nature. The person who first invented clothes, for example, observed how nature clothes growing things and followed her example. This is a very long way from the interpretation of the divine image in humanity and the human dominion over the world as a kind of participation in the divine creativity by which human beings can recreate the world. Only the latter would lead to the modern technological project.

Fourthly, it must be remembered that, although this tradition of thought offers a highly anthropocentric interpretation of the world, the anthropocentricity belongs within a broader theocentricity. This allowed the Stoic notion that all other creatures exist only for human benefit to be combined with a rather different theme in Christian tradition: that nature reflects and exists for the glory of God.[47] From this point of view the natural world serves humanity not only in the Stoic, utilitarian sense, but also by revealing its Creator and assisting human contemplation of God. Thus when Thomas Aquinas spells out the sense in which all corporeal creatures have been created for humanity's sake, he says: '[T]hey serve man in two ways, first as sustenance of his bodily life, secondly, as helping him to know God, inasmuch as man sees the invisible things of God by the things that are made' (*Summa theologiae* 3.91.1). This sense of the contemplative value of nature as revelation of God was to be lost in the transition to the purely utilitarian attitude to nature as a resource to be exploited which informed the modern project of dominating nature.

Fifthly, there is another sense in which the anthropocentricity of the traditional Christian view was qualified. For there were believed to be a vast number of created beings superior to humanity: the angels.[48] Although the rest of the corporeal creation was made for humanity's sake, this did not by any means make humanity the summit of

---

history of interpretation of human dominion. For the first time, he claims, Genesis 1:28 is understood as an imperative to restore dominion over the earth by technological innovation. But I can find no evidence for this view in the text of the *Didascalion*.

[47] For this theme in patristic and medieval writers, see Wallace-Hadrill, *Greek Patristic View*, pp. 120–1, 128–30; Glacken, *Traces*, chapter 5. There are some classical precedents, e.g. Xenophon, *Mem.* 4.3.14.

[48] Cf. Santmire, *Travail*, pp. 83, 90–1.

creation as such, for the purely spiritual beings ranked higher than humanity. The pure anthropocentricity which treats humanity as the summit and goal of all things arose not from the traditional Christian world-view, but from the Renaissance exaltation of humanity above the angels and the Enlightenment rejection of both angels and God.

Sixthly, as the previous two points indicate, the anthropocentric view that the world existed for humanity could not obscure the more fundamental doctrine of creation: that angels, humans and other creatures are all creatures of God the Creator. This came to expression perhaps most clearly in the belief that all creation worships God and that human worship is participation in that worship of God by all creation. This theme was more familiar in the medieval period than in the modern partly because of the frequent liturgical use of the *Benedicite*,[49] the canticle which calls on each and every creature, in a long catalogue of invocation, to worship the Creator. The *Benedicite* is taken from the Greek version of the book of Daniel (3:52–90), where it is one of the Greek additions to the Hebrew/Aramaic text of Daniel. It was therefore part of the canon of the Old Testament for the medieval western (as also the eastern) church and included in the Vulgate version, whereas it was not part of the canon of the Jewish Scriptures and would therefore be relegated to the Apocrypha by the Protestant Reformers. But Lynn White, who remarks that it 'contradicts the historically dominant Judeo-Christian anthropocentrism', is quite wrong in supposing that it shows the influence of Hellenism or was ever thought in the least heretical.[50] On the contrary, it merely develops at length the theme of nature's praise of God to be found in the Psalms (especially Psalm 148). Medieval Christians familiar with it in regular worship would have acquired thereby a strong sense of their horizontal relationship to the rest of creation as fellow-creatures, all existing for the glory of God.

Seventhly, awareness that the creatures over whom humanity exercises dominion are God's creatures could balance and modify the trend to understand dominion as a human right to use them in whatever way

---

[49] For its use in the Irish church, see Thomas Owen Clancy and Gilbert Márkus, *Iona: The Earliest Poetry of a Celtic Monastery* (Edinburgh: Edinburgh University Press, 1995), pp. 89–90; Mary Low, *Celtic Christianity and Nature* (Belfast: Blackstaff Press/Edinburgh: Edinburgh University Press, 1996), pp. 173–4. While the use of the Benedicite has not disappeared altogether in modern liturgy, it is often regarded as tediously repetitious and sometimes used in abbreviated form.

[50] Lynn White, 'Continuing the Conversation,' in *Western Man* (ed. Barbour), pp. 61–2.

serves human needs. This is particularly clear in relation to cruelty to animals. The view cited above that human beings have no duty of kindness to animals was far from universal.[51] For example, the early fifteenth-century treatise on the Ten Commandments, *Dives and Pauper*, though allowing the slaughter of animals for food, clothing or protection, warns that unnecessary harm or cruelty to animals is a very serious abuse of God's creatures.[52] Similarly Calvin, while taking the view that all creatures were made for the sake of humanity, nevertheless insisted that when God subjected the animals to human rule, he did so on condition that we treat them considerately, avoiding cruelty, because they are God's creatures.[53] Whether this acknowledgment that animals, as God's creatures, have certain rights we must respect is strictly consistent with the view that they exist only for our benefit is doubtful, but it does set some limit to human dominion. The interpretation of dominion as the right to use the rest of creation for human benefit is unchanged, but it is limited by another principle. A more radical step, which no one seems to have taken before the seventeenth century, would be to reinterpret dominion as stewardship over God's creation. On this view human beings have been given by God the responsibility of caring for the creation.[54] But this was a step decisively beyond the view which dominated Christian thought up to the early modern period.

In summary, the dominant theological tradition before the modern period did articulate a strongly anthropocentric view of the human dominion, largely as a result of imposing on the biblical texts understandings of the human relationship to nature which were of Greek, rather than biblical, origin. However, the facts that the dominion was understood as a static fact, not a mandate for extension, and the world was understood as created ready and adapted to human use, not requiring large-scale technological modification, distinguish this view sharply from the interpretation of the dominion which accompanied the rise of the modern project of technological domination of nature. They show that the medieval view was not itself sufficient to authorize that project. Moreover, the anthropocentricity of the dominant tradition was also significantly qualified by other convictions about the relationship between God, humanity and the rest of creation: that

---

[51] Thomas, *Man*, pp. 152–5.
[52] Quoted in Thomas, *Man*, pp. 152–3.
[53] Sermons on Deuteronomy, quoted in Thomas, *Man*, p. 154.
[54] Thomas, *Man*, p. 155; Glacken, *Traces*, pp. 480–2.

human beings are part of God's creation, which itself is theocentric, existing for the glory of God; that not humans, but angels, were the summit of creation; and that all creatures worship God and have the value of creatures created by God. Such qualifications meant the vertical relationship in which the dominion over nature placed humanity to the rest of creation was complemented by a real aware- ness of the horizontal relationship in which humans relate to their fel- low-creatures as all creatures of the one Creator. As we shall see, all these qualifications fell away in the Renaissance interpretation of the human dominion that paved the way for the modern subjugation of nature. When any sense of the value of creation for God and of a com- mon creatureliness in which humans share was lost, the idea of human dominion would acquire quite new significance.

However, what we have called the dominant view was never com- pletely dominant, and there is one major pre-modern tradition of Christian attitudes to the non-human creation that, while having some affinity with the dominant view, also diverged significantly from it. Though it has been comparatively neglected in studies of the history of Christian attitudes to nature, it deserves to be taken just as seriously as the dominant view that we have so far described.

An Alternative Tradition: Saints and Nature

As well as the work of the theologians and exegetes, on which our previous section focused, there is another tradition of Christian lit- erature in which Christian attitudes to the natural world are expressed and the idea of human dominion over nature interpreted. This is the tradition of stories of hermits, holy men and women who went to live (permanently or temporarily) apart from human socie- ty in order to devote themselves entirely to God. Because they delib- erately sought out places remote from human habitation, they lived amid wild nature, closer than most people to nature unmodified by human use. There are hundreds of stories of the relationships of these saints to the natural environment in which they lived, espe- cially their relations with wild animals.[55] The tradition of these

---

[55] Helen Waddell, *Beasts and Saints* (London: Constable, 1934) is a collection of some of the best of the Latin stories in translation, while David N. Bell, *Wholly Animals: A Book of Beastly Tales* (Cistercian Studies 128; Kalamazoo: Cistercian Publications 1992) overlaps with Waddell's collection but also includes many stories from other sources. Many of the stories about the desert fathers can be found in

stories runs from the desert fathers of the fourth century to the Franciscan saints of the thirteenth and fourteenth centuries: the same period as that covered by the dominant theological tradition surveyed in our previous section. Moreover, the tradition has not only a wide chronological range, but also a wide geographical range: from Egypt to Belgium, from Georgia[56] to Ireland. Those who know some of these stories, for example in Helen Waddell's collection of some of the most attractive,[57] have perhaps tended to think of them simply as charming stories. But they are much more than that. They express attitudes to the natural world which, through the considerable popularity of these stories, must have been very influential throughout the medieval Christian world, surely at least as influential at the popular level as the views expressed in works of academic theology and technical exegesis. Nor is the importance of these stories much affected by the view we take of the relation between fact and fiction in the tradition. The tradition must certainly be rooted in the real experiences of many Christian hermits.[58] But the themes certainly also became conventional and many of the actual stories are probably legendary to some degree. Modern readers will find some of the stories plausible and others obviously tall, but in many cases will be unable to judge their historicity. But this

---

translation in Norman Russell and Benedicta Ward, *The Lives of the Desert Fathers* (London/Oxford: Mowbray/Kalamazoo, Michigan: Cistercian Publications, 1981). Some of the stories of the Celtic saints are retold in Robert van de Weyer, *Celtic Fire: An Anthology of Celtic Christian Literature* (London: Darton, Longman & Todd, 1990). Studies of the stories include Susan P. Bratton, 'The Original Desert Solitaire: Early Christian Monasticism and Wilderness', *Environmental Ethics* 10 (1988): pp. 31–53; Roger D. Sorrell, *St. Francis of Assisi and Nature* (New York/Oxford: OUP, 1988), pp. 19–27; Allison Goddard Elliott, *Roads to Paradise: Reading the Lives of the Early Saints* (Hanover/London: University Press of New England, 1987), pp. 144–67, 193–204; Susan P. Bratton, 'Oaks, Wolves and Love: Celtic Monks and Northern Forests', *Journal of Forest History* 33 (1989): pp. 4–20; and especially William J. Short, *Saints in the World of Nature: The Animal Story as Spiritual Parable in Medieval Hagiography* (900–1200) (Rome: Gregorian University, 1983) (I am grateful to Dr Short for providing me with a photocopy of this book, which is unobtainable in Britain). Surprisingly, such stories are not discussed in Low, *Celtic Christianity and Nature*, though cf. pp. 111, 136–7. I am also grateful to James Bruce for comment on my treatment of these stories.

56 See the stories about David of Garesja in David Marshall Lang, *Lives and Legends of the Georgian Saints* (London: Allen & Unwin/New York: Macmillan, 1956), chapter 5.

57 Waddell, *Beasts*.

58 Cf. Bratton, 'Original Desert Solitaire', pp. 40–1.

need not at all affect their value as witness to a view of the human relationship with nature.[59]

The Christian ascetic tradition has often been blamed for fostering negative attitudes to the natural world. It is true that parts of that tradition in the medieval period were heavily influenced by a Greek dualism of spirit and matter, which denigrated the physical and aspired to spiritual detachment from the physical world to which the human body is akin. But the stories of hermits and nature reveal a quite different side to the ascetic tradition, largely unaffected by Platonic dualism. In some of the stories there is a different kind of dualism: a strong sense of the world as a scene of conflict between good and evil. The hermits who went out into the wilderness in order to encounter and defeat the forces of evil sometimes understood aspects of the natural world, such as snakes and scorpions, as emblems of the demonic.[60] But more prominent is their positive appreciation of their natural surroundings. In a period when most people's appreciation of nature was largely limited to nature as cultivated, ordered and otherwise improved by human art, it was the hermits who, from their experience of living alone in the wild, learned to appreciate the beauty of wild nature and to love the natural world for its own sake as God's creation.[61]

Perhaps the most 'conservationist' of all the stories of saints and nature is one of the stories about the Irish saint, Kevin (Coemgen, d. 618), who more than any of the early Irish saints was remembered in later traditions for his love of animals. An angel was sent to tell Kevin that he and his monks were to move to a new place, where the monastery he was to found would be home to thousands of monks until the day of judgment. But the place the angel indicates is well-nigh inaccessible. Kevin protests: 'It is impossible for monks to live in

---

[59] No attempt is made here to plot any chronological development in the attitudes to nature expressed by the stories. They are, of course, evidence primarily of such attitudes at the time of composition or recension of the stories, which is often much later than the time of the saints they describe. Where I have indicated the period in which the saint lived, no implication as to the date of the stories about him is intended.

[60] Cf. Louis Leloir, 'Anges et démons chez les Pères du Desert', in *Anges et Démons: Actes du Colloque de Liège et de Louvain-La-Neuve 25–26 novembre 1987* (ed. Julian Ries and Henri Limet; Louvain-La-Neuve: Centre d'Histoire des Religions, 1989), pp. 330–1; Bratton, 'Original Desert Solitaire', pp. 41–2; Sorrell, *St. Francis*, p. 21; Short, *Saints*, chapters 6–7.

[61] See Wallace-Hadrill, *Greek Patristic View*, pp. 87–91 (on Basil of Caesarea); Short, *Saints*, pp. 25–7.

that valley, hemmed in by mountains, unless God assists them by his power.' The angel promises that God will supply all they need, and goes on to picture the future glories of the monastery:

> [T]his place shall be holy and revered. The kings and the great ones of Ireland shall make it glorious to the glory of God because of you, in lands, in silver and gold, in precious stones and silk raiment, in treasures from over the seas . . . A great city shall rise there. And the burial place of your monks shall be most sacred, and none that lie beneath its soil shall know the pains of hell. Indeed, if you should wish that these four mountains that hem the valley in should be leveled into rich and gentle meadow lands, beyond question your God will do that for you.

But Kevin replies: 'I have no wish that the creatures of God should be moved because of me. My God can help that place in some other fashion. And moreover, all the wild creatures on these mountains are my house mates, gentle and familiar with me, and what you have said would make them sad.'[62]

Implicit in the whole tradition of these stories – and occasionally explicit – is an understanding of the human dominion over nature. Because the hermits are exemplary righteous people, they relate to nature in the way that God originally intended human beings to do.[63] Submitting themselves wholly to God's will, they recover the human dominion over the rest of creation in its ideal form. In their relationships with wild nature, paradise is regained and the coming restoration of paradise in the kingdom of God is anticipated.[64]

What this means in practice can sometimes remind us of the theological tradition of hierarchical order. The animals acknowledge the saints as those who have the right to rule and command them. Dangerous animals become tame and revere the saint.[65] They obey the saint's orders. Often they willingly serve the saint.[66] Abba Helle, one of the desert fathers, had only to call out to a herd of wild asses, requiring that one carry his burden for him, and one of them willingly

---

[62] Waddell, *Beasts*, 134–6 (translation adapted).

[63] It is notable that none seem to have thought this required complete vegetarianism, even though they protected animals from the hunters.

[64] Glacken, *Traces*, 310–11; George Hunston Williams, *Wilderness and Paradise in Christian Thought* (New York: Harper, 1962), pp. 42–6; Sorrell, *St. Francis*, p. 20; Elliott, *Roads*, p. 167; Short, *Saints, passim*.

[65] E.g. Short, *Saints*, pp. 11, 13, 33, 35, 51.

[66] Short, *Saints*, chapter 2.

trotted up to undertake the task.[67] For the sixth-century Breton saint, Leonoris, when he and his monastic brothers were worn out from working the fields without oxen, twelve stags appeared and spontaneously ploughed for thirty-eight days.[68] The Italian saint William of Montevergine (d. 1085) recruited two wolves to protect his garden from a wild boar.[69] As often, the most attractive stories are of the Celtic saints. Colman's three friends – the cock, the mouse and the fly – each assisted his devotions: the cock crowed in the middle of the night to wake him for prayer, the mouse woke him in the morning by nibbling his eyes, and the fly would keep his place on the page of the Scriptures as he meditated on the words.[70] After Cuthbert had prayed all night submerged to his neck in the sea, two otters warmed his feet with their breath and tried to dry him with their fur.[71] Not only the animals, but even the sea served Cuthbert, throwing up on the shore a plank of exactly the length he needed for the shelter he was constructing. His biographer Bede draws out the significance explicitly in this case: 'it is hardly strange that the rest of creation should obey the wishes and commands of a man who dedicated himself with complete sincerity to the Lord's service. We, on the other hand, often lose that dominion over creation which is ours by right through neglecting to serve its Creator.'[72]

Such stories presuppose a hierarchical order in which those human beings who obey God have a right to be obeyed by the rest of creation. But this is portrayed as a state of harmony in which the animals willingly serve but are certainly not exploited. Moreover, it is not implied that they exist only for the use of humans. As other stories make clear, the hierarchical order is understood as a state of harmony which benefits all God's creatures. The animals are not the saint's slaves, but are frequently portrayed as friends and companions of the saint, and as objects of the saint's care and concern. In these respects the stories step right outside the theological and exegetical tradition.

---

[67] Waddell, *Beasts*, p. 19; Bell, *Wholly Animals*, p. 73; *Historia Monachorum* 12.5, translated in Russell and Ward, *Lives*, p. 90.

[68] Short, *Saints*, pp. 53–4.

[69] Short, *Saints*, p. 46.

[70] Waddell, *Beasts*, pp. 145–7; cf. Kenneth (Canice) and the stag whose antlers he used as a lectern: Bell, *Wholly Animals*, p. 37.

[71] Bede, *De Vita et Miraculis S. Cudberti* 10, translated in James Francis Webb, *Lives of the Saints* (Harmondsworth: Penguin, 1965), pp. 84–5; Waddell, *Beasts*, pp. 59–61; Bell, *Wholly Animals*, pp. 49–51.

[72] Bede, *De Vita et Miraculis S. Cudberti* 21, translated in Webb, *Lives*, pp. 98–9.

Although some of the desert fathers can appear rather severe in their treatment of animals,[73] others took pleasure in the friendly companionship of wild creatures.[74] Several stories of the Celtic saints represent the saint as the abbot of a small monastery of wild animals, who keep him company in the wilderness and obey him as their abbot.[75] This picture puts rather well the ideal relationship the stories envisage: the monks must obey the abbot, but they are also, as fellow-monks, his brothers and companions in the service of God, and his rule over them is a matter of pastoral care. The care and concern of the saints for wild animals are the theme of many stories. The famous story of Kevin and the blackbird is an extreme example. As Kevin knelt in prayer with his hand outstretched, a blackbird built her nest on his hand and laid her eggs in it. Kevin kept his hand open until the chicks were hatched.[76] The twelfth-century English hermit Godric of Finchale is another saint remembered, probably with more historical basis, for his habit of caring for animals in need.[77]

Two themes recur frequently as forms of the saints' care for animals. One is their feeding of wild animals. Several of the desert fathers provided food and water for the animals of the Egyptian desert: lions, wolves, antelope, wild asses, gazelles.[78] In the later, European stories, birds are the most common recipients of food.[79] That timid birds feed from the saint's hand is seen as evidence of his gentleness, as in the case of William Firmat (d. 1179) of Mantilly in France,

---

[73] E.g. Abba Bes in *Historia Monachorum* 4.3, translated in Russell and Ward, *Lives*, p. 66; Abba Helle and the crocodile: *Historia Monachorum* 12.6–9, translated in Russell and Ward, *Lives*, pp. 90–1; cf. Waddell, *Beasts*, pp. 20–1; Bell, *Wholly Animals*, p. 74. Harsh treatment of animals can also be found in some stories of the Celtic saints.

[74] E.g. Theon: *Historia Monachorum* 6.4, translated in Russell and Ward, *Lives*, p. 68; Bell, *Wholly Animals*, p. 120; Macarius and the hyena: *Historia Monachorum* 21.15–16, translated in Russell and Ward, *Lives*, p. 110; cf. Waddell, *Beasts*, pp. 13–15; Bell, *Wholly Animals*, p. 93.

[75] For the Cornish saint, Piran, see Van de Weyer, *Celtic Fire*, pp. 60–1; for the Irish saint, Ciaran of Saighir, see Waddell, *Beasts*, pp. 104–6; Bell, *Wholly Animals*, pp. 40–2.

[76] Waddell, *Beasts*, p. 137. Another extreme example is the concern of David of Garesja for a monstrous dragon which was attacking the deer he had befriended: Lang, *Lives*, pp. 85–6. Note also the theme of the blessing of animals by saints: Bratton, 'Original Desert Solitaire', p. 37; Van de Weyer, *Celtic Fire*, p. 60.

[77] Bell, *Wholly Animals*, pp. 69–70, 156–7. Sadly, this aspect of Godric does not feature in Frederick Buechner's novel *Godric* (London: Chatto & Windus, 1981).

[78] *Historia Monachorum* 6.4, translated in Russell and Ward, *Lives*, p. 68; Bratton, 'Original Desert Solitaire', pp. 36, 38–9.

[79] But for other examples, see Bell, *Wholly Animals*, pp. 94–5, 96, 100.

who also sheltered birds from the cold under his clothes and fed breadcrumbs to the fish in the local pond.[80] The account is surely in this case an accurate reminiscence of a man who loved God's creatures, but it also portrays the ideal harmonious relationship of humans and animals: the gentleness of the saint is reciprocated by the tameness of the animals. Sometimes a saint shares his own food with birds, recognizing their common creaturely dependence on the Creator's provision.[81] We are reminded of the biblical stress on the Creator's provision of food for birds (Job 38:41; Ps. 147:9; Matt. 6:26; Luke 12:24). The saints both recognize their common creatureliness with the birds and reflect the Creator's own caring provision for his creatures the birds.

The other recurrent theme is that of the saint's protection of animals from hunters.[82] Wild boars, bears, partridges, stags, rabbits and foxes are all saved from the hunters pursuing them when they enter the sanctuary of the hermit's dwelling.[83] The hermitage and its environs are understood as a paradise where all creatures are safe and the violence of the hunt may not intrude. Once again the ideal relationship of humans and animals is envisaged as peaceful harmony, rather than as the human right to make use of animals, with which the dominant theological tradition underpinned the practice of hunting.

In summary, we may say that the tradition of stories of hermits and animals understands the human dominion over the rest of creation as a hierarchical relationship of mutual service and care: the animals willingly serve those who serve God, but the servants of God care for and protect the animals. Moreover, the sense of hierarchy is strongly qualified by a sense of common creatureliness. The animals are friends and companions. The saints delight in their company. They recognize their common dependence on their common Creator. When a partridge took refuge with the Georgian saint David of Garesja and its hunters asked him who looked after and fed him there in the uninhabited wilderness, David said: 'He whom I believe in and worship looks after and feeds all his creatures, to whom he has given birth. By Him are brought up all men and all animals and all plants, the birds of the sky and the fishes of the sea.'[84]

---

[80] Short, *Saints*, p. 16.
[81] E.g. Short, *Saints*, pp. 18–19; cf. Bratton, 'Original Desert Solitaire', p. 39.
[82] Short, *Saints*, chapter 3.
[83] Short, *Saints*, pp. 79–87, 95–100; Lang, *Lives*, pp. 88–9.
[84] Lang, *Lives*, p. 89.

Rarely but significantly, this shared creatureliness is perceived as the common worship of God. The Saxon saint Benno of Meissen (d. 1106) was disturbed in his contemplation by the loud croaking of a frog, and so he commanded it to be silent. But he then remembered the words of the *Benedicite*, which, among its exhortations to all creatures to worship God, includes: 'bless the Lord you whales and all that swim in the waters' (Daniel 3:79). Reflecting that God might prefer the singing of the frogs to his own prayer, he commanded the frogs to continue praising God in their own way.[85]

Francis of Assisi as Representative of the Alternative Tradition

Lynn White proposed Francis of Assisi as 'a patron saint for ecologists'.[86] The proposal is entirely appropriate. No other figure in Christian history so clearly, vividly and attractively embodies a sense of the world, including humanity, as a community of God's creatures, mutually interdependent, existing for the praise of their Creator, or has so effectively inspired in Christians an attitude of appreciation, gratitude, respect and love for all God's creatures.[87] However, when White portrays Francis as a completely exceptional figure in Christian history, he both misrepresents Francis's own views and neglects the extent to which they are anticipated in the tradition of stories of saints and nature. On the one hand, it is not true that 'Francis tried to depose man from his monarchy over creation and set up a democracy of all God's creatures' or that he 'tried to substitute the equality of all creatures, including man, for the idea of man's limitless rule of creation'.[88] Francis did not reject the notion of human dominion over the rest of creation, but interpreted it in the way that we have seen that the tra-

---

[85] Waddell, *Beasts*, pp. 71–2; Bell, *Wholly Animals*, pp. 25–6. (See also Chapter 7 in this volume.) Note also the quotation from the *Benedicite* in the *Voyage of St Brendan*, discussed by Sorrell, *St. Francis*, pp. 24–5.

[86] White, 'Historical Roots', p. 30.

[87] The definitive study is now Sorrell, *St. Francis*; but see also Edward A. Armstrong, *Saint Francis: Nature Mystic* (Berkeley/Los Angeles/London: University of California Press, 1973); Eloi Leclerc, *Le Chant des Sources* (3rd edn; Paris: Editions Franciscaines, 1975).

[88] White, 'Historical Roots,' pp. 28, 29. Leonardo Boff, *Saint Francis: A Model for Human Liberation* (London: SCM Press, 1982), p. 34, who speaks of 'the cosmic democracy', comes rather close to this mistake, though his insights into Francis's confraternity with all creatures are very valuable.

dition of stories of saints and nature interpreted it. On the other hand, White misrepresents the latter tradition when he says that the legends of the saints (referring especially to the Irish saints) do not provide a precedent for the stories about Francis, because they told of the saints' dealings with animals only in order 'to show their human dominance over creatures'.[89] White cannot have read many of the legends of the Irish saints if he has not noticed how much more striking are the saints' delight in the companionship of animals and their loving care for animals. This is not to say that there are not relatively new aspects and emphases in Francis's teaching and behaviour, but the novelty emerges from his continuity with the tradition in which he stood.[90] Francis is the climax of a tradition reaching back to the desert fathers. He transcends it only through deep dependence on it.

Many of the stories of Francis's relationships with animals and other creatures continue the theme of the restoration of the paradisal relationship of humans to the rest of creation,[91] and they portray this relationship in much the same ways as the tradition of the stories of the saints had done. Francis frequently acts with authority to command the animals,[92] illustrating Bonaventura's conclusion that 'Francis had power not only over men, but also over the fishes of the sea, the birds of the air and the beasts of the field'.[93] The fierce wolf that was terrorizing the town of Gubbio was tamed and became friendly under Francis's influence.[94] Animals serve Francis, like the falcon, which during his residence in his hermitage at La Verna used

---

[89] White, 'Historical Roots', p. 29.

[90] Even Sorrell, who carefully establishes Francis's continuity with the tradition before attempting to specify the really novel elements in his life and message (see the summary: *St. Francis*, pp. 138–9), perhaps fails to show sufficiently how the relatively novel elements develop out of the traditional. Bratton, 'Oaks', pp. 17–20, helpfully compares and contrasts Francis with the desert fathers and the Celtic saints.

[91] According to Bonaventura, *Legenda Maior* 8.1, Francis returned 'to the state of primeval innocence by restoring man's harmony with the whole of creation' (translation in Marion A. Habig, *St. Francis of Assisi: Writings and Early Biographies: English Omnibus of the Sources for the Life of St. Francis* [Chicago: Franciscan Herald Press, 1983], p. 688). Translations from Francis's works and the early biographies are taken from Regis J. Armstrong, J.A. Wayne Hellmann and William J. Short, eds, *Francis of Assisi: Early Documents*, vol. 1: *The Saint* (New York: New City Press, 1999) when the texts are included in this volume, in other cases from Habig, *St. Francis*.

[92] Examples listed in Sorrell, *St. Francis*, p. 43.

[93] Habig, *St. Francis*, p. 1880.

[94] *Fioretti* 1.21 (Habig, *St. Francis*, pp. 1348–51).

to wake him in time for matins, but showed such consideration for the saint that when Francis was tired or ill it would delay waking him until dawn.[95] Like many of the stories in the earlier tradition, this one emphasizes the affectionate friendship between the saint and the bird. The creatures respect Francis's authority, but they do so lovingly and willingly, as friends rather than slaves.

Many stories show Francis's care for animals in relatively traditional ways. Like other saints, he fed and protected his fellow-creatures. He wanted Christmas Day, a festival of special importance to Francis, to be honoured by the provision of abundant food for birds and more than the usual amount of food for domestic animals.[96] He saw to it that bees were provided with honey or wine lest they die of cold in the winter.[97] Though he is not said to have saved animals from hunters, several stories portray him saving animals from danger or harm, freeing animals that had been caught and brought to him, returning fish to the water, even removing worms from the road lest they be trampled.[98] (But it should be noted that Francis was not a vegetarian, and so cannot have thought the catching of fish and trapping of animals was always wrong.) Such stories are both continuous with the tradition and sufficiently distinctive of Francis to convince us that we are not dealing with a literary topos, but with genuine reminiscences of Francis's concern for creatures, which stemmed from his eremitical experience of living closely with wild nature, as many hermits had before him. Like some of the stories in the earlier tradition, those about Francis frequently emphasize the reciprocity of his relationships with animals: they are tame and friendly as he is gentle and concerned. The friendly and non-violent harmony of paradise is restored.

Francis is reported as saying that 'every creature says and proclaims: "God has created me for you, O man!"' Although this reflects the medieval theological commonplace that the rest of the material creation was made for humanity, the context should be noted. Francis was telling the brother gardener not to plant vegetables everywhere, but to reserve part of the garden for plants whose scent and flowers 'might invite all men who looked at them to praise God'.[99] Thus

---

[95] Celano, *Vita Secunda* 168 (Habig, *St. Francis,* pp. 497–8).

[96] Celano, *Vita Secunda* 200 (Habig, *St. Francis,* p. 522).

[97] Celano, *Vita Prima* 80 (Habig, *St. Francis,* p. 296; Armstrong, R. J. et al., eds, *Francis of Assisi,* p. 250).

[98] Listed in Sorrell, *St. Francis,* p. 44.

[99] *Legenda Perugina* 51 (Habig, *St. Francis,* p. 1029).

Francis refuses to limit the value of the rest of creation for humanity to its practical usefulness but sees it as consisting also in its assisting humanity's praise of God. But Francis's principle (to be expressed most fully and beautifully at the end of his life in the *Canticle of Brother Sun*) was that because the 'creatures minister to our needs every day', and 'without them we could not live', therefore we should appreciate them and praise God for them.[100] Thus the theme of human dominion is understood theocentrically rather than anthropocentrically. The creatures' service of humanity is properly received only as cause for praise and thankfulness to God. Therefore the human dominion over the creatures becomes for Francis primarily a matter of dependence on the creatures, with whom humanity shares a common dependence on the Creator. The creatures on whose service we depend are not to be exploited, but to be treated with brotherly/sisterly respect and consideration.

This means that in Francis the sense in which humanity has been given a superior status in creation is only to be understood in relationship to his overwhelming sense of the common creatureliness which makes all creatures his 'sisters' and 'brothers'.[101] This usage seems to be distinctive of Francis. The Celtic saints had called the animals who befriended them their brothers in the monastic sense. Francis regards all the creatures (not only animals, but also fire and water, sun and moon, and so on) as brothers and sisters, because they are fellow-creatures and fellow-members of the family of those who serve God. The terms denote affection and especially affinity. Thus, while there is a residual element of hierarchy in the relationship (humans and other creatures are not regarded as equal members of a democracy), this does not negate the common creatureliness of humans and other creatures. One concept, which helped Francis, as a man of the thirteenth century, to understand the relationship of humans and other creatures in terms not of domination but of mutuality, was the chivalric notion of 'courtesy'.[102] Courtesy is the magnanimous, deferential, respectful attitude which enables love to be shown up and down the social hierarchy. In the community of creation, brothers and sisters on different levels of the hierarchy can interact with mutual respect and loving deference. With the chivalric notion of courtesy Francis fused the traditional monastic virtues of obedience and humility,[103] so that he can say that obedience 'is subject and

---

[100] *Legenda Perugina* 43 (Habig, *St. Francis*, p. 1021).

[101] Sorrell, *St. Francis*, pp. 66, 127–8.

[102] See Sorrell, *St. Francis*, pp. 69–75.

submissive to everyone in the world, not only to people but to every beast and wild animal as well[,] that they may do whatever they want with it insofar as it has been given them from above by the Lord'.[104] Here the hierarchy is virtually subverted by mutuality: the obedience which the creatures owe to humanity is reciprocated by an obedience of humanity to the creatures. What Francis envisages, in the end, is a kind of mutual and humble deference in the common service of the creatures to their Creator.

Another theme which has roots in the tradition, as we have seen, but which Francis also made very characteristically his own is that of the duty of all creatures to praise their Creator and of the participation of humans in the worship given by all creation to God. The influence of the psalms and the *Benedicite* is unmistakable in Francis's own liturgical compositions which call on all creatures to praise God.[105] Francis was original in that he translated this liturgical usage into an actual practice of addressing the creatures themselves. This began with the famous sermon to the birds in 1211,[106] which initiated a regular practice: 'From that day on, he carefully exhorted all birds, all animals, all reptiles, and also insensible creatures, to praise and love their Creator, because daily, invoking the name of the Savior, he observed their obedience in his own experience.'[107]

In this way Francis put into practice a conviction that every creature has its own God-given worth (as he said to the birds: 'God made you noble among His creatures')[108] that should be returned to its source in praise of the Creator. We should also remember Francis's habit of

---

[103] On the relationship of humility (and poverty) to Francis's confraternity with creatures, see Boff, *Saint Francis*, pp. 38–40.

[104] *The Praises of the Virtues* (Habig, *St. Francis*, p. 134; Armstrong, R.J. et al., eds, *Francis of Assisi*, p. 165).

[105] *The Exhortation to the Praise of God* (translation in Sorrell, *St. Francis*, p. 109; Armstrong, R.J. et al., eds, *Francis of Assisi*, p. 138) and *The Praises of God before the Office* (Habig, *St. Francis*, pp. 138–9; Armstrong, R.J. et al., eds, *Francis of Assisi*, pp. 161–2). These works echo the psalms that call on all creatures to praise God, the *Benedicite*, and Revelation 5:13. The latter was to be used by the friars before each hour of the office. The influence of Psalm 148 and the *Benedicite* can also be seen in *The Canticle of Brother Sun*: see Sorrell, *St Francis*, pp. 99, 102–5.

[106] Celano, *Vita Prima* 58 (Habig, *St. Francis*, pp. 277–8; Armstrong, R.J. et al., eds, *Francis of Assisi*, p. 234); *Fioretti* 1.16 (Habig, *St. Francis*, pp. 1336–7).

[107] Celano, *Vita Prima* 58 (Habig, *St. Francis*, p. 278; Armstrong, R.J. et al., eds, *Francis of Assisi*, p. 234); cf. 80-1 (Habig, *St. Francis*, pp. 296–7; Armstrong, R.J. et al., eds, *Francis of Assisi*, p. 250–1).

[108] Celano, *Vita Prima* 58 (Habig, *St. Francis*, p. 278; Armstrong, R.J. et al., eds, *Francis of Assisi*, p. 234).

singing along with cicadas or birds in what he understood as their praise of their Creator.[109] In this way he translated the sentiments of the *Benedicite* into a real human solidarity with the rest of creation understood as a theocentric community existing for the praise and service of God.[110]

In the famous *Canticle of Brother Sun* or *Canticle of the Creatures*, written at the end of his life, Francis summed up much of his attitude to creation. It is important to appreciate fully the opening two stanzas that praise God before reference is made to the creatures:

> Most High, all-powerful, good Lord,
> Yours are the praises, the glory, and the honor, and all blessing,
> To You alone, Most High, do they belong,
> and no human is worthy to mention Your name.[111]

That God surpasses the creatures in such a way as to be the only praiseworthy one could not be clearer. So, when the next stanza continues: 'Praised be You, my Lord, with all Your creatures', the praising of the creatures can only be a way of praising their Creator, from whom their praiseworthy features derive. This praise of God *with* the creatures (stanzas 3–4) is a transition from the praise of God without the creatures (stanzas 1–2) to the praises of God *for* the creatures, which occupy stanzas 5–13. In these stanzas the various qualities of the creatures are lovingly detailed, so that God may be praised for them. Each of these stanzas begins (in Francis's Italian original): '*Laudato si, mi Signore, per* . . .' followed by reference to one or more of the creatures. There has been controversy over whether the meaning is 'Be praised, my Lord, by . . ."' Be praised, my Lord, through . . .' or 'Be praised, my Lord, for . . .'. Divergent interpretations of the phrase go back to soon after Francis's death,[112] and any would be consistent with his thinking about the creation. But the latest detailed study by Sorrell argues very convincingly for the translation: 'Be praised, my Lord, for . . .'.[113] In that case the canticle does not call on Sister Moon, Brother Wind, Sister Water and the rest to praise God, even though

---

[109] Celano, *Vita Secunda* 171 (Habig, *St. Francis*, pp. 499–500); Bonaventura, *Legenda Maior* 8.9 (Habig, *St. Francis*, pp. 695–6); J.R.H. Moorman, *A New Fioretti* 57 (Habig, *St. Francis*, pp. 1881–2).

[110] Cf. Boff, *Saint Francis*, pp. 37–8.

[111] Armstrong, R.J. et al., eds, *Francis of Assisi*, p. 113.

[112] Sorrell, *St. Francis*, pp. 116–17, 119.

[113] Sorrell, *St. Francis*, pp. 118–22.

Francis, as we have seen, could well have done this. Rather the canticle takes up Francis's conviction, which we have also noticed, that human beings should praise God for their fellow-creatures. The creatures are appreciated in three ways: for their practical usefulness in making human life possible and good, for their beauty, and for the way their distinctive qualities reflect the divine being (in particular 'Sir Brother Sun', in his beauty and radiance, resembles God). This is an appreciation of the God-given value of creation which goes far beyond a purely utilitarian, anthropocentric view. It celebrates the interdependent harmony of creation. The canticle is designed to teach people to think of creation with gratitude, appreciation and respect.[114]

We have considered various aspects of Francis's attitude to and relationships with the non-human creation, but we have still to register the intensity of delight in the creatures that frequently raised Francis to ecstatic rejoicing in their Creator. Some comments from his early biographers will illustrate this:

> He used to extol the artistry of [the bees'] work and their remarkable ingenuity, giving glory to the Lord. With such an outpouring, he often used up an entire day or more in praise of them and other creatures.[115]

> He had so much love and sympathy for [the creatures] that he was disturbed when they were treated without respect. He spoke to them with a great inner and exterior joy, as if they had been endowed by God with feeling, intelligence, and speech. Very often it was for him the occasion to become enraptured in God.[116]

> [H]e caressed and contemplated [the creatures] with delight, so much so that his spirit seemed to live in heaven and not on earth.[117]

This aspect of Francis's relationship to the creatures seems unprecedented in the Christian tradition and warrants speaking of Francis's creation mysticism.[118]

---

[114] Sorrell, *St. Francis*, p. 124.
[115] Celano, *Vita Prima* 80 (Habig, *St. Francis*, p. 296; Armstrong, R J. et al., eds, *Francis of Assisi*, p. 250).
[116] *Legenda Perugina* 49 (Habig, *St. Francis*, p. 1027).
[117] *Legenda Perugina* 51 (Habig, *St. Francis*, p. 1029).
[118] See also Chapter 9 in this volume.

Creating the Modern Tradition

Italian Renaissance humanists

A major development in the understanding of the human dominion over nature occurred in the Italian humanist writers of the Renaissance. It was a development which could hardly have taken place except on the basis of the dominant theological tradition of the patristic and medieval periods, which we have already outlined, but it was also a major step beyond that tradition, which has been little enough noticed in discussions of our subject.[119] It is this step which can be said to have created the ethos within which the modern project of aggressive domination of nature has taken place.

The Renaissance humanists were preoccupied with the theme of the supreme dignity of humanity, which they not infrequently expounded as exegesis of Genesis 1:26.[120] Even where reference to the text is not explicit, it is frequently implicit. Moreover, the traditional understanding of the human dominion, which these writers knew not only from the theological tradition but also from the classical sources that had influenced that tradition, is taken entirely for granted. The rest of creation was made for humanity (it was, says Petrarch, 'dedicated to nothing but your uses, and created solely for the service of man').[121] The unique superiority of human nature over the rest of creation equips human beings to rule the world.[122] But these traditional themes are given unprecedented emphasis and at the same time developed in a novel direction.

A striking feature of the Renaissance humanist idea of humanity is that the vertical relationship of humanity to nature – human beings as rulers over the rest of creation – is emphasized to the virtual exclusion of the horizontal relationship of humanity to nature – human beings as creatures who share with other creatures a common creaturely relationship to the Creator. Humanity's place within creation is abolished in favour of humanity's exaltation above creation. While this takes to an extreme one aspect of the traditional hierarchical thinking, other aspects of the medieval hierarchical view of creation are left aside.

---

[119] Wybrow, *Bible*, pp. 166–71, is one of the few discussions to give it serious attention.

[120] See especially Charles Trinkaus, *In Our Image and Likeness: Humanity and Divinity in Italian Humanist Thought* (London: Constable, 1970).

[121] *De remediis utriusque fortunae* (1357), quoted in Trinkaus, *In Our Image*, p.180.

[122] Cf. Trinkaus, *In Our Image*, p. 192.

Human beings are no longer regarded as occupying a metaphysical status below that of the angels, but are exalted above the angels, if not by virtue of their creation, then at least by virtue of their deification in Christ.[123] With this is connected a rejection of the idea that humanity occupies a given, fixed place within the created order. Human beings are understood as uniquely free to make of themselves what they will and to transcend all limits. In effect, humanity becomes a kind of god in relation to the world. Human creatureliness is forgotten in the intoxication with human godlikeness. The Renaissance humanist vision of humanity is of a creative and sovereign god over the world.

In writers such as Giannozzo Manetti, Marsilio Ficino and Pico della Mirandola, the image of God in human nature is understood not simply as the rational or moral capacity that distinguishes humans from other creatures, as the dominant theological tradition had understood it, but as likeness to God in the divine activity of creating and mastering the world. The rather traditional theme, inherited from classical antiquity, of stress on humanity's ingenuity and inventiveness is heightened and emphasized in the typical Renaissance adulation of the artistic and technological achievements of humanity. As Manetti commented:

> After that first, new and rude creation of the world, everything seems to have been discovered, constructed and completed by us out of some singular and outstanding acuteness of the human mind . . . The world and all its beauties seems to have been first invented and established by Almighty God for the use of man, and afterwards gratefully received by man and rendered much more beautiful, much more ornate and far more refined.[124]

This is a relatively restrained adumbration of the idea that humanity's likeness to God consists in a creative ability to reshape the world, fashioning a kind of second creation out of the raw materials of the first. The idea that we noticed in Cicero here finally comes into its own, with its implication that, as Manetti quotes from Cicero, human beings, in their special capacity for knowing and doing, act in their dominion over the world 'as though a certain mortal god'.[125]

---

[123] Trinkaus, *In Our Image*, pp. 188–92, 212–13, 511–12.

[124] *De dignitate et excellentia hominis* (1542/3), quoted in Trinkaus, *In Our Image*, p. 247.

[125] Quoted in Trinkaus, *In Our Image*, p. 250.

This new sense of the godlike creativity of humanity should be contrasted with the traditional concept, which we have seen in the work of Hugh of St Victor, according to which human beings can do neither the work of God nor that of nature, but can only imitate nature. According to Ficino: 'Human arts make by themselves whatever nature itself makes, so that we seem to be not servants of nature but competitors . . . Man at last imitates all the works of divine nature and perfects, corrects and modifies the works of lower nature.'[126] Human sovereignty over the world in knowing and creating is such that the human soul must be termed divine:

> The mind in comprehending conceives of as many things in itself as God in knowing makes in the world. By speaking it expresses as many in the air; with a reed it writes as many on paper. By making it constructs as many in the material of the world. Therefore he would be proven mad who would deny that the soul, which in the arts and in governing competes with God, is divine.[127]

It is clear here that Ficino's aim is to envisage humanity in terms of the attributes traditionally restricted to God as Creator and Ruler of the world.[128] The human relationship to the world is therefore described in terms that, for all the magnificence of the vision, are ludicrously hyperbolic. All creaturely limitations are deliberately suppressed, as in the following passage, which is worth quoting at length:

> In these industrial arts . . . man everywhere utilises all the materials of the universe as though all were subject to man. He makes use . . . of all the

---

[126] Quoted in Trinkaus, *In Our Image*, p. 482.

[127] Quoted in Trinkaus, *In Our Image*, p. 484.

[128] Cf. Jürgen Moltmann, *God in Creation* (trans. Margaret Kohl; London: SCM Press, 1985), pp. 26–7; Jürgen Moltmann, *God for a Secular Society* (trans. Margaret Kohl; London: SCM Press, 1999), pp. 98–9. Moltmann sees the fundamental problem as a one-sided emphasis, in Nominalism and the Renaissance, on God's absolute power. Human beings, as the image of such a God, are therefore bound to strive for power and sovereignty over the world. However, if this concept of God were, as Moltmann argues (as an alternative to Lynn White's thesis), the source of the modern project to subjugate nature, why did the latter not arise in Islamic societies? The problem posed for Christian theology by the Renaissance and the modern culture derived from it is not only a matter of getting the understanding of God right, but also of conceiving human likeness to God in a properly creaturely way, such that human self-understanding is formed by contrast as well as resemblance to God.

elements, the stones, metals, plants and animals, and he transforms them into many shapes and figures, which animals never do. Nor is he content with one element or few, as animals, but he uses all as though he were master of all. He tramps the earth, he sails the water, he ascends in the air by the highest towers . . . He acts as the vicar of God, since he inhabits all the elements and cultivates all . . . Indeed he employs not only the elements but all the animals of the elements, terrestrial, aquatic, and flying, for food, comfort and pleasure, and the supernal and celestial ones for learning and the miracles of magic. He not only uses the animals but he rules them . . . He does not only use the animals cruelly, but he also governs, fosters and teaches them. Universal providence is proper to God who is the universal cause. Therefore man who universally provides for all things living is a certain god. He is the god without doubt of the animals since he uses all of them, rules them, and teaches some of them. He is established also as god of the elements since he inhabits and cultivates them all.[129]

If we understand Renaissance humanism as in some sense giving birth to the spirit of the modern project of unlimited domination of nature, then it is extremely instructive to see how explicit Ficino is in connecting a human aspiration to subjugate all things to human control with a human aspiration to divinity: '[Man] will not be satisfied with the empire of this world, if, having conquered this one, he learns that there remains another world which he has not yet subjugated . . . Thus man wishes no superior and no equal and will not permit anything to be left out and excluded from his rule. This status belongs to God alone. Therefore he seeks a divine condition.'[130]

The gap between such a view and the traditional Christian view of the human dominion is vast. Anthropocentric as the latter was, it nevertheless understood the human dominion in static and very limited terms, and qualified it by a consciousness of humanity's creatureliness in common with the rest of creation. In Ficino, on the other hand, human beings are godlike in their restless will to power. Human dominion over the world has become a limitless aspiration. The attitudes that have led to the contemporary ecological crisis can be traced back to this source, but no further.

A final quotation, from the sixteenth-century Italian pantheist philosopher Giordano Bruno, will illustrate just how far the idea of humanity's divine creativity could be taken:

---

[129] Quoted in Trinkaus, *In Our Image*, pp. 483–4.
[130] Quoted in Trinkaus, *In Our Image*, p. 491.

The gods have given man intelligence and hands, and have made him in their image, endowing him with a capacity superior to other animals. This capacity consists not only in the power to work in accordance with nature and the usual course of things, but beyond that and outside her laws, to the end that by fashioning, or having the power to fashion, other natures, other courses, other orders by means of his intelligence, with that freedom without which his resemblance to the deity would not exist, he might in the end make himself god of the earth.[131]

This idea of humanity's capacity to refashion the world at will into whatever form of new creation we desire has provided, as it were, the ethos of much of the modern project. It has been one of the myths by which modern western civilization has lived. But, of course, the scientific and technological means by which modern society has attempted to put this myth into practice could not relate to nature in quite the way Bruno (inspired by Renaissance magic) envisaged. Science and technology cannot act outside nature's laws. Much as they might aspire to refashion nature, their ability to do so depends on their mastery of nature's laws. To find a version of the Renaissance humanist aspiration which recognized this and thereby provided more precisely the ideology of the modern scientific movement in its attempt to subjugate nature to human use, we must turn to Bruno's English contemporary, Francis Bacon.

Francis Bacon

The extraordinary achievement of Francis Bacon (1561–1626) was to set out in advance a programme for the modern scientific enterprise which can still stand as a classic statement of the ideology which has inspired and governed scientific research and technological innovation from the seventeenth to the twentieth centuries.[132] His contribution to

---

[131] *Spacio de la Bestia Trionfante*, quoted in Benjamin Farrington, *The Philosophy of Francis Bacon: An Essay on its Development from 1603 to 1609 with New Translations of Fundamental Texts* (Liverpool: Liverpool University Press, 1964), p. 27. It is ironical that Bruno is one of the heroes of Matthew Fox's bizarre reading of Christian history: Matthew Fox, *Original Blessing* (Santa Fe, New Mexico: Bear, 1983), pp. 10, 312.

[132] Relevant studies of Bacon include Farrington, *Philosophy of Francis Bacon*; Paolo Rossi, *Francis Bacon: From Magic to Science* (trans. Sacha Rabinovitch; London: Routledge & Kegan Paul, 1968); Leiss, *Domination*, ch. 3; James Samuel Preus, 'Religion and Bacon's New Learning: From Legitimation to Object', in *Continuity and Discontinuity in Church History: Essays Presented to George Huntston Williams*

the modern scientific method has been frequently discussed and debated, but methodology was not in reality his main contribution to modern science. This lay rather in his vision of organized scientific research with a utopian goal to be realised through scientific innovation and progress. It was this dream that inspired the pioneering scientists of seventeenth- and eighteenth-century England. Central to Bacon's vision of scientific progress was his understanding of the goal of science as the implementation of the God-given human dominion over nature, which Bacon himself presented as the meaning of Genesis 1:28.[133]

Taking entirely for granted the traditional view that the rest of creation exists for the sake of humanity, Bacon understands the human dominion as humanity's right and power to use nature for human benefit.[134] This human dominion was severely impaired at the fall, but it can be recovered: 'Man by the fall fell at the same time from his state of innocency and from his dominion over creation. Both of these losses can in this life be in some part repaired; the former by religion and faith, the latter by arts and sciences.'[135]

The words of God to Adam after the fall – that 'in the sweat of thy face shalt thou eat bread' (Gen. 3:19, AV) – Bacon takes to mean that 'by various labours' the earth can be 'at length and in some measure subdued to the supplying of man with bread; that is, to the uses of human life'.[136] These labours are primarily the intellectual labours of scientific research which make possible the technological exploitation of nature for human benefit.[137] The human task is to recover the dominion over the earth to its fullest extent.[138] This is 'the real business and

---

(ed. F. Forrester Church and Timothy George; Leiden: Brill, 1979); Jerry Weinberger, *Science, Faith, and Politics: Francis Bacon and the Utopian Roots of the Modern Age* (Ithaca/London: Cornell University Press, 1985); Robert Kenneth Faulkner, *Francis Bacon and the Project of Progress* (Lanham: Rowman & Littleford, 1993). For a critique from a feminist and green theological perspective, see Catharina J.M. Halkes, *New Creation: Christian Feminism and the Renewal of the Earth* (trans. C. Romanik; London: SPCK, 1991), pp. 27–32, 56–58.

[133] For exegetical argument against Bacon's (and Baconians') interpretations of this and other texts in Genesis, see Wybrow, *Bible*, ch. 5.

[134] Cf. Rossi, *Francis Bacon*, pp. 102–3.

[135] *Novum Organon* 12.52, in Francis Bacon, *The Works of Francis Bacon* (ed. James Spedding, Robert Leslie Ellis, Douglas Denon Heath; London: Longman, 1857–8) IV: 247–8.

[136] Bacon, *Works* IV: 248.

[137] Bacon, *Works* III: 222–3.

[138] *New Atlantis*, quoted in Preus, 'Religion', p. 269: 'the enlargement of the bounds of Human Empire, to the effecting of all things possible'.

fortunes of the human race.'[139] It is also the central goal of Bacon's own work, which is devoted to 'my only earthly wish, namely to stretch the deplorably narrow limits of man's dominion over the universe to their promised bounds'.[140]

Hence the title of Bacon's projected masterpiece, which he never completed but which was to sum up all his work, was to be 'The Great Instauration'. By this term he means precisely the restoration of the human dominion over nature which was promised in Genesis 1: 'that right over nature which belongs to [the human race] by divine bequest'.[141] This restoration of dominion is a vast enterprise, not to be accomplished quickly. It is to be the work of dedicated scientific labour over many generations.[142]

Thus, much more clearly than in the Italian humanists, in Bacon the human dominion becomes a historical task, to be progressively accomplished. Indeed, it is the great task of the human race, to which all its best efforts should be directed. The restoration of the human dominion is not, as in the tradition of stories of saints and nature, given by God to those who live according to his will. It is not, in that sense, a concern of religion, though Bacon does expect the exercise of dominion to be 'governed by sound reason and true religion'.[143] He effectively drew a very firm distinction between the restoration of human innocence, which was the province of religion, and the restoration of human dominion, which would be accomplished by science and technology.

The task is very explicitly that of subjecting nature to human use. The language of domination comes readily to Bacon's pen: 'I am come in very truth leading you to Nature with all her children to bind her to your service and make her your slave.'[144]

In a revealing passage, Bacon refers to three sorts of ambition. Those who desire to increase their own power in their own country are not to be admired. The desire to increase one's own country's power over other nations is more admirable, but still culpable. By contrast, the endeavour 'to extend the power and dominion of the human race itself over the universe' is wholly admirable: 'a work truly divine'.[145] This is

---

[139] Bacon, *Works* IV: 32.
[140] *The Masculine Birth of Time*, in Farrington, *Philosophy of Francis Bacon*, p. 62.
[141] *Novum Organon* 1.129, in Bacon, *Works* IV: 115.
[142] Bacon, *Works* IV: 21.
[143] Bacon, *Works* IV: 115.
[144] *The Masculine Birth of Time*, in Farrington, *Philosophy of Francis Bacon*, p. 62.
[145] *Valerius Terminus*, in Bacon, *Works* III: 223; cf. *Novum Organon* 1.129, in Bacon, *Works* IV: 114.

because it is unselfishly directed to the benefit of all humanity. Bacon equates 'the instigator [i.e. restorer] of man's domination of the universe' with 'the champion of freedom' and 'the conqueror of need'.[146] This is, appearing probably for the first time, the modern vision of the scientific and technological enterprise as dedicated to the good of humanity by acquiring power over nature and using it to liberate humanity from all the ills of the human condition. It has a high ethical motivation and goal. But the ethical limit it places on human domination of nature is solely that of the love of humanity: the scientific enterprise should be governed, not by desire for personal gain or glory, but by love of humanity.[147] No limit is imposed by any sense that nature has intrinsic value for itself or for God. Because Bacon assumes that nature exists solely for human benefit, it is not only right, but a prime human duty to exploit it for human benefit as far as possible.

As well as an ethical limit, there is a practical limit to human power to dominate nature. This limit is imposed by the facts of nature. Nature has been constituted by its Creator in a certain way which human beings must understand if they are to be able to use nature to the fullest possible extent for human benefit.[148] This is the point at which Bacon so significantly does what the Italian humanists had not been able to do: he gives the vision of human dominion its connection with the empirical science he advocated and inspired. Nature's laws cannot be ignored or set aside or breached. They must be understood if humanity is to exercise realistic power over nature.[149] This is Bacon's famous doctrine that 'knowledge is power':[150]

> For man is but the servant and interpreter of nature: what he does and what he knows is only what he has observed of nature's order in fact or in thought . . . For the chain of causes cannot by any force be loosed or broken, nor can nature be commanded except by being obeyed. And so those twin objects, human Knowledge and human Power, do really meet in one: and it is from ignorance of causes that operation fails.[151]

---

[146] *De Interpretatione Naturae Prooemium*, in Bacon, *Works* III: 518, translated in Rossi, *Francis Bacon*, p. 193.

[147] Cf. Bacon, *Works* III: 217–18; IV: 21.

[148] Cf. Rossi, *Francis Bacon*, p. 18.

[149] Cf. Rossi, *Francis Bacon*, p. 130.

[150] Farrington, *Philosophy of Francis Bacon*, p. 51; Rossi, *Francis Bacon*, p. 21.

[151] Bacon, *Works* IV: 32.

In this sense, Bacon advocates a kind of humility,[152] which sounds a different note from the rather more Promethean vision of some of the Italian humanists. It is the humility of the believing scientist, who respects the way God has made nature, studies its laws, and thereby gains the power over it that God intends humanity to have. In this sense, 'nature cannot be conquered except by obeying her'.[153] But the aim is certainly to conquer nature, and Bacon's vision of what it is possible for human power over nature to achieve is far from the limited medieval concept of imitating nature. He attacks the error 'of looking upon art [i.e. technology] as a kind of supplement to nature; which has power enough to finish what nature has begun or correct her when going aside, but no power to make radical changes, and shake her in the foundations'.[154]

The language of 'conquering' nature is not the least of Bacon's enduring bequests to modern western culture – a metaphor that came to be used standardly and unreflectively until the quite recent development of ecological consciousness made it questionable. As a typical expression of the nineteenth-century view, the following quotation from Thomas Carlisle is plainly in direct descent from Bacon: 'We war with rude nature; and, by our resistless engines, come off always victorious, and loaded with spoils.'[155]

It is significant that Bacon does not speak, like the Italian humanists, of human deification or of humanity as a kind of god over the world. He accuses traditional natural philosophy of the sin of pride in wanting to be god, because in his view it constructed an idea of nature out of the philosopher's imagination. The traditional natural philosopher created the world as he would have liked it to be – thereby playing God – instead of humbly observing the world that God has actually made, as Bacon's empirical scientist does.[156] In this sense, Bacon set the tone for the early modern scientific enterprise. Bacon's scientist is not a god who can recreate the world in any way he will, but he can by mastering the laws of nature subject it to the purpose for which God created it: human benefit. Bacon's achievement was to transfer the Renaissance vision of unlimited dominion away from its association with magic and alchemy, harnessing it instead to the practical pursuit

---

[152] *Valerius Terminus*, in Bacon, *Works* III: 224.
[153] *Thoughts and Conclusions*, in Farrington, *Philosophy of Francis Bacon*, p. 93.
[154] *Sketches of the Intellectual World*, in Bacon, *Works* V: 506.
[155] Quoted in Trevor Blackwell and Jeremy Seabrook, *The Revolt against Change* (London: Vintage, 1993), p. 24.
[156] *Historiae Naturalis*, in Bacon, *Works* V: 132–3.

of scientific knowledge and technological innovation, and to relate it to biblical and religious ideas in a way more congenial to Protestant England. But it is also significant that Bacon's formulation of the idea of human mastery of nature turned out to be easily secularized as the cultural impact of Christian belief steadily diminished in the centuries after his time. As Leiss puts it: '[Bacon's] contention that science shared with religion the burden of restoring man's lost excellence helped create the climate in which earthly hopes flourished at the expense of heavenly ones.'[157]

By comparison with the tradition, there seems a total loss of any sense that human beings belong within creation alongside other creatures: Bacon's humanity simply stands above nature, mastering it by knowledge and power. As in the Italian humanists, the vertical relationship entirely replaces the horizontal. Also by comparison with the tradition, the value of nature has become purely utilitarian: the notion that all creatures exist for the glory of God and thereby assist humanity's contemplation of God has disappeared in favour of nature's usefulness for practical human needs. Despite the continued reference to God the Creator, this is the point at which western attitudes to nature became exclusively anthropocentric rather than theocentric. Therefore it made little practical difference when atheistic scientists eventually took their place alongside believing scientists in the Baconian tradition.

The 'Judeo-Christian tradition' has often been praised or blamed for the so-called de-sacralization of nature in the western tradition. It has been praised for this by those who think the achievements of modern science were thereby made possible, and blamed by those who think the modern exploitation of nature – the root of the ecological crisis – was thereby made possible.[158] But we need to be clearer about the meaning of 'de-sacralization'.[159] The Judeo-Christian tradition certainly de-divinized nature. Nature is not reverenced as divine in a pantheistic or animistic sense. But deeply rooted in the Judeo-Christian tradition is the sense that all creatures exist for the glory of God and reflect the glory of God. Human beings both praise God along with the rest of creation and praise God for the beauty and

---

157 Leiss, *Domination*, p. 53.
158 White, 'Historical Roots,' p. 25; Toynbee, 'Religious Background,' pp. 145–8, who ascribes the ecological crisis to 'the monotheistic disrespect for nature' and recommends a return to pantheism as a remedy.
159 Cf. Passmore, *Man's Responsibility*, pp. 10–11; Wybrow, 'Old Testament,' pp. 80–3, who rightly argues that in the Old Testament nature is 'De-divinized but not De-animated'.

worth of the rest of creation in which they see the Creator's glory reflected. Only with the loss of this non-utilitarian sense of the value of creation for and in relation to God, in favour of an exclusively utilitarian view of nature as given by God for human beings to exploit for human benefit, can we properly speak of a de-sacralization of nature. This happened in the Baconian understanding of the relation of humanity to the rest of creation. Significantly, it is in the seventeenth-century Christian scientist Robert Boyle that we find a call for the de-sacralization of nature, explicitly linked with a Baconian understanding of the human dominion: 'The veneration wherewith men are imbued for what they call nature has been a discouraging impediment to the empire of man over the inferior creatures of God: for many have not only looked upon it, as an impossible thing to compass, but as something of impious to attempt.'[160]

Without the Baconian de-sacralization of nature, a scientific enterprise would have been possible, but not the actual scientific and technological enterprise of aggressive domination of nature which has been so significant a feature of modern western history.

Reading Bacon is to experience frequent shocks of recognition as one finds all too familiar features of the modern scientific enterprise already clearly stated by him. For example, Bacon already expressed the conviction so often voiced by contemporary scientists that scientific work itself is value-free and only its use can be right or wrong (with the implication, in contemporary discourse, that scientists are absolved of any responsibility for the use made of their discoveries):[161] 'light is in itself pure and innocent; it may be wrongly used, but cannot in its nature be defiled.'[162] Leiss comments: 'This clear separation of natural knowledge and moral knowledge gradually became a cardinal principle of modern thought: it echoes in the fashionable contemporary distinction between "facts" and "values," according to which questions of values constitute a unique discourse outside the scope of "scientific" knowledge.'[163]

---

[160] Quoted in Passmore, *Man's Responsibility*, p. 11.

[161] This argument is a smokescreen disguising the fact that most scientific work is commercially driven and directed to specific ends which those funding and usually those doing the research judge desirable. The effort devoted to discovering and developing techniques of cloning animals, for example, would not have been exerted by the scientists involved had they been convinced that such techniques could never rightly be used.

[162] *Thoughts and Conclusions*, in Farrington, *Philosophy of Francis Bacon*, p. 92, quoted in Leiss, *Domination*, p. 50.

[163] Leiss, *Domination*, p. 52.

Another instance has only recently become observable. In his scientific utopia, the *New Atlantis*, Bacon anticipates scientific manipulation of animals such as has only now become possible through genetic engineering:

> By art, likewise, we make them greater or taller than their kind is; and contrariwise dwarf them, and stay their growth: we make them more fruitful and bearing than their kind is; and contrariwise barren and not generative. Also we make them differ in colour, shape, activity, many ways. We find means to make commixtures and copulations of different kinds, and them not barren, as the general opinion is . . . Neither do we do this by chance, but we know beforehand of what matter and commixture what kind of those creatures will arise.[164]

Reading this one realises that the *ideology* of the modern project, as already fully propounded by Bacon, *entailed* such results. Bacon had no notion of the means by which these results would be achieved four centuries later, but he could anticipate the results because he coined the ideology that still inspires the scientists in our twenty-first-century laboratories of biotechnology. In this chapter I am attaching huge importance for the historical transformation of ideas of human dominion to the work of this one man, but it seems that the scale and enduring impact of his influence really does justify this.

At this point it may be useful to summarize what the historical evidence we have examined implies with regard to Lynn White's thesis. I have argued that the ideological roots of the modern western project of aggressive domination of nature are to be found in a traditional interpretation of the human dominion over nature which drew on Greek rather than biblical sources and which was subsequently, in the Renaissance, removed from its broader context in a Christian understanding of creation. The dominant theological interpretation of the dominion in patristic and medieval times in some respects prepared the way for the modern scientific and technological project of conquering nature for human benefit, but it could not itself have provided the ideological support and motivation for that project. Only the

---

[164] Francis Bacon, *The Great Instauration and New Atlantis* (ed. Jerry Weinberger; Arlington Heights, Illinois: AHM Publishing, 1980), p. 73. On biotechnology as fulfilling Bacon's project, see David F. Noble, *The Religion of Technology: The Divinity of Man and the Spirit of Invention* (New York: Penguin, 1999), ch. 11.

significantly new interpretations given to the human dominion in Renaissance humanism and English Baconianism accomplished that. The crucial new elements were the understanding of the human dominion as a historical task, not a static condition of things but a mandate for progressive achievement of mastery over nature, to be accomplished by scientific discovery and technological innovation; the loss of an effective doctrine of creation, such that the human relationship to other creatures as fellow-creatures gave way to an exclusively vertical relationship of humans to nature; and the reduction of the value of nature to the purely utilitarian, orientated only to practical human benefit.

Domination of Nature after Bacon

A history of the idea of 'mastery of nature' after Bacon remains to be written.[165] It certainly passed through the Baconianism of seventeenth-century English scientists into general modern thinking about science, technology and their place in the utopian idea of human progress that developed at the time of the European Enlightenment and became *the* ideology of the modern west. As we have already indicated, essentially Bacon's ideas prevailed. It was as though he had already expressed all that the modern age felt it necessary to be thought about this concept. According to Leiss:

> No outstanding thinker after Bacon devoted comparable attention to the concept of mastery over nature. In the ensuing period it undergoes little further development, even though it is more and more frequently employed. The measure of Bacon's achievement is that most of those who followed him have found the form in which he cast this concept to be sufficient for their own purposes. So definitive was his work that the history of all subsequent stages in the career of this idea down to the present can be arranged as a set of variations on a Baconian theme.[166]

There is, for example, a frequently quoted passage from Descartes' *Discourse on Method* (1637) in which he adopts a thoroughly Baconian

---

[165] Probably Leiss, *Domination*, ch. 4, is the nearest we yet have to this, though he admits it is no more than a 'fragmental biography of the idea' (p. 95). The main concern of Leiss's book is the way in which the domination of nature developed the domination of other humans as a corollary. This is a very important aspect which cannot, unfortunately, be investigated in our present context.

[166] Leiss, *Domination*, p. 71, cf. p. 79.

approach to 'practical philosophy', by which humans will 'render ourselves masters and possessors of nature',[167] but the passage is unique in Descartes' works. It was apparently an idea to which he felt no need to give more detailed attention, so thoroughly was he ready to take it over and to take it for granted.

However, one very important 'variation on a Baconian theme' which has emerged more recently and could only have emerged much later than Bacon's own time, because it depends on the nineteenth- and twentieth-century idea of the evolution of life, is the notion that scientists are becoming masters of the evolutionary process (not least human evolution), taking control of it and directing it. This idea has become especially plausible with the rapidly emerging possibilities of manipulating genes and changing the genetic basis of species. This particular variation of Baconianism makes sense in the context, as we have already noticed, of biotechnological research deeply imbued with and motivated by the Baconian ideology of dominion.

We have already noted that, despite its religious colouring, Bacon's vision could easily enough be secularized, and the same could be said for the explicitly more Promethean Renaissance humanist one. For both, God enters into the human relationship with nature only in that he is believed to have granted humanity dominion. God sets no limits to the dominion, so that in effect humans play the role of God in relation to the world. The loss of truly divine transcendence left the human quasi-divine transcendence over the world in place. Whether as creative gods or as conquerors through knowledge, human beings were already thought to have the destiny of subjecting nature wholly to their will. With the Enlightenment they merely took for themselves the destiny they had previously received from God. In doing so, however, they rejected altogether the Christian doctrine of creation, with its potential for a quite different perception of the human relationship to nature.

Leiss argues that the secularization of the notion of human dominion freed it from moral constraints:

> Lynn White's argument must be qualified to this extent, namely, that Christian doctrine sought to restrain man's earthly ambitions by holding him accountable for his conduct to a higher authority. So long as Christianity remained a vital social force in Western civilization, the

---

[167] *The Philosophical Works of Descartes*, vol. 1 (trans. E. Haldane and G. Ross; New York: Dover Books, 1955), p. 119, quoted in Leiss, *Domination*, p. 81.

notion of man as lord of the earth was interpreted in the context of a wider ethical framework. Religion's declining fortunes, however, led to the gradual secularization of this notion in imperceptible stages, and in contemporary usage it reveals few traces of its Judaeo-Christian background.[168]

This may not be entirely accurate. In Bacon's idea the achievement of human dominion is motivated, as we have seen, by an ethic of service to humanity, which has retained its force in scientific endeavour alongside other ideals and motivations. But the ethic in this case is purely humanistic, entirely subjecting nature to the good of humanity. There is no sense of the value of the natural world in itself or an ethical obligation to respect this value. This is what was lost with the loss of a doctrine of creation.

Moreover, in stepping outside a religious doctrine of creation, the western project of dominating nature sidestepped not only the issue of ethical obligation to nature but also that of limits given in the created order of things. Both Bacon's recognition that nature's laws must be understood if nature is to be exploited (so that presumably nature's laws set limits to the kind of exploitation that is possible) and the Renaissance sense that humanity has unlimited creative power to unleash nature's potentialities have fed into the modern project, investing science with hugely utopian expectations and also inspiring the hubris that overreaches its capacities and brings unforeseen and disastrous consequences into being. In the late twentieth century it became more and more obvious that the Baconian dream had a powerful element of unreason hidden in its apparent rationality. This 'cunning of unreason', as Leiss calls it, is revealed in the persistent illusion that the undertaking known as 'the mastery of nature' is itself mastered.[169]

Finally, we should note that the secularization of the project of domination left it exposed to commercialization and consumerization. It is this that has fatally compromised the humanist ethical goal to be found in its more admirable versions. The satisfaction of human needs and the curing of human ills have proved too limited as goals for the exploitation of nature. Descartes envisaged 'the invention of an infinity of arts and crafts which enable us to enjoy without any trouble the fruits of the earth and all the good things which are to be found

---

[168] Leiss, *Domination*, pp. 34–5, cf. p. 54.
[169] Leiss, *Domination*, p. 23.

there'.[170] But he did not recognize how human desires would have to be manufactured to require the unlimited products of technology. Insatiable desires must match unlimited dominion in a spiral that makes the direction of causality quite obscure. This is where ethical as well as other limits fall away and disregard of nature's own inherent limits finally makes them disastrously evident.

An Alternative Modern Tradition: Dominion as Stewardship

The understanding of the human dominion over nature that has become most popular among Christians in the context of the contemporary ecological crisis, representing a new consciousness of ecological responsibilities in the churches, is the idea of stewardship. This is often thought to be more thoroughly rooted in the Christian tradition than it really is. A recognition that the world is God's creation and that this imposes ethical limits on human dominion over it (for example, inhibiting cruelty to animals) had, as we have seen, a place in the Christian tradition, however much in tension it might seem to be to the dominant view. But where the medieval and even Reformation commonplace that the rest of creation was created by God for human benefit held sway, we cannot speak of stewardship. The latter idea means rather that human beings have been entrusted by God with the care of creatures not primarily existing for human benefit. This is not just a restraint on dominion but a different idea of dominion, which it is hard to find clearly expressed before the late seventeenth century.[171]

The stewardship concept seems to have been a response to the growing sense of human control over nature, which had also prompted the Italian humanist and Baconian interpretations of the dominion. Consciously or unconsciously, it provided an alternative, in the

---

[170] Descartes, *Philosophical Works*, vol. 1, p. 119, quoted in Leiss, *Domination*, p. 81.

[171] Cf. Passmore, *Man's Responsibility*, pp. 28–31. Attfield, 'Christian Attitudes', and *Ethics*, ch. 3, argues against Passmore and claims to offer evidence for a strong tradition of stewardship through the patristic and medieval periods. But his definition of stewardship seems to me unhelpfully vague, and the fact that he can apparently include even Francis Bacon within a stewardship tradition seems to undermine his case considerably. Calvin's use of the image of stewardship for the way humans should treat all their possessions (quoted in Lawrence Osborn, *Guardians of Creation* [Leicester: Apollos, 1993], pp. 141–2) does not imply the inherent value of these things and does not contradict his belief that God created all things for human use and benefit; it merely limits the individual's use of what God intended for the benefit of all people.

England of the Royal Society, to the excessively anthropocentric Baconian view. Those who espoused it shared the contemporary enthusiasm for the extension of human control over nature, but instead of thinking purely of a human right to use nature for human benefit, they maintained also a human responsibility to care for nature, since, as George Hughes put it, man's rule is 'subordinate and stewardly, not absolutely to do as he list with God's creatures'.[172] In other words, almost for the first time, the dominion was being interpreted in a way that acknowledged ethical obligations arising from nature's inherent value.

Although this idea seems to have been relatively popular in religious writers of the second half of the seventeenth century,[173] it was the eminent English lawyer Matthew Hale (1609–76) who gave it fullest expression. Hale, like some of his contemporaries, is clear that the world was not created solely for human benefit, but for God's glory.[174] Humanity is 'the Steward and Tenant of Almighty God',[175] appointed to manage the earth on God's behalf, responsible to God for their treatment of it:

> In relation . . . to this inferior World of Brutes and Vegetables, the End of Man's Creation was, that he should be the Vice-Roy of the great God of heaven and earth in this inferior World; his Steward, Villicus, Bayliff or Farmer of this goodly Farm of the lower World, and reserved to himself the supreme Dominion, and the Tribute of Fidelity, Obedience, and Gratitude, as the greatest recognition or Rent for the same, making his Usufructuary of this inferior World to husband and order it, and enjoy the Fruits thereof with sobriety, moderation, and thankfulness.
>
> And hereby Man was invested with power, authority, right, dominion, trust, and care, to correct and abridge the excesses and cruelties of the fiercer Animals, to give protection and defence to the mansuete and useful, to preserve the Species of divers Vegetables, to improve them and others, to correct the redundance of unprofitable Vegetables, to preserve the face of the Earth in beauty, usefulness, and fruitfulness.[176]

Hale presupposes that nature left to itself would be chaotic: fierce animals would render the gentler and more useful animals extinct, the

---

[172] Quoted in Thomas, *Man*, p. 155.
[173] Cf. Thomas, *Man*, pp. 154–5, 180, 359 n. 23.
[174] Glacken, *Traces*, p. 405.
[175] Quoted in Glacken, *Traces*, p. 405.
[176] Quoted in Glacken, *Traces*, p. 481.

earth would be submerged in marsh and overgrown with trees and weeds. The earth needs a superior creature to keep it in order. Humanity's duty is therefore to keep things in balance, to prevent the wilder aspects of nature from creating chaos. Human beings are to control the earth for the earth's sake as well as for their own sake.[177] The prejudice that nature controlled and managed by humanity is preferable to wilderness, a prejudice from which since classical times few except the hermits had been free, is still dominant here. Human control improves nature. Technology is justified as an instrument of humanity's beneficent stewarding of the world. As yet there is no admission that human control of nature might be destructive, that wilderness might be better left alone, that nature might have its own order which human interference turns to chaos and its own balance that technology might upset.

The value of the notion of stewardship was that it formally intro-duced the notion of justice into the human relationship to nature. It is no accident that Hale was a lawyer. As steward responsible to the divine King, humanity has legal obligations to administer the earth justly and without cruelty.[178] If the concept of stewardship did nothing to preserve wild nature from human interference, it was significantly linked with an apparently growing Christian sensitivity about cruelty to animals.[179] Matthew Hale himself was one of those who thought it unjustified to chase and to kill animals for mere sport.[180] He decided to put his aged horses out to graze, rather than selling them to the knackers.[181] Other living creatures have a value in themselves and a right to life that human beings, as their responsible superintendents, must respect and protect.[182] Even the right of human beings to kill ani-mals for food was being doubted by the late seventeenth century, and Hale, though he maintained that right, admitted that the sight of sheep grazing always made him feel God must have intended 'a more innocent kind of food for man'.[183]

The appeal of the notion of stewardship is that it recognizes value in the non-human creation other than its usefulness to humanity and gives humanity obligations to treat the non-human creation accordingly, while

---

[177] Glacken, *Traces*, pp. 480–2.
[178] Glacken, *Traces*, p. 481.
[179] Thomas, *Man*, pp. 173–81.
[180] Thomas, *Man*, p. 162.
[181] Thomas, *Man*, p. 190.
[182] Thomas, *Man*, p. 279.
[183] Thomas, *Man*, p. 293.

at the same time recognizing the unique degree of power over the rest of creation which human beings wield in modern times. However, it should be noticed that it sets human beings over nature just as emphatically as Italian humanism and Baconianism did. In that sense it shares not only the early modern period's exclusively positive evaluation of human control over nature but also its concentration on the vertical relationship of 'superior' humanity to 'inferior' nature at the expense of the horizontal relationship of human beings to their fellow-creatures.

In the recent Christian revival of the notion of stewardship,[184] it seems to be a rather flexible term. It is, for example, employed on all sides of the debate about biotechnology. For some, deeply involved in the recent development in genetic science and technology, such as Francis Collins, director of the Human Genome Project, Donald Munro and V. Elving Anderson, stewardship seems to be the Christian notion that authorizes an uninhibitedly Baconian project.[185] It mandates the scientific task of unlimited improvement of creation. On the other hand, in the *Evangelical Declaration on the Care of Creation*[186] the role of human stewards is not portrayed as improving nature, but as preserving and protecting it. (The stress therefore comes close to Lawrence Osborn's preferred image of 'guardians' of creation,[187] Loren Wilkinson's 'earthkeeping'[188] or even Andrew Linzey's 'servants' of creation.)[189] Here the emphasis is more on the givenness of the created order rather than on human intervention to change nature. It is not that nature needs human protection from its own destructiveness, but that it needs protection and healing from human abuse of it. Stewardship here has acquired a late-twentieth-century content, along with somewhat chastened and humbled aims by comparison with the technological confidence it expressed in the seventeenth century. But the fact that, in the words of others, it retains precisely that original force shows that without further definition, involving relationship to other

---

[184] See, e.g. Douglas John Hall, *Imaging God: Dominion as Stewardship* (Grand Rapids: Eerdmans, 1987); Cooper, *Green Christianity*, ch. 2; *Earthkeeping in the Nineties: Stewardship of Creation* (ed. Loren Wilkinson; Grand Rapids: Eerdmans, 1991; rev. edn of *Earthkeeping: Christian Stewardship of Natural Resources*, 1980); Osborn, *Guardians*, ch. 8; C.A. Russell, *The Earth, Humanity and God* (London: UCL Press, 1994), pp. 146–8.

[185] Noble, *Religion*, pp. 194–200.

[186] Berry, *Care*, pp. 18–22.

[187] Osborn, *Guardians*. The image comes from Heidegger.

[188] Wilkinson, *Earthkeeping*.

[189] Andrew Linzey, *Animal Theology* (London: SCM Press, 1994), ch. 3.

biblical and Christian themes, the idea of stewardship itself may not be very helpful.

One problem with the concept of stewardship[190] today may be highlighted by referring to the now widespread agreement that we urgently need to protect wilderness, nature free from human interference insofar as any part of nature still remains that. Of course, it is true that wilderness can now survive only if humans protect it from human interference. But, unlike nature farmed and modified by humans, the value of wilderness is wholly independent of any human part in it. Protecting the last great wildernesses – Antarctica and the depths of the oceans, not to speak of the moon – is a challenge humans have scarcely faced before in history. Until recently wildernesses were just always there outside the sphere of human habitation, feared by most, loved by the remarkable few, the hermits and the monks, who chose to live with wild nature. The question now is whether, now that humans have the power to interfere everywhere on earth (and even beyond), we can learn to care without interfering, simply to keep away and to keep our hands off, and to do so not so that we still have wildernesses to visit as eco-friendly tourists, but actually because God's other creatures have their own value for God and for themselves, quite independently of us. For this purpose it may be that the image of stewardship is still too freighted with the baggage of the modern project of technological domination of nature. Can we entirely free it of the implication that nature is always better off when managed by us, that nature needs our benevolent intrusions, that it is our job to turn the whole world into a well-tended garden inhabited by well-cared-for pets? The problem is in part that stewardship remains, like most interpretations of the Genesis 'dominion' and as we have already suggested, an image that depicts the human relationship to the rest of creation in an entirely 'vertical' way. It sets humans above the rest of creation, sharply differentiated from it, in God-given charge of it. As far as the resources of Christian history goes, it needs at least to be supplemented by the medieval Christian awareness, vividly expressed in many of the stories of saints and animals and never more fully realized than by Francis of Assisi, of mutuality, interdependence, friendliness and confraternity between human beings and the other creatures of God.

---

[190] For criticisms of the idea of stewardship, cf. Northcott, *Environment*, p. 129; Worster, *Wealth*, pp. 187–8; Hugh Spanner, 'Tyrants, Stewards – or Just Kings?,' in Linzey and Yamamoto, *Animals*, pp. 222–3.

3.

Reading the Synoptic Gospels Ecologically

Few of those who have written about the ecological dimension of the Bible have found much to say about the Synoptic Gospels.[1] It may be that, as Robert Murray comments, Jesus' relationship to the non-human creation is not 'a salient theme in the gospels',[2] but, alternatively, it may be that, especially when the Gospels are read with their relation to the Old Testament in view, there are significant references to the non-human creation that have not been given the attention they deserve. It may be that, in the case of the Gospels, the eyes of modern urban readers still need to be opened to that dimension of human life, our relationship to the non-human environment and its creatures, that to the biblical writers was self-evidently of huge importance.

In this chapter I shall explore two approaches to identifying the ecological dimensions of the story of Jesus in the Synoptic Gospels. (I shall not be concerned to distinguish 'the historical Jesus' from the Jesus of the Gospels, but with the way in which the Gospels depict Jesus and his story.) The first approach attempts to make explicit the Palestinian ecological context that the Gospels largely take for granted, in the hope of discovering something of Jesus' relationship with it. The second approach works with the theme of the kingdom of God,

---

[1] Notable exceptions include Robert Faricy, *Wind and Sea Obey Him* (London: SCM Press, 1982), pp. 40–8; Northcott, *Environment*, pp. 224–5; Adrian M. Leske, 'Matthew 6.25–34: Human Anxiety and the Natural World', in *The Earth Story in the New Testament* (ed. Norman C. Habel and Vicky Balabanski; Earth Bible 5; Sheffield: Sheffield Academic Press, 2002), pp. 15–27; William Loader, 'Good News – For the Earth? Reflections on Mark 1.1–15', in Habel and Balabanski, *Earth Story in the New Testament*, pp. 28–43; and some other essays in the same volume.

[2] Murray, *Cosmic Covenant* (Heythrop Monographs 7; London: Sheed & Ward, 1997), p. 126.

unquestionably the central theme of Jesus' teaching and ministry in the Synoptic Gospels, in order to show that the kingdom includes the whole of creation and that some of the acts in which Jesus anticipated the coming kingdom point to the redemption of the human relationship with the rest of creation.

Jesus in His Ecological Context

In a chapter called 'Jesus and the Ecology of Galilee',[3] Sean Freyne has recently characterized the 'micro-ecologies' that distinguished the three regions of Galilee – Lower (including Nazareth), the Valley (including Capernaum and the lakeside) and Upper (including Caesarea Philippi) – along with the 'different modes of human interaction with, and different opinions about the natural world'[4] that the three different environments produced. Freyne sees Jesus' ministry as taking place successively in these three regions, and suggests ways in which the ecological character of each may have influenced Jesus' thought and teaching. It has to be said that many of these suggestions are very speculative, while some are illuminating and others at least plausible.

It is probable, for example, that the term 'the sea', used by Mark and Matthew to refer to the lake of Galilee, reflects the usage of those who lived beside it and were unconcerned with the Mediterranean, while the story of the stilling of the storm reflects the threat of the mythological abyss on the part of people whose lives were dominated by water, its possibilities and dangers. It is also plausible that Jesus' faith in the Creator God of the Hebrew Scriptures, who cares for his creation and overcomes the ever-threatening chaos, engaged at this point with the consciousness, at once realistic and mythic, of the local fishermen who were his disciples.[5] (The stilling of the storm will be discussed further in the last main section of this chapter.)

On the other hand, I am not tempted by this suggestion: 'One is tempted to ask whether Jesus' healing ministry, attested in all the gospels, might have given him a special appreciation of the climatic

---

[3] Sean Freyne, *Jesus, a Jewish Galilean: A New Reading of the Jesus-Story* (London: T&T Clark [Continuum], 2004), ch. 2.

[4] Freyne, *Jesus*, p. 40.

[5] Freyne, *Jesus*, p. 53.

conditions of the Lake area, and the quality of its water, prompting a visit to its source [Mount Hermon].'[6] Nothing in the stories of Jesus' healings offers the slightest hint of a regard for the health-giving quality of the water of the lake. There is nothing like Elisha's command to Naaman to wash in the Jordan (2 Kgs. 5:10) or the Johannine Jesus' command to the blind man to wash in the pool of Siloam (John 9:7). Freyne does not answer the question he says 'one is tempted to ask', but one may also question whether such an excessively speculative question is even worth asking. It seems to be a strained attempt to forge a link between Jesus and some aspects of the lake of Galilee and Mount Hermon that we know interested some ancient writers. This example is among the least plausible of Freyne's suggestions.

Freyne is surely right in general to argue that Jesus' thought and teaching were influenced by his natural environment, its diversity and the various ways Galileans made a living from it. He was not a bookish intellectual but a man consciously embedded in his rural environment. But Freyne is also right to insist that we need not play off Jesus' direct experience of his environment against the rootedness of his beliefs in the Hebrew Scriptures and Jewish religious tradition (especially, in this case, faith in God as Creator of all things). The parables, he says, 'are the product of a religious imagination that is deeply grounded in the world of nature and the human struggle with it, and at the same time deeply rooted in the traditions of Israel which speak of God as creator of heaven and earth and all that is in them'.[7]

It is also important to note that Freyne does not, like some nineteenth-century writers,[8] depict Jesus' relationship to nature as a romantic idyll. Many of Jesus' references to the non-human world are to the hard work of making a living from the soil or the lake, and the parables also show awareness of the increasingly precarious state of small landowners, hard pressed or deprived of their land as large estates became more numerous.[9]

---

[6] Freyne, *Jesus*, p. 56.

[7] Freyne, *Jesus*, p. 59; cf. also p. 48. Similarly, Edward P. Echlin, *Earth Spirituality: Jesus at the Centre* (New Alresford: Arthur James, 1999), p. 76: Jesus' 'sensitivity to nature, so vivid in his parables, derived from living close to the natural world and from familiarity with the Jewish Scriptures and their metaphors of cosmic order.'

[8] See especially Ernest Renan, *Renan's Life of Jesus* (trans. William G. Hutchinson; London: Walter Scott, 1905), pp. 42–4.

[9] Freyne, *Jesus*, pp. 45–6. On this point with regard to the parables, see also V. George Shillington, 'Engaging with the Parables,' in *Jesus and His Parables: Interpreting the Parables of Jesus Today* (ed. V. George Shillington; Edinburgh: T&T Clark, 1997), pp. 1–20, here 9–11.

Freyne's method is a historical one, drawing on archaeology and literary sources to reconstruct the ecology of Galilee in Jesus' time. As in much historiography, historical imagination is required to make the links with Jesus. But Edward Echlin's approach is more creatively imaginative. He speaks of 'imaginative contemplation' in which we can make the 'implicit' in the Gospels (as in the rest of the Bible) 'explicit.'[10] 'When we contemplate the testimonies to Jesus looking for insights we will catch glimpses in the depths, in the small print, in what is hidden, between the lines, tacit and silent.'[11]

The following passage, imagining Jesus' early years in Nazareth, shows how Echlin takes up hints in the Gospels to paint the sort of picture they make no attempt to provide, but which Echlin, a former Jesuit, aptly places in the tradition of the imaginative meditations in Ignatius Loyola's *Spiritual Exercises*:

> With imagination we may place ourselves in hilly Nazareth with its few hundred families and their sheep and goats, oxen, cattle and donkeys. In those green and brown and stony hills we may imaginatively observe the growing Jesus (Lk. 2.40, 52) learning, especially from his mother, about the useful elder trees, the scattered Tabor oaks and Aleppo pine, the nettle, bramble, mallow, and startling yellow chrysanthemums of April, the galaxy of weeds and herbs and wild flowers which he later compared to Solomon's attire. Grapes grow and grew in Nazareth's old town, their branches nourished by the everlasting vine. Jesus wondered at their rapid growth, their ripening in the burning sun, and their harsh winter pruning, he learned about apples, almonds and pomegranates, he saw figs swarming from rocks offering two, even three crops of dripping sweetness. When they began to put out leaves, as did the other trees, he knew that summer was here (Lk. 21.20).[12]

This may seem novelistic, but something like this must indeed have been the case for Jesus, as for any boy growing up in the villages of Lower Galilee. In principle, this kind of filling in of the environmental context of Jesus that the Gospels take for granted or ignore is no different from the way that historical Jesus scholars routinely fill in the social, economic, political and religious contexts of first-century

---

[10] Echlin, *Earth Spirituality*, pp. 26–7, 30, 32, 54–5.

[11] Echlin, *Earth Spirituality*, p. 29, cf. p. 54.

[12] Echlin, *Earth Spirituality*, p. 55. It is interesting to compare this account of Jesus' environment in his early years in Nazareth with Renan's: Renan's, *Life of Jesus*, pp. 17–18. Renan's is more romantically aesthetic, Echlin's more ecological.

Jewish Palestine to which events of the gospel narratives relate. Imaginative as it is, an exercise like this could, paradoxically perhaps, also be an exercise in historical realism.

The wealth of references to flora, wild and cultivated, and fauna, wild and domesticated, as well as to common farming practices, in the synoptic teaching of Jesus has, of course, often been taken to indicate Jesus' closeness to the natural and rural world of Galilee, but I know of no systematic study of the matter. In an admittedly rapid survey, I find the following animals mentioned, each at least once: bird, camel, chicken (cock and hen), dog, donkey, dove, fish, fox, gnat, goat, moth, ox, pig, raven, scorpion, sheep, snake, sparrow, viper, vulture, wolf (21). Of these, eight are domestic animals. None is especially surprising in a rural Palestinian environment. The following are the plants to which the synoptic teaching of Jesus refers: bramble, fig tree, herbs (mint, dill, cummin, rue and others), mulberry, mustard plant, reed, thorn, vine, weed, wheat, wild flower. Methods of making a living from this environment, mentioned in Jesus' teaching, include arboriculture, viticulture, shepherding, trapping animals, netting birds, and the various stages of growing and processing wheat and other grains. Of course, this basic information could be expanded to include the frequency of mention of the various items, and evidence of familiarity with natural and farming processes, animal behaviour and so forth. References to the weather and its bearing on the farming activities of Jesus' Galilean contemporaries are another such topic for which the information could be assembled and discussed.

Most of these references, of course, function in the teaching of Jesus, not as literal references, but as figurative comparisons, and even the factual references are made for the sake of a religious point. Broadly similar phenomena are common in the prophets, the psalms and wisdom literature. So the question arises whether such material in the teaching of Jesus derives from direct observation of nature and farming or from the scriptural and oral traditional sources of Jesus' reflection and teaching. Vincent Mora, writing specifically about the animals in Matthew's Gospel, argues that almost all of these are used as symbols with deep roots in the Hebrew Scriptures.[13] This is, course, true for some of the material, such as the image of shepherd and sheep, but certainly not for all. To take just two examples of Matthean animals, that foxes have holes (8:20) and that pigs can be savage (7:6)

[13] Vincent Mora, *La Symbolique de la Création dans l'Évangile de Matthieu* (Lectio Divina 144; Paris: Cerf, 1991), pp. 18492.

are not observations to be found in the Hebrew Bible or in Jewish traditions known to us. As we have already noted that Freyne observes, there is no need to think of direct observation and traditional usage as exclusive alternatives.

With the range and frequency of allusions to nature in the synoptic teaching of Jesus it is perhaps instructive to compare the comparative rarity of such allusions in the Pauline letters. In the whole Pauline corpus (including the Pastorals) these animals occur: dog, lion, ox, snake, sheep (and Passover lamb), viper, wild animals, along with a general reference to birds, animals and reptiles. Only the following plants occur: olive tree, vine, wheat and other grains. Although ancient cities were much more closely connected with the natural and cultivated environment outside them than modern cities are, it does seem likely that the contrast between Jesus and Paul in this respect reflects the urban context of both Paul and his readers and hearers, by contrast with the mostly rural context of Jesus' life and ministry. The contrast shows that the range and frequency of allusions to nature in the synoptic teaching of Jesus are not merely what one might expect from any Jewish teacher acquainted with the Scriptures and Jewish religious traditions.

This whole issue merits much closer and more careful study. But, even if we suppose that Jesus' teaching drew extensively on his own close familiarity with the nature and farming practices of rural Galilee, we may still ask what the significance of this might be. With few exceptions, all these references have a figurative function: they do not seem to function to teach Jesus' hearers anything about the natural world itself or human relationships with it, but serve to make points about God and human life. However, there are some suggestions in the literature that could indicate otherwise. C.H. Dodd, having observed that the parables are realistic stories, true to nature and to life,[14] rather than artificial allegories, writes:

> There is a reason for this realism of the parables of Jesus. It arises from a conviction that there is no mere analogy, but an inward affinity, between the natural order and the spiritual order; or as we might put it in the language of the parables themselves, the Kingdom of God is intrinsically *like* the process of nature and of the daily life of men. Jesus

---

[14] On the realism of the parables, see especially Charles W. Hedrick, *Parables as Poetic Fictions: The Creative Voice of Jesus* (Peabody, Massachusetts: Hendrickson, 1994), ch. 3.

therefore did not feel the need of making up artificial illustrations for the truths He wished to teach. He found them ready-made by the Maker of man and nature.[15]

Claus Westermann understands the way parables work differently from Dodd, but he also argues that, like the 'comparisons' in the Old Testament with which he compares them, the parables of Jesus, by drawing their comparisons from the world of creation, 'assign great significance to God's creation in the context of what the Bible says about God'.[16] These are claims that need much fuller investigation before they can be confidently accepted or rejected.

Sean Freyne makes a related but somewhat different point:

> Part of the genius of Jesus' parable-making is his ability to take everyday experiences, such as sowing and reaping and weave these into narratives that are at one and the same time highly realistic in terms of his hearers' world and their experiences *and* deeply resonant of Yahweh's activity on behalf of Israel as this had been described in the psalms and the prophets. For peasant hearers their everyday work and experiences were being elevated to a symbolic level with reference to God's caring presence to Israel, as was the case also with the proverbial wisdom in the Hebrew Scriptures. The element of surprise and dislocation that many of these stories contain was intended to challenge the hearers to reconsider their understanding of God and his dealings with Israel, and to experience his presence in the world of the everyday, the world of home, village, field, sky and mountain.[17]

This feature of the parables of Jesus could be highlighted by a comparison with the rabbinic parables. Though these share motifs with the parables of Jesus, they are much less connected with the everyday world (natural and occupational) of ordinary people. This down-to-earth and small-scale character of the stories Jesus told could also be associated with Jesus' miracles (healings, exorcisms and nature miracles) and significant acts (such as eating with sinners): both in his teaching and his activity Jesus proclaimed and embodied the kingdom of God in small-scale instances within the lives of ordinary

---

[15] Charles Harold Dodd, *The Parables of the Kingdom* (rev. edn; Glasgow: Fontana [Collins], 1961), p. 20.

[16] Claus Westermann, *The Parables of Jesus in the Light of the Old Testament* (Edinburgh: T&T Clark, 1990), p. 202.

[17] Freyne, *Jesus*, p. 59.

people. These people's relationship to the natural world was a constant and determining feature of their lives, and this is reflected both in Jesus' parables and in his nature miracles.

Closeness and sensitivity to the natural environment would not, of course, make Jesus a modern ecologist. Echlin is clear about this: 'What emerges from the gospels is a villager within the Jewish tradition of holistic compassion and sustainable organic husbandry with people and animals on the land, working with and not against the ways of nature.'[18]

In other words, Echlin sees Jesus as embodying the best of the Jewish tradition, informed by the Hebrew Bible, with regard to attitudes to other living creatures and the environment. But this requires that we look for signs of the creation theology of the Hebrew Scriptures within the Synoptic teaching of Jesus. This is the starting-point for the next section of this chapter, in which we shall ask how creation theology might relate to the central theme of Jesus' teaching and ministry: the kingdom of God.

The Kingdom of God as the Renewal of Creation

Jesus presupposed the creation theology of the Hebrew Bible, centred on the belief that God created all things (cf. Matt. 19:9; Mark 10:6) and, as 'Lord of heaven and earth' (Luke 10:21; Matt. 11:25), cared for the whole of his creation. As we shall see, this was the presupposition of his teaching about the kingdom of God. But creation theology also appears explicitly at a number of key points in Jesus' theology:

1. To support his command to love enemies, Jesus uses the notion of imitation of God: 'so that you may be children of your Father in heaven; for he makes his sun rise on the evil and on the good, and sends rain on the righteous and on the unrighteous' (Matt. 5:45).[19] The God who generously and mercifully pours his blessings on all people without distinction is the Creator who, according to Psalm 145, 'is good to all, and his compassion is over all that he has made' (Ps. 145:9). He is the source of all the blessings of the natural world, including sun (Ps. 19:4–6) and rain (Pss. 65:9–11; 104:13; 147:8; Lev. 26:4).

---

[18] Echlin, *Earth Spirituality*, p. 78.
[19] Biblical quotations in this chapter are from the NRSV unless otherwise stated.

2. 'Are not two sparrows sold for a penny? Yet not one of them will fall to the ground unperceived by your Father. And even the hairs of your head are all counted. So do not be afraid; you are of more value than many sparrows' (Matt. 10:29–31; cf. Luke 12:6–7). While the point of this saying is to reassure the disciples of God's providential care for them, this rests on the assertion that God's providence embraces even the sparrows, whom humans value so cheaply that a pair costs a penny in the market. It is God who preserves each sparrow's life, and so not one sparrow can be caught in a hunter's net without his knowledge and consent. Jesus' words here reflect the view of the Hebrew Scriptures that God's caring responsibility embraces each living creature he has made (Job 12:10; Pss. 36:6; 104:29–30).[20]

3. 'Look at the birds of the air; they neither sow nor reap nor gather into barns, and yet your heavenly Father feeds them. Are you not of more value than they? . . . Consider the lilies of the field, how they grow; they neither toil nor spin, yet I tell you, even Solomon in all his glory was not clothed like one of these. But if God so clothes the grass of the field, which is alive today and tomorrow is thrown into the oven, will he not much more clothe you . . .?' (Matt. 6:26,28–30; cf. Luke 12:24,27–8). Again, this is an argument from the lesser (wild flowers and birds) to the greater (human), but again the lesson for Jesus' hearers cannot be had without the premise that God cares for birds and wild flowers. That God feeds the birds (as he does all living creatures) is explicit in the Hebrew Bible (Ps. 147:9; Job 38:41; cf. Pss. 104:27–8; 145:15–16). Humans can trust in God's provision because they too are members, even if eminent members, of the community of God's creatures for whom he generously provides.

4. Probably Jesus' hearers would also have understood his parables of growth (Mark 4:3–8,26–32; and parallels) in terms of Jewish creation theology. They would not have supposed the growth of grain or mustard plants to be some kind of autonomous natural process, but as due to the blessing of God (cf. 1 Cor. 3:6). Only through the blessing of God is his creation fruitful (Deut. 7:12; 26:15; 28:4–5; Pss. 65:9–11; 67:6; 107:38; cf. Gen. 1:22,28). So in these parables the comparison is between God-given growth in creation and the God-given growth of the kingdom of God, or, we might say, between the divine work of creation and the divine work of salvation and

---

[20] On this passage, and the Lukan parallel, see Chapter 4.

renewal. Also worth noticing at this point is the fact that the Psalms feature so prominently among the biblical sources of Jesus' creation theology. They would, of course, have been among the Scriptures best known to both Jesus and his hearers.

From these indications of the importance of creation theology to Jesus the question arises as to its relationship to his proclamation of the coming kingdom of God, which the Synoptic Gospels consider the overriding theme of his mission and teaching. Misunderstanding at this point has been fostered both by the tendency of scholars (enshrined in the so-called 'criterion of dissimilarity') to stress only what appears to be novel in the teaching of Jesus vis-à-vis Judaism, and also by the perception of some kind of opposition between creation and eschatology, as though the eschatological kingdom comes to abolish and replace creation. Instead, we should recognize the continuity between Jesus' teaching and the Scriptures and traditions of Judaism, without which what was novel in his teaching cannot be understood, and, crucially, that the kingdom of God in the teaching of Jesus represents not the abolition but the renewal of creation.

Just as Jesus' creation theology seems rooted especially in the Psalms, so also is his understanding of the kingdom of God, though Isaiah and Daniel are also important in this case. Most treatments of the background to the kingdom of God in the Gospels give no great prominence to the Psalms, but Bruce Chilton's work especially remedies this failure.[21] The kingship and rule of God are more prominent in the Psalms than in most other parts of the Hebrew Bible, and they are closely related to creation. It is as Creator that God rules his whole creation (Ps. 103:19–22). His rule is over all that he has made, human and otherwise (Pss. 95:4–5; 96:11–13), and it is expressed in the kind of caring responsibility for creation that we have already seen reflected also in the teaching of Jesus (Ps. 145). All non-human creatures acclaim his rule now (Pss. 103:19–22; 148) and all nations must come to do so in the future (Ps. 97:1), for God is coming to judge the world, that is, both to condemn and to save (Pss. 96:13; 98:9). His own people Israel's role is to declare his kingship to the nations (Pss. 96:3,10; 145:10–12). When God does come to judge and to rule, all creation will rejoice at his advent (Pss. 96:11–12; 98:7–8). (These last three sentences show how close these Psalms are to the message of Isa. 40 – 66, where the rule of God is also central.)

---

[21] Bruce Chilton, *Pure Kingdom: Jesus' Vision of God* (Grand Rapids: Eerdmans/London: SPCK, 1996), ch. 2.

The kingship and rule of God in the Psalms have both a spatial and a temporal dimension. They are cosmic in scope, encompassing all creation, by no means confined to human society. They are also eternal, established at creation and set to last forever (Pss. 93; 145:13; 146:10). Yet God's rule is widely flouted and rejected by the nations, and so it is still to come in the fullness of power and in manifest glory. The God who rules from his heavenly throne (Pss. 11:4; 103:19) is coming to establish his rule on earth. It is this coming that Jesus proclaims. His distinctive phrase, 'the kingdom of God comes', stands for the expectation of the psalms and the prophets that God himself is coming to reign.[22]

The cosmic scope of the kingdom can be seen in the opening three petitions of the Lord's Prayer in Matthew's version:

> Our Father in heaven,
>> hallowed be your name.
>> your kingdom come.
>> your will be done,
>>> on earth as it is in heaven (Matt. 6:9–10).

The phrase 'on earth as it is in heaven' should probably be understood to qualify all three of the petitions. Presently, God's name is perfectly hallowed, his rule perfectly obeyed, and his will absolutely done in heaven, but all are neglected or contested on earth. Probably the emphasis is on humans coming to hallow God's name, to acknowledge God's rule and to do his will, but we should recall that in the Hebrew Bible non-human creatures also do these things, often when humans fail to do so (e.g. praising God's name: Ps. 145:5,13; acclaiming his rule: Pss. 103:19–22; 145:10–11; doing his will: Jer. 8:7). Moreover, the coupling of 'heaven' and 'earth' cannot fail to evoke the whole creation, everything God created at the beginning (Gen. 1:1; 2:1,4). God, it was standardly said, is the Creator of heaven and earth, and this is the basis on which his kingdom must come on earth as it is in heaven. The kingdom does not come to extract people from the rest of creation, but to renew the whole creation in accordance with God's perfect will for it.

As well as proclaiming and explaining the kingdom of God, Jesus instantiated it in the many activities of his ministry. These included

---

[22] John P. Maier, *A Marginal Jew: Rethinking the Historical Jesus*, vol. 2: *Mentor, Message, and Miracles* (New York: Doubleday, 1994), pp. 298–9.

the miracles of healing, exorcisms and the so-called 'nature' miracles. They also included significant acts such as his demonstration in the temple, sharing meals with sinners, blessing children, washing the disciples' feet, and riding a donkey into Jerusalem. All these activities are to be understood as proleptic instances of the coming of the kingdom, helping to define how Jesus understood the rule of God, but more than just symbols of its coming. In such activities the kingdom was actually coming, but in anticipatory fashion, in small-scale instances. Their small-scale nature comports with the way most of the parables represent the kingdom by events set in the ordinary world of Jesus' hearers. Just as a mustard plant, in the parable, grows to the dimensions of the mythical world tree, so, when Jesus stills the storm, a squall on the lake evokes the vast destructive power of the mythical abyss. Just as the extraordinary generosity of God in his coming kingdom is figured, in the parable, when a master serves dinner to his slaves, so it takes place when Jesus pronounces the forgiveness of a notorious sinner who washed his feet.

The activities of Jesus were small-scale anticipations of the kingdom that heralded its universal coming in the future. What is notable about them, for our purposes, is the way that their holistic character points to the coming of the kingdom in all creation. Jesus brought wholeness to the lives of the people he healed and delivered: reconciling them to God, driving the power of evil from their lives, healing diseased bodies, making good crippling disabilities, restoring social relationships to those isolated by their misfortune, while of those who had everything he required much. Some at least of the nature miracles anticipate the transformation of human relationships with the non-human world in the renewed creation. In the feeding miracles God's generous provision for his people through the gifts of creation takes place even in the barren wilderness, as had happened in the first exodus (Ps. 78:15–16, 23–5) and was expected for the new exodus (Isa. 35:1,6–7;[23] 41:18–19; 51:3; cf. Ezek. 34:26–39). When Jesus walks on the water and stills the storm, God's unique sovereignty over the waters of chaos is evoked, with the expectation that in the renewed creation the destructive powers of nature will be finally quelled. While most of Jesus' activities focused on humans and human society in relation to God, there are sufficient indications that Jesus and the evangelists also

---

[23] It is noteworthy that in Isa. 35, the transformation of nature accompanies the healing of the blind, the deaf, the lame and the dumb (a passage to which Matt. 11:6 and Luke 7:22 allude).

embraced the fully inclusive understanding of God's rule over all creation that is so prominent in the Psalms.

Jesus and the Peaceable Kingdom

In the Hebrew Bible the desirable relationship between humans and other creatures is sometimes portrayed as peace. As Robert Murray points out, this may be either peace *from* or peace *with*.[24] Both speak to the threat that dangerous animals posed both to human life and to human livelihood (in the form of domestic animals). Peace *from* is the more pragmatic possibility, secured in the covenant with Noah by the fear of humans that came to characterize other creatures (Gen. 9:2). Peace *from* could also be secured simply by the absence of dangerous animals, like the absence of invading armies that is sometimes linked with it (Lev. 26:6; Ezek. 34: 25,28; cf. Hos. 2:18). The more positive state of peace *with* wild animals is a return to paradisal conditions. This is the relationship with dangerous animals that is portrayed in the well-known description of the messianic kingdom in Isaiah 11:6–9. This passage has often been misunderstood by modern readers as a picture simply of peace between animals. In fact, it depicts peace between the human world, with its domesticated animals (lamb, kid, calf, bullock, cow), and those wild animals (wolf, leopard, lion, bear, poisonous snakes) that were normally perceived as threats both to human livelihood and to human life. Humans appear in their most vulnerable form, as children, just as most of the domestic animals do (lamb, kid, etc.). This is a picture of reconciliation of the human world with the wild world, healed of the fear and violence that had been accepted, as a pragmatic compromise, in the Noahic covenant.

It is likely that the ecotopia envisaged in Isaiah 11 is the key to understanding the reference to wild animals in Mark's brief account of Jesus in the wilderness:

> He was in the wilderness forty days, tempted by Satan;
> and he was with the wild animals;
> and the angels ministered to him. (Mark 1:13, my translation)

Here Jesus goes into the wilderness, the realm outside of human habitation, in order to establish his messianic relationship with the

---

[24] Murray, *Cosmic Covenant*, pp. 34, 105.

non-human creatures. The order in which the three categories of them appear is significant. Satan is simply an enemy of Jesus and the angels simply his friends, but the wild animals, placed by Mark between the two, are enemies of whom Jesus makes friends. Jesus in the wilderness enacts, in an anticipatory way, the peace between the human world and wild nature that is the Bible's hope for the messianic future. Mark's simple but effective phrase ('he was with the wild animals') has no suggestion of hostility or resistance about it. It indicates Jesus' peaceable presence with the animals. The expression 'to be with someone' frequently has, in Mark's usage (3:14; 5:18; 14:67; cf. 4:36) and elsewhere, the sense of close, friendly association. (It may also be relevant that Genesis describes the animals in the ark as those who were 'with' Noah: Gen. 7:23; 8:1,17; 9:12.) Mark could have thought of the ideal relationship between wild animals and humans, here represented by their messianic king, as the restoration of dominion over them or as recruiting them to the ranks of the domestic animals who are useful to humans. But the simple 'with them' can have no such implication. Jesus befriends them. He is peaceably with them.[25]

A passage that evokes a very different aspect of messianic peace with the non-human world is the story of the stilling of the storm. According to Mark's version (4:35–41), Jesus 'rebuked the wind, and said to the sea, "Peace! Be still!" Then the wind ceased, and there was a dead calm' (4:39). The story evokes a mythical image that is widely reflected in the Hebrew Bible: the primeval waters, the destructive powers of nature imaged as a vast tempestuous ocean, which God in creation reduced to calm and confined within limits so that the world could be a stable environment for living creatures. These waters of chaos were not abolished by creation, only confined, always ready to break out and endanger creation, needing to be constantly restrained by the Creator. For ancient Israelites the waters of the mythical abyss were not simply a metaphysical idea. In something like a storm at sea, the real waters of the sea became the waters of chaos, threatening life and controllable only by God. In the case of this story, a squall on the lake of Galilee is enough to raise the spectre of elemental chaos.

When Mark says that Jesus 'rebuked the wind and said to the sea, "Peace! Be still!"', he recalls the most characteristic ways in which the Hebrew Bible speaks of God's subduing the waters of chaos. The

---

[25] I have argued at length for this interpretation in Chapter 5 of this volume. Among recent studies, this view is also taken by Joel Marcus, *Mark 1-8* (AB 27; New York: Doubleday, 1999), pp. 167–8.

'rebuke' is God's powerful word of command, as in Psalm 104:7: 'at your rebuke [the waters] flee.' The word that silences the storm occurs, among other places, in Job 26:12: 'By his power he stilled the Sea.' What Jesus enacts, therefore, is the Creator's pacification of chaos. In this small-scale instance he anticipates the final elimination of all forces of destruction that will distinguish the renewed creation from the present (cf. Isa. 27:1; Rev. 21:1).

A third instance in which Jesus anticipated the peaceable kingdom is his entry into Jerusalem riding a donkey (Mark 11:1–10 and parallels). As Matthew (21:5) makes explicit, Jesus here enacts the prophecy of Zechariah 9:9–10.[26] According to the prophecy, following the Messiah's victory ride on the donkey, he will 'command peace to the nations'. The peace is among humans, but a peaceable animal, the donkey, helps to bring it about.[27] In ancient Near Eastern cultures, horses were associated with war, but a king in peacetime might be expected to ride a mule, not a donkey (cf. 1 Kgs. 1:33).[28] Jesus rides the animal that was every peasant farmer's beast of burden.

Michael Northcott writes that, in the Gospels, 'Jesus is portrayed as one who lives in supreme harmony with the natural order.'[29] This is not entirely true. The harmony is marred by the destruction of the Gerasene pigs (Mark 5:10–13 and parallels) and by the cursing of the unfruitful fig tree (Mark 11:12–14,20–21; Matt. 21:18–21). It is, of course, the demons who destroy the pigs, but Jesus lets them do so, presumably because the destruction of the pigs was of lesser concern than the deliverance of a man from demon-possession.[30] The fig tree suffers from symbolizing the failure of the temple authorities to do the good that God expected of them. In both cases we are reminded that Jesus anticipates the kingdom within a still unredeemed and unrenewed world. The glimpses of paradisal harmony are no more than small-scale instances pointing to the eschatological future. They do, however, show that the Gospels take seriously the

---

[26] There may also be allusion to Genesis 49:10–11, interpreted as a reference to the Davidic Messiah. Here the Messiah's donkey occurs within a context of paradisal plenty.

[27] Cf. Eric F.F. Bishop, *Jesus of Palestine* (London: Lutterworth, 1955), p. 212: 'In this case both animal and Rider implied the same idea of peaceable progress.'

[28] William David Davies and Dale C. Allison, *A Critical and Exegetical Commentary on the Gospel according to Saint Matthew*, vol. 3 (Edinburgh: T&T Clark, 1997), pp. 116–17, provide relevant references but seem curiously unable to distinguish a donkey from a mule.

[29] Northcott, *Environment*, p. 224.

[30] On the story of the Gerasene demoniac, see Chapter 4 in this volume.

Messiah's task of healing the enmity between humans and the rest of God's creation.

Concluding Comment

This exploration of the ecological dimension of the Synoptic Gospels has remained within their first-century Jewish thought world. I have not attempted the further hermeneutical task of relating this to the very different ecological context in which twenty-first-century people find themselves. The suggestions made here do not have direct ethical implications, but may contribute to the formation of a Christian theological understanding, rooted in the whole canon of Scripture, of what it means for God's human creatures to be part of God's whole creation. The earthly Jesus, his teaching and story, can hardly be irrelevant to such an understanding. But the enterprise of reading the Gospels ecologically has barely begun.

4.

Jesus and Animals

A cursory reading of the Gospels might well leave the impression that there is very little to be said about Jesus and animals. This impression would seem to be confirmed by the fact that modern New Testament scholarship, which has left rather few stones unturned in its detailed study of Jesus and the Gospels, has given virtually no attention to this subject. However, this chapter will show that there is in fact a good deal to be learned from the Gospels about Jesus' understanding of the relationship between humans and other living creatures. This will only be possible by relating Jesus and his teaching to the Jewish religious tradition in which he belonged. All aspects of Jesus' ministry and teaching, even the most innovatory, were significantly continuous with the Jewish tradition of faith, especially, of course, with the Hebrew Bible. Many features of this religious tradition Jesus presupposed. He did not argue, for example, that the God of Israel is the one true God, but everything he did and said presupposed this. Similarly, he presupposed the religious and ethical attitudes to animals that were traditional and accepted, both in the Old Testament and in later Jewish tradition. In his teaching, he adopts such attitudes, not for the most part in order to draw attention to them for their own sake, but in order to base on them teaching about the relation of humans to God. But this does not imply that he took them any the less seriously than other aspects of Jewish faith and religious teaching that he endorsed and developed. But it does mean that, in order to appreciate the full implications of Jesus' references to animals in his teaching, we must investigate the context of Jewish teaching to which they belong.

Compassionate Treatment of Animals

A duty to treat animals humanely and compassionately, not causing unnecessary suffering and whenever possible relieving suffering, was well established in Jewish tradition by Jesus' time, though it was applied largely to domestic animals – those animals owned by humans as beasts of burden, working animals, sources of milk and food, and therefore also offered in sacrifices to God. These were the animals for which humans had day-to-day responsibility. They were not simply to be used and exploited for human benefit, but to be treated with respect and consideration as fellow-creatures of God. Proverbs 12:10 states the general principle:

> A right-minded person cares for his beast,
> but one who is wicked is cruel at heart. (REB)[1]

In later Jewish literature, an interesting instance is the *Testament of Zebulon*,[2] which is much concerned with the duty of compassion and mercy to all people, exemplified by the patriarch Zebulon himself, and understood as a reflection of the compassion and mercy of God.[3] Compassion is probably here an interpretation of the commandment to love one's neighbour (Lev. 19:18), taken to be the central and comprehensive ethical commandment of God and interpreted as requiring compassion for all people. In other words, the love commandment is interpreted much as Jesus interpreted it. But in Zebulon's general statement of the ethical duty of compassion he extends it not only to all people but also to animals: 'And now, my children, I tell you to keep the commands of the Lord: to show mercy to your neighbour, and to have compassion on all, not only human beings but also irrational animals. For on account of these things the Lord blessed me' (*T. Zeb.* 5:1–2).

Another interesting, if not perhaps very representative, passage from the Jewish literature of Jesus' time occurs in *2 Enoch* (the *Slavonic*

---

[1] On this verse, see especially Murray, *Cosmic Covenant*, p. 113.

[2] The majority scholarly opinion is that this, like the other *Testaments of the Twelve Patriarchs*, is an originally Jewish work, which has received some Christian editing. But the argument of H.W. Hollander and M. de Jonge, *The Testaments of the Twelve Patriarchs: A Commentary* (SVTP 8; Leiden: Brill, 1985), pp. 82–5, that the Testaments as we have them are a Christian work, whose Jewish sources cannot be reconstructed, should also be noted.

[3] See Hollander and De Jonge, *Testaments*, pp. 254–5.

Apocalypse of Enoch) in a context of ethical teaching that again has many points of contact with the ethical teaching of Jesus. Chapters 58 – 59 deal with sins against animals. Uniquely, it teaches that the souls of animals will be kept alive until the last judgment, not, apparently, for the sake of eternal life for themselves,[4] but so that they may bring charges, at the last judgment, against human beings who have treated them badly (58:4–6). There seem to be three kinds of sins against animals: failing to feed domestic animals adequately (58:6),[5] bestiality[6] (59:5), and sacrificing an animal without binding it by its four legs (59:2–4). This third sin may seem at first sight to be purely a matter of not observing what the author understood to be the proper ritual requirements for sacrificial slaughter, and it is not obvious why it should be considered a sin against the animal. The reason may be that an animal not properly bound would struggle and die with unnecessary suffering. More probably, the idea is that if the animal struggled, the knife used to cut its throat might slip and damage the animal in some other way.[7] The animal would then not satisfy the ritual requirement that a sacrificial victim be without blemish, and could not be a valid sacrifice. In that case, its life would have been taken to no purpose. This passage of 2 *Enoch* is evidence that some Jews gave serious thought to human beings' ethical duties towards animals.[8]

Of more direct relevance to material in the Gospels (as we shall see) are Jewish legal traditions, in which the law of Moses was interpreted as requiring compassion and consideration for animals. Later rabbinic

---

[4] The point is not quite clear, because of the difference between the two recensions of the work: see the translations of 58:4–6 in manuscripts J and A in Francis I. Andersen, '2 (Slavonic Apocalypse of) Enoch', in *The Old Testament Pseudepigrapha*, vol. 1 (ed. James H. Charlesworth; London: Darton, Longman & Todd, 1983), pp. 184–5.

[5] This may also be the sin to which Pseudo-Phocylides 139 refers. Pieter W. van der Horst translates: 'Take not for yourself a mortal beast's ration of food.' But the Greek is very obscure: see Pieter W. van der Horst, *The Sentences of Pseudo-Phocylides* (Leiden: Brill, 1978), p. 206. Cf. also *b. Gitt.* 62a; *b. Ber.* 40a.

[6] For this interpretation, see Andersen, '2 (Slavonic Apocalypse of) Enoch', pp. 184–5 n. a. For Jewish condemnation of bestiality, see Exod. 22:18; Lev. 18:23; 20:15–16; Deut. 27:21; Philo, *Spec.* 3.43–50; *Sib. Or.* 5:393; *T. Levi* 17:11; *Ps.-Phoc.* 188; *m. Sanh.* 7:4; *m. Ker.* 1:1; *m. 'Abod. Zar.* 2:1; *b. Yeb.* 59b.

[7] Cf. Targums Pseudo-Jonathan and Neofiti to Gen. 22:10, where Isaac asks Abraham to bind him well for precisely this reason. I owe this point to Philip Alexander.

[8] It should be noted that the date and provenance of 2 *Enoch* are uncertain. I think it most likely to date from the late Second Temple period.

traditions understood a whole series of laws in this way (Exod. 22:30; 23:4–5; Lev. 22:27,28; Deut. 22:1–4,6–7,10; 25:4).[9] In many of these cases, it is not obvious that the point of the law is compassion for the animals, and modern Old Testament exegetes often understand them differently.[10] Ancient Jews could also do so. For example, the law of Deuteronomy 22:6–7, which requires someone taking the young birds from a nest (for food) to let the mother bird go, was evidently understood (probably correctly) by the Jewish writer known as Pseudo-Phocylides (lines 84–5) as a conservation measure: 'leave the mother bird behind, in order to get young from her again.'[11] But it was also commonly understood as a matter of compassion for the bird (Josephus, *C. Ap.* 2.213; *Lev. Rab.* 27:11; *Deut. Rab.* 6:1). The rabbis deduced from such laws a general principle that all living beings should be spared pain (the principle of *a'ar ba'aley ayyim*).[12] The rabbinic material, of course, post-dates the New Testament, but there are enough pieces of early evidence of the same kind of interpretation for us to be sure that this way of interpreting the law, as concerned with compassion for animals, was well established by Jesus' time. For example, Josephus, in a remarkable passage in which he is trying to represent the law of Moses in the ways most calculated to appeal to Gentile critics of Judaism, explains that Moses required that the Jews treat strangers and even national enemies with consideration, and then argues that Moses even required consideration for animals:

> So thorough a lesson has he given us in gentleness and humanity that he does not overlook even the brute beasts, authorizing their use only in accordance with the Law, and forbidding all other employment of them [cf. Exod. 20:10; Deut. 5:14; 22:10]. Creatures which take refuge in our houses like suppliants we are forbidden to kill.[13] He would not suffer us to take the parent birds with the young [Deut. 22:6–7], and bade us even in an enemy's country to spare and not to kill the beasts

---

[9] See, e.g. *b. Ber.* 33b; *b. B. Mets.* 31a–32b, 87b; *b. Shabb.* 128b; *Lev. Rab.* 27:11; *Deut. Rab.* 6:1.

[10] For a recent discussion, see Murray, *Cosmic Covenant*, pp. 114–19.

[11] Van der Horst's discussion (*Sentences*, pp. 172–3) seems to overlook the fact that the law is not here interpreted as a matter of kindness to the bird, as it is in other Jewish sources.

[12] Elijah Judah Schochet, *Animal Life in Jewish Tradition* (New York: Ktav, 1984), p. 151.

[13] This otherwise unknown law is also found in a lost work of Philo (*Hypothetica*), quoted in Eusebius, *Praep. Evang.* 8.7.

employed in labour [perhaps cf. Deut. 20:19]. Thus, in every particular, he had an eye to mercy, using the laws I have mentioned to enforce the lesson (*C. Ap.* 2.213–214).[14]

Here the principle of compassion for animals apparently leads to the formulation of laws not to be found in the written Torah at all.

A very similar treatment, though restricted to laws actually found in the Torah, is given by Philo of Alexandria, who sees the gentleness and kindness of the precepts given by Moses in the fact that consideration is extended to creatures of every kind: to humans, even if they are strangers or enemies, to irrational animals,[15] even if they are unclean according to the dietary laws, and even to plants and trees (*Virt.* 160; cf. 81, 125, 140). He expounds in detail the laws which he understands to be motivated by compassion for animals: Leviticus 22:27 (*Virt.* 126–133); Leviticus 22:28 (134–142); Exodus 23:19; 34:26; Deuteronomy 14:21 (142–144); Deuteronomy 25:4 (145); and Deuteronomy 22:10 (146–147).

This line of interpretation of the law cannot be explained merely as an apologetic for the law of Moses by diaspora Jews concerned to impress Gentiles. Not only can it be paralleled in later rabbinic literature.[16] One striking instance, which may well go back to New Testament times, is found in the Palestinian Targum. It concerns the law of Leviticus 22:28, which forbids the slaughter of an animal and its young together (one of the laws discussed by Philo, though not by Josephus, as an instance of compassion for animals). According to the Targum of Pseudo-Jonathan, which frequently preserves Jewish exegetical traditions from the Second Temple period,[17] God, when

---

[14] Translation from Henry St John Thackeray, *Josephus*, vol. 1 (LCL; London: Heinemann/New York: Putnam, 1926), p. 379.

[15] Philo adopted the Stoic view that animals are distinguished from humans by their lack of reason. For Philo's views of animals and his relationship on this point to Hellenistic philosophy, see Terian, *Philonis Alexandrini De Animalibus*.

[16] See n. 9 above.

[17] For the probably early date of this particular tradition, see Martin McNamara, *The New Testament and the Palestinian Targum to the Pentateuch* (AnBib 27; Rome: Pontifical Biblical Institute, 1966), pp. 136–7. It was later criticized and censured by rabbis who objected to the giving of reasons for commandments of the Torah, because this reduced the ordinances of God to mere acts of mercy: *m. Ber.* 5:3; *b. Ber.* 33b; *y. Ber.* 5,3,9c; *y. Meg.* 4,9,75c. See Efraim Elimelech Urbach, *The Sages: Their Concepts and Beliefs* (Jerusalem: Magnes Press, 1975), pp. 382–5, 452; Schochet, *Animal Life*, pp. 179–83; E. Segal, 'Justice, Mercy and a Bird's Nest,' *JJewishS* 42 (1991): pp. 176–95.

giving this commandment, says to his people: 'just as I in heaven am merciful, so shall you be merciful on earth' (cf. Luke 6:36). Behind this statement probably lies Psalm 145:9: 'The LORD is good to all, and his compassion is over all that he has made.'[18] God's compassion for all his creatures is to be imitated by his people, and the laws requiring consideration for animals are given to this end.

The idea that compassion for animals is a general principle of the Torah explains why acts of compassion for animals were permitted on the Sabbath, even though they involved what would otherwise be considered work, which is prohibited on the Sabbath. On three occasions in the Gospels Jesus refers to such generally recognized exceptions to the prohibition of work on the Sabbath. He does so in the context of debate about his practice of performing healings on the Sabbath, to which the Pharisees (Matt. 12:10–14; Luke 14:3) and others (Luke 13:14; 14:3) objected. In each case his point is to argue that, since his opponents agreed that relieving the suffering of domestic animals was lawful on the Sabbath, how much more must relieving the suffering of human beings be lawful. The statements are:

> Matthew 12:11–12: Suppose one of you has only one sheep and it falls into a pit on the sabbath; will you not lay hold of it and lift it out? How much more valuable is a human being than a sheep! So it is lawful to do good on the sabbath.

> Luke 14:5: If one of you has a child[19] or an ox that has fallen into a well, will you not immediately pull it out on a sabbath day?[20]

> Luke 13:15–16: Does not each of you on the sabbath untie his ox or his donkey from the manger, and lead it away to give it water? And ought not this woman, a daughter of Abraham whom Satan bound for eighteen long years, be set free from this bondage on the sabbath day?

---

[18] Biblical quotations in this chapter are from the NRSV, unless otherwise stated.

[19] The best manuscript evidence is divided between *huios* (child) and *onos* (donkey, as in Luke 13:15). The textual question is discussed by I. Howard Marshall, *The Gospel of Luke* (NIGTC; Exeter: Paternoster Press, 1978), pp. 579–80; Joseph A. Fitzmyer, *The Gospel According to Luke (X–XXIV)* (AB 28A; New York: Doubleday, 1985), pp. 1041–2. Both accept *huios*, as the harder reading.

[20] Matt. 12:11 and Luke 14:5 are probably variant forms of the same saying, though probably not derived by Matthew and Luke from the same source. Of course, Jesus could well have made the same point in the context of two debates about his practice of healing on the Sabbath.

Not all Jews would have agreed with Jesus' account of what it was permitted to do for animals on the Sabbath.[21] The written Torah, of course, makes no such explicit exceptions to the Sabbath commandment. Therefore the Qumran sect, whose interpretation of the Sabbath laws was extremely strict, categorically forbade such acts of mercy: 'No man shall assist a beast to give birth on the Sabbath day. And if it should fall into a cistern or pit, he shall not lift it out on the Sabbath' (CD 11:12–14).[22] On this latter question, addressed in Matthew 12:11 and Luke 14:5, later rabbinic opinion was divided as to whether it was permissible to help the animal out of the pit or only to bring it provisions until it could be rescued after the Sabbath (*b. Shabb.* 128b; *b. B. Mets.* 32b). We may take the Gospels as evidence that the more lenient ruling was widely held in Jesus' time. As to the example given in Luke 13:15, it is very much in line with the Mishnah's interpretation of Sabbath law in relation to domestic animals, though not explicitly stated as a rabbinic ruling. The point is that tying and untying knots were defined as two of the types of activity that constituted work and were generally unlawful on the Sabbath (*m. Shabb.* 7:2), but provision for domestic animals was one kind of reason for allowing exceptions (*m. Shabb.* 15:1–2; cf. *b. Shabb.* 128a–128b; cf. also *m. Erub.* 2:1–4, where it is taken for granted that cattle are watered on the Sabbath).

These exceptions to the prohibition of work on the Sabbath are remarkable. They are not cases in which the lives of the animals were in danger, and so they cannot be understood as motivated by a concern to preserve the animals as valuable property. Rather they are acts of compassion, intended to prevent animal suffering. It was only because the law was understood as generally requiring considerate treatment of animals that the Sabbath commandment could be interpreted as not forbidding such acts of mercy to animals on the Sabbath. Moreover, it is clear that Jesus understood the issue in this way. His argument is that, since his hearers agreed that acts of compassion, designed to relieve the suffering of animals, are lawful on the Sabbath, surely acts of compassion, designed to relieve human suffering, are also lawful. According to Matthew 12:12–13, rescuing a sheep from a pit on the Sabbath is 'doing good', and so healing a man's withered hand on the Sabbath is also doing good.

---

[21] For differences in interpretation of the Sabbath law in New Testament times, see Ed P. Sanders, *Jewish Law from Jesus to the Mishnah* (London: SCM Press/ Philadelphia: Trinity Press International, 1990), pp. 6–23.

[22] Translation from Geza Vermes, *The Dead Sea Scrolls in English* (3rd edition; London: Penguin, 1987), p. 95.

Of course, in all three texts, the law's requirement of compassion for animals is only the presupposition for the point Jesus is making. But his argument is certainly not merely *ad hominem*. He is arguing from a presupposition that is genuinely agreed between him and his opponents. Jesus, in his recorded teaching, does not teach compassion for animals, but he places himself clearly within the Jewish ethical and legal tradition that held that God requires his people to treat their fellow-creatures, the animals, with compassion and consideration.

An Apocryphal Story

A practically unknown apocryphal story about Jesus is unique in showing Jesus engaged in an act of compassion for an animal:

> It happened that the Lord left the city and walked with his disciples over the mountains. And they came to a mountain, and the road that led up it was steep. There they found a man with a pack-mule. But the animal had fallen, because the man had loaded it too heavily, and now he beat it, so that it was bleeding. And Jesus came to him and said, 'Man, why do you beat your animal? Do you not see that it is too weak for its burden, and do you not know that it suffers pains?' But the man answered and said, 'What is that to you? I may beat it as much as I please, since it is my property, and I bought it for a good sum of money. Ask those who are with you, for they know me and know about this.' And some of the disciples said, 'Yes, Lord, it is as he says. We have seen how he bought it.' But the Lord said, 'Do you then not see how it bleeds, and do you not hear how it groans and cries out?' But they answered and said, 'No, Lord, that it groans and cries out, we do not hear.' But Jesus was sad and exclaimed, 'Woe to you, that you do not hear how it complains to the Creator in heaven and cries out for mercy. But threefold woes to him about whom it cries out and complains in its pain.' And he came up and touched the animal. And it stood up and its wounds were healed. But Jesus said to the man, 'Now carry on and from now on do not beat it any more, so that you too may find mercy.'[23]

---

[23] My translation from the German translation of the Coptic in Julius Boehmer, *Neutestamentliche Parallelen und Verwandte aus altchristlicher Literatur* (Stuttgart: Greiner & Pfeiffer, 1903), pp. 26–7. There is also an English translation in Bernhard Pick, *Paralipomena: Remains of Gospels and Sayings of Christ* (Chicago: Open Court, 1908), pp. 58–9, but the story does not appear in any other collection of apocryphal literature, and, as far as I know, it has not been referred to or discussed anywhere else.

Since nothing is known of the source of this story, preserved in Coptic,[24] it is impossible to know whether it derives from an early gospel tradition. However, it does seem to presuppose the Jewish legal tradition that we have discussed in the last section. Specifically, it relates to the commandment to relieve an animal that has fallen under its burden (Exod. 23:4; Deut. 22:4), interpreted as requiring compassion for an overburdened animal.[25] So the story might go back to a Jewish Christian source in which Jesus' teaching that love is the overriding principle in interpreting the law was extended, as it is not explicitly in the canonical Gospels, to concern for animals as well as people. Jesus' final saying in the story extends to the treatment of animals: Jesus' general principle that 'the measure you give will be the measure you get' (Matt. 7:2; Luke 6:38), as well as the thought of the beatitude: 'Blessed are the merciful, for they will receive mercy' (Matt. 5:7). If people do not show mercy to their animals, they cannot expect mercy from God.[26] Whatever its source, the story is at least a kind of testimony to the impression the figure of Jesus in the Gospels can make on their readers. This – we may agree – is how the Jesus portrayed in the Gospels would have behaved in such a situation.

God's Provision for His Creatures

> Matthew 6:26: Look at the birds of the air; they neither sow nor reap nor gather into barns, and yet your heavenly Father feeds them. Are you not of more value than they?

> Luke 12:24: Consider the ravens: they neither sow nor reap, they have neither storehouse nor barn, and yet God feeds them. Of how much more value are you than the birds!

In this saying, as in the corresponding exhortation to consider the wild flowers (Matt. 6:28; Luke 12:27), Jesus adopts the style of a Jewish wisdom teacher, inviting his hearers to consider the natural

---

24 Boehmer gives its source merely as 'Coptic Bible'.

25 For this interpretation of these texts, see *b. B. Mets.* 31a–32b; *b. Sanh.* 128b.

26 There is a remarkable parallel in the saying attributed to the second-century Rabbi Gamaliel III: 'Whosoever has compassion upon his fellow-creatures, upon him will God have compassion' (*b. Shabb.* 77b; *y. Ber.* 9,3,13c; quoted in Schochet, *Animal Life*, p. 164). See also the story of Rabbi Judah ha-Nasi, of which this is the moral: Schochet, *Animal Life*, p. 164.

world, God's creation, and to draw religious lessons from it (cf. Job 12:7–8; 35:4; Prov. 6:6; Sir. 33:15; *1 Enoch* 2:1–3; 3:1; 4:1; 5:1,3). What he asks them to notice – that God feeds the birds/ravens – is drawn directly from the creation theology of the Hebrew Bible, especially the Psalms, in which it is a commonplace that God the Creator supplies all his living creatures with food.[27] In the following passages, I have italicized the references to God feeding his creatures in general and to God feeding specifically the birds or the ravens, in order to show how relatively often the example of God's provision which Jesus uses occurs:

Ps. 147:9:   He *gives* to the animals *their food*,
                 and to the young ravens when they cry.
Ps. 104:10–11: You make springs gush forth in the valleys . . .
                 giving drink to every wild animal . . .
        14:     You cause the grass to grow for the cattle,
                 and plants for people to use,
                 to bring forth food from the earth . . .
        21:     The young lions roar for their prey,
                 seeking their food from God . . .
        27–8:   These all look to you
                 to give them their food in due season;
                 when you *give to them*, they gather it up;
                 when you open your hand, they are filled with
                 good things.
Job 38:39–41:   Can you hunt the prey for the lion,
                 or satisfy the appetite of the young lions,
                 when they crouch in their dens,
                 or lie in wait in their covert?
                 Who *provides for the raven* its prey,
                 when its young ones cry to God,
                 and wander about for lack of food?
Ps. 145:15–16: The eyes of all look to you,
                 and *you give them their food* in due season.
                 You open your hand,
                 satisfying the desire of every living thing.

---

[27] M.F. Olsthoorn, *The Jewish Background and the Synoptic Setting of Mt 6,25–33 and Lk, 12,22–31* (Studium Biblicum Franciscanum Analecta 10; Jerusalem: Franciscan Printing House, 1975), p. 36, calls this 'one of the most common beliefs of listeners . . . familiar with the Jewish tradition'.

It is probably impossible to tell whether, in Jesus' saying, Matthew's 'the birds of the air' or Luke's 'the ravens' is more original, but the latter gives a more precise Old Testament allusion to Job 38:41 or Psalm 147:9. The reason why both these Old Testament texts single out the ravens for mention is that the cry of the young ravens, to which they both refer, was especially raucous. Young ravens 'squawk for food with louder and longer cries than almost any other species'.[28] In the context of Jesus' saying, it might also be significant that, according to the dietary laws, the raven is an unclean animal (Lev. 11:15; Deut. 14:14). The point would then be that God takes care to provide even for an unclean bird like the raven.[29] (We have already noticed that Philo, *Virt.* 160, extols the Mosaic law's compassion for animals by pointing out that it extends even to unclean animals.)

The Old Testament creation theology, which Jesus here echoes, includes humans among the living creatures for whom God provides. The great creation psalm – 104 – where humans are included among all the creatures who look to God for food (vv. 27–8), is notable for its depiction of humans as one species among others in the community of creation for which the Creator provides. Psalm 145:15, which echoes Psalm 104:27–8, does so, as the context makes clear, in order especially to highlight God's provision for humans. Like Jesus, the psalmist points to God's care for all his living creatures in order to assure humans who turn to God in need that he provides for them. The same point is made, in dependence on these psalms, in a later Jewish psalm (from the first century BCE):

> For if I am hungry, I will cry out to you, O God,
> and you will give me (something).
> You feed the birds and the fish
> as you send rain in the wilderness that grass may sprout
> to provide pasture in the wilderness for every living thing,
> and if they are hungry, they will lift their eyes up to you.
> You feed kings and rulers and peoples, O God,
> and who is the hope of the poor and needy, if not you, Lord?
>
> (*Pss. Sol.* 5:8–11)[30]

---

[28] Virginia C. Holmgren, *Bird Walk through the Bible* (2nd edn; New York: Dover, 1988), p. 146.

[29] Ravens were also generally disliked: *1 Enoch* 90:8–19; *Jub.* 12:18–21; *b. Sanh.* 108b; *t. Shabb.* 6:6; *Barn.* 10:4 (where precisely their idleness is the point). Cf. Olsthoorn, *Jewish Background*, p. 35.

[30] Translation from R.B. Wright, 'Psalms of Solomon', in *The Old Testament Pseudepigrapha*, vol. 2 (ed. James H. Charlesworth; London: Darton, Longman & Todd, 1985), p. 657.

Clearly, in arguing from the Creator's provision for birds to his provision for people, Jesus' words belong firmly within Jewish tradition. The point that is not from the tradition is Jesus' observation that birds do not sow or reap or store their food in barns. This observation has been variously interpreted. Jesus has sometimes been thought to contrast the birds who do not work with people who do: if God feeds even the idle birds, how much more will he provide for people who work hard for their living. He has also been thought to compare the birds who do not work with disciples who do not work either, but as wandering preachers depend on God's provision by way of receiving charity. It is improbable that either of these alternatives is the real point. Rather the point is that, because the birds do not have to labour to process their food from nature, their dependence on the Creator's provision is the more immediate and obvious.[31] Humans, preoccupied with the daily toil of supplying their basic needs by sowing and reaping and gathering into barns, may easily suppose that it is up to them to provide themselves with food. Focusing on their necessary efforts to process their food, they neglect the fact that, much more fundamentally, they are dependent on the divine provision, the resources of creation without which no one could sow, reap or gather into barns. The birds, in their more immediate and obvious dependence on the Creator, remind humans that ultimately they are no less dependent on the Creator.

Once again, as in the Sabbath healing discussions, what Jesus says about animals is a presupposition from which to argue something about humans. But it is a necessary presupposition. It is not, as some modern readers tend to assume, just a picturesque illustration of Jesus' point, as though the point could stand without the illustration. Rather Jesus' argument depends on the Old Testament creation theology evoked by his reference to the birds. Humans can trust God for their basic needs, treating the resources of creation as God's provision for these needs, only when they recognize that they belong to the community of God's creatures, for all of whom the Creator provides. Only those who recognize birds as their fellow-creatures can appreciate Jesus' point. It is noteworthy that, although the argument, like that in the discussions of Sabbath law, is an argument from the lesser to the

---

[31] The point is therefore rather different from that in *m. Qidd.* 4:14 (quoted below), where R. Simeon ben Eleazar observes that animals and birds do not have to work to gain a living, whereas humans do. His point is that humans would be sustained without effort, had they not forfeited this right through sin (cf. Gen. 3:17–19).

greater (since God provides for the birds, he will certainly also provide for humans who are of more value than birds), it is not an argument which sets humans on a different plane of being from the animals. On the contrary, it sets humans within the community of God's creatures for all of whom he provides. Apparently, they are regarded as particularly eminent members of that community (a point to which we shall return), but they are members of it, nonetheless.

God's Concern for Every Creature

> Matthew 10:29–31: Are not two sparrows sold for a penny? Yet not one of them will fall to the ground unperceived by your Father. And even the hairs of your head are all counted. So do not be afraid; you are of more value than many sparrows.

> Luke 12:6–7: Are not five sparrows sold for two pennies? Yet not one of them is forgotten in God's sight. But even the hairs of your head are all counted. Do not be afraid; you are of more value than many sparrows.

Evidently sparrows were sold in the market, either in pairs or in fives (which for Jewish counting in tens would be equivalent to our half-dozen), as food for the poor, who would probably rarely be able to afford any other form of meat. That sparrows were the cheapest birds for sale in the market – and for this reason selected by Jesus to make his point – is confirmed by a decree of Emperor Diocletian (late third century CE) that fixes maximum prices for all kinds of items and lists sparrows as the cheapest of all the birds used for food.[32] The cheapness of birds, in general, is interestingly confirmed by a passage in the Mishnah relating to the law of Deuteronomy 22:6–7, which, as we have already noticed, forbids taking the mother bird together with her young from a nest. The rabbis were struck by the fact that, very unusually, this law specifies a reward for keeping it: 'that it may go well with you and you may live long' (Deut. 22:7). They concluded that if such a reward attaches to 'so light a precept concerning what is

---

[32] Adolf Deissmann, *Light from the Ancient East* (4th edition; London: Hodder & Stoughton, 1927), pp. 273–4; Otto Bauernfeind in *TDNT* 7.730 n. 10, 732 n. 19. I. Howard Marshall, *Luke*, p. 514, appears to be mistaken when he says that sparrows were not in fact eaten for food and that *strouthion* here must mean any small bird eaten for food.

worth but an *issar'*, then how much more will a similar reward be given for observing 'the weightier precepts of the law' (*m. Ḥull.* 12:5). The commandment is here considered trivial, compared with others,[33] because it concerns only a bird, which is worth only an *issar*. The *issar* is the same small copper coin as Matthew's and Luke's 'penny' (*assarion*).[34]

Thus Jesus has selected a creature that is valued very cheaply by humans, of course on the basis of its limited usefulness to them. Even a creature that humans think so unimportant is important enough to God for it never to escape his caring attention. Matthew's and Luke's versions of the saying make the point in slightly different ways. Matthew's is the more specific and relates to the capture of sparrows for food. The sparrow's fall to the earth is not, as modern readers often suppose, its death,[35] but what happens when the hunter's throw-net snares it and brings it to the ground (cf. Amos 3:5).[36] It will then be sold in the market. The sparrow's capture cannot happen 'without (*aneu*) your Father' (Matt. 10:29), i.e. without his knowledge and consent.

There is a remarkably close parallel, not only to this point but also to the moral which Jesus draws from it with regard to God's care for the disciples, in a later rabbinic story, which must show that Jesus is drawing on traditional Jewish teaching. The story concerns Rabbi Simeon ben Yohai (mid-second century CE), who at the end of the second Jewish war spent thirteen years hiding in a cave with his son.

> At the end of this period he emerged and sat at the entrance of the cave and saw a hunter engaged in catching birds. Now whenever R. Simeon heard a heavenly voice exclaim from heaven, 'Mercy!' [i.e. a legal sentence of release] it escaped; if it exclaimed, 'Death!' it was caught. 'Even a bird is not caught without the assent of Providence,' he remarked;

---

[33] Cf. *Deut. Rab.* 6:2, which calls it the least weighty of the commandments, whereas Exod. 20:12, for which the same reward is specified, is the weightiest.

[34] The Romans reckoned an *assarion* (Latin *as*) as one sixteenth of a denarius, the rabbis as one twenty-fourth of a denarius: see Hermann Leberecht Strack and Paul Billerbeck, *Kommentar zum Neuen Testament aus Talmud und Midrasch*, vol. 1 (Munich: Beck, 1922), p. 291.

[35] E.g. William David Davies and Dale C. Allison, *A Critical and Exegetical Commentary on the Gospel according to Saint Matthew*, vol. 2 (Edinburgh: T&T Clark, 1991), p. 208.

[36] See the comments on Amos 3:5 in William Rainey Harper, *A Critical and Exegetical Commentary on Amos and Hosea* (ICC; Edinburgh: T&T Clark, 1905), pp. 70–1; James Luther Mays, *Amos* (OTL; London: SCM Press, 1969), p. 61.

'how much more then the life of a human being!' Thereupon he went forth and found that the trouble had subsided. (*Gen. Rab.* 79:6)[37]

Rabbi Simeon realizes that his fate is in the hands of God, to whom he can therefore entrust himself, when he realises that this is even true of each bird.

If Jesus drew on traditional Jewish teaching, this teaching was itself rooted in the Old Testament, which says that:

> In his hand is the life of every living thing
>> and the breath of every human being (Job 12:10)

and:

> You save humans and animals alike, O LORD (Ps. 36:6).

It is God who preserves the life of each of his creatures, animal and human, and who likewise allows that life to perish when it does.

Luke's version makes the more general point that not a single sparrow ever escapes God's attention ('forgotten in the sight of God' is a Jewish reverential periphrasis for 'forgotten by God'; cf. Matt. 18:14). But in both versions the point is God's caring providence for each individual creature. God does not concern himself only with the species, but with each individual of the species. Nor does he simply superintend what happens to each without concern for the welfare of each: this would provide no basis for Jesus' assurance that the disciples need have no fear. The point is that since God actually cares about and takes care of each sparrow, how much more must he care about and take care of Jesus' disciples. Of course, Jesus does not raise the problems of such a doctrine of providence:[38] Why does God let one sparrow escape and another be captured and killed? Why does he allow righteous people to suffer? Here Jesus is content to affirm that the disciples, like all God's creatures, are in the hands of God who cares for all he has made.

---

[37] Translation from Harry Freedman, *Midrash Rabbah: Genesis*, vol. 2 (London: Soncino Press, 1939), p. 730. The story also appears in *y. Sheb.* 9,22,38d; *Eccles. Rab.* 10:8; *Midr. Ps.* 17:13.

[38] For a modern discussion of this issue in relation to animal suffering, which takes Jesus' saying as its starting-point, see Jay B. McDaniel, *Of God and Pelicans: A Theology of Reverence for Life* (Louisville, Kentucky: Westminster/John Knox Press, 1989), ch. 1.

Humans are of More Value than Animals

All the references to animals in the sayings of Jesus that we have considered belong to a form of argument from the lesser to the greater (*a minore ad maius*, or, in rabbinic terminology, *qal va-homer*). Since, it is stated or assumed, humans are of more value than animals, if something is true in the case of animals, it must also be true in the case of humans. If acts of compassion for animals are lawful on the Sabbath, then acts of compassion for humans must also be lawful. If God provides for birds, then he can be trusted to provide for humans also. If not even a sparrow escapes God's caring attention, then Jesus' disciples can be sure they are in God's care.

This form of argument is used in rabbinic literature, and so we can probably conclude that it was already an established form of Jewish religious argument in Jesus' time. In addition to the passage quoted (from *Gen. Rab.* 79:6) in the previous section,[39] the following are examples of this form of argument:

> *m. Qidd.* 4:14: R. Simeon b. Eleazar says: Hast thou ever seen a wild animal or a bird practising a craft? – yet they have their sustenance without care and were they not created for naught else but to serve me? But I was created to serve my Maker. How much more then ought not I to have my sustenance without care? But I have wrought evil, and [so] forfeited my [right to] sustenance [without care].[40]

> *b. Qidd.* 82b: R. Simeon b. Eleazar said: In my whole lifetime I have not seen a deer engaged in gathering fruits, a lion carrying burdens, or a fox as a shopkeeper, yet they are sustained without trouble, though they were created only to serve me, whereas I was created to serve my Maker. Now, if these, who were created only to serve me are sustained without trouble, how much more so should I be sustained without trouble, I who was created to serve my Maker! But it is because I have acted evilly and destroyed my livelihood, as it is said, your iniquities have turned away these things [Jer. 5:25].[41]

> *y. Ber.* 9,3,13c: Elijah asked Rabbi Nehorai, Why had God created in his world tiny insects and worms? He replied, 'When human beings sin,

---

[39] Cf. also *Mekilta* to Exod. 12:1, quoted in Olsthoorn, *Jewish Background*, p. 37.

[40] Translation from Herbert Danby, *The Mishnah* (Oxford: Clarendon Press, 1933), p. 329.

[41] Translation from Harry Freedman, *The Babylonian Talmud: Kiddushin* (London: Soncino Press, 1936), p. 425. See also *y. Qidd.* 4,11,66d.

He looks on the lower forms of creation and says: "If I sustain these tiny useless creatures, how much more must I preserve human beings who are useful." [42]

Deut. Rab. 6:5: Another comment [on Deut. 22:6–7]: R. Hiyya said: If a bird that has neither ancestral merit nor covenants nor oaths to rely upon, can be atoned for by her children, how much more will the children of Abraham, Isaac, and Jacob who have ancestral merit to rely on, if any of them sin, be atoned for by their children in the time to come. [43]

All of these passages use the phrase 'how much more', which Jesus also uses in other examples of *qal wa-homer* argument in his teaching (Matt. 6:30 par. Luke 12:28; Matt. 7:11 par. Luke 11:13; Matt 10:25: *pos mallon* in all cases except Matt. 6:30). But this expression is not used in the arguments from animals to humans (except in Luke 12:24). Instead, expressions employing the verb *diapherein* are used:

Matthew 12:12: How much more valuable (*pos diapherei*) is a human being than a sheep!
Matthew 6:26: Are you not of more value (*mallon diapherete*) than they [the birds of the air]?
Luke 12:24: Of how much more value are you (*pos . . . mallon diapherete*) than the birds!
Matthew 10:31: You are of more value (*diapherete*) than many sparrows!
Luke 12:7: You are of more value (*diapherete*) than many sparrows.

It might be a preferable translation of *diapherein* to say that humans 'are superior to' animals. The reference is probably to the kind of hierarchical superiority that is implied in the Old Testament's notion of human dominion over the animals (Gen. 1:26–8; Ps. 8:5–8). Humans are of superior status in the sense that a king is superior to his subjects. At least in biblical thought, a king is not of greater value than his subjects. However, we cannot rule out the idea of a difference in intrinsic value. Certainly the law of Moses treats human life as more valuable than animal life. A human being or even a domestic animal that kills a human being is subject to death, but a human being who

---

[42] Quoted in Gerald Friedlander, *The Jewish Sources of the Sermon on the Mount* (London: Routledge/New York: Bloch, 1911), p. 194.
[43] Translation from Joseph Rabbinowitz, *Midrash Rabbah: Deuteronomy* (London: Soncino Press, 1939), p. 124.

kills a domestic animal is required only to make financial restitution
to its owner (Exod. 21:28–35; Lev. 24:17–21; cf. Gen. 9:5–6). In these
laws animals seem to be treated only as property, but it should also be
noted that the prohibition on eating meat with blood in it (Gen. 9:4;
Lev. 3:17; 7:26; 17:10; Deut. 12:16,23; 15:23) is a kind of recognition that
animal life is valuable (it is the gift of God and must be returned to
him), even though there are permissible reasons for taking it. Jesus'
arguments certainly presuppose that animals have intrinsic value for
God. Otherwise it could make no sense to say that humans are more
valuable.[44]

Two observations on Jesus' arguments from animals to humans are
appropriate. In the first place, they do not employ certain ideas that
we find in some of the rabbinic passages quoted above. In the saying
of Rabbi Simeon b. Eleazar (*m. Qidd.* 4:14; *b. Qidd.* 82b), animals are
said to have been created only to serve humans. This non-biblical idea
– which is certainly not implied in Genesis 1 – 2 and is clearly refuted
by Job 39 – entered both Jewish and Christian thought from
Aristotelian and Stoic philosophy.[45] There is no reason to think that it
is presupposed in Jesus' sayings. The saying attributed to Rabbi
Nehorai may well reflect the kind of discussions that the Stoic notion
that all other creatures exist for the sake of their usefulness to humanity provoked. Many creatures seemed of no obvious use to humanity
at all, and ingenious explanations of their usefulness had to be
found.[46] Rabbi Nehorai admits that some tiny creatures are useless
(presumably to human beings), but gives them a kind of use in
reminding God that he should preserve human beings, who, by contrast, are useful (presumably to God). The only point at which Jesus
refers to the value of creatures by the standard of their usefulness to
human beings is when he cites the price of sparrows in the market
(Matt. 10:29; Luke 12:6), but he does so in order to contrast this human
estimate of the value of sparrows with their importance to God. Thus,
if Jesus' sayings do imply a kind of hierarchical superiority of humans
to animals, it is not the kind of hierarchy implied in these two rabbinic

---

[44] This point is neglected in the following *non sequitur*: 'Men and women are worth
more than the birds or the grass of the field. The real value of beasts and trees lies
in how far they enrich human life, for nourishment, protection or beauty' (E.
Marshall, 'Jesus and the Environment: How Green is Christianity?,' *Modern
Churchman* 33 [1992], p. 4).

[45] E.g. Aristotle, *Pol.* 1.8; Cicero, *Nat. D.* 2. See also Chapter 2 in this volume.

[46] See Terian, *Philonis Alexandrini De Animalibus*, p. 51; Glacken, *Traces*, pp. 57, 61. For
a rabbinic example, see *b. Shabb.* 77b.

sayings, in which animals exist solely to serve humanity and humans to serve God. It is a hierarchy within the community of creation, in which humans and animals alike exist for God's glory, and in which there is a mutuality in fellow-creatureliness, such that, if some animals do serve humans, humans also have responsibilities of care towards those animals (Matt. 12:11; Luke 13:15; 14:5).

The second observation is very important. It is that Jesus never uses the superiority of humans to animals in order to make a negative point about animals. He does not argue, as some later Christian theologians influenced by Greek philosophy did,[47] that because animals are inferior to humans, therefore humans have no ethical responsibilities towards animals. He does not argue that because animals are inferior to humans, therefore God does not take as much trouble to provide for animals as he does for humans. He does not argue that because animals are inferior to humans, therefore God's providence does not extend to individual animals, but only to species.[48] On the contrary, in every case, his argument is that because such-and-such is true in the case of animals, it must also be true in the case of humans. The arguments actually depend more on the idea that humans and animals are all creatures of God, than they do on the idea of a hierarchical difference between them.

Perhaps this is the appropriate point at which to mention the incident of the Gerasene (or Gadarene) swine (Matt. 8:28–34; Mark 5:1–20; Luke 8:26–39), since, at least since Augustine, this has often been understood to demonstrate that Jesus set little value on animal life. Augustine argued, against the Manicheans, that it is not wrong to slaughter animals, since Jesus himself did so when he sent the demons into the herd of pigs. But Augustine shows the presupposition on which his reading of the story depends, when he says that Jesus did this 'on the ground that there is no community of rights between us and brutes' (*Mor. Manich.* 17.54).[49] This is the Stoic doctrine that, because humans are rational and animals irrational, there can be no question of justice or injustice in human relationships with animals.[50] Animals have no rights which can affect human treatment of them. This Stoic principle was to have a long history in Christian thought,[51] but it would not have influenced Jesus.

---

[47] See Chapter 2 in this volume.
[48] As Maimonides argued: Schochet, *Animal Life*, pp. 204–6.
[49] Augustine is followed by E. Marshall, 'Jesus and the Environment', p. 4, who takes the story to show that Jesus put humans 'in a class apart from other living creatures'.
[50] See Terian, *Philonis Alexandrini De Animalibus*, p. 52.
[51] E.g. Thomas Aquinas, *Summa theologiae* 2.65.3.

We should observe that in the Markan and Lukan versions of the story Jesus permits the demons to enter the pigs, in response to their begging him to let them (Mark 5:12–13; Luke 8:32), and although Matthew makes the permission into a command of Jesus, it is still a command to do what they have begged to be allowed to do (Matt. 8:31–2). The story can only be properly understood in terms of the ideas of the demonic prevalent in Jesus' time. The demons fear being without a living being to inhabit, and would certainly not have remained without a habitation for long. According to contemporary Jewish ideas on the subject, if they could not readily find an alternative home, they would be liable to return to the one they had left (Matt. 12:43–5; Mark 9:25). Moreover, demons were thought to be associated with particular locations, and would naturally see the nearby pigs as a suitable refuge.[52] Their destruction of the pigs manifests the inherent tendency of the demonic to destroy whatever it possesses (cf. Mark 5:5; 9:22). Finally, although only Matthew's version attributes to the demons when they first encounter Jesus the alarmed question, 'Have you come here to torment us before the time?' (Matt. 8:29; cf. Mark 1:24), the thought implied in this question is certainly implicit in all three versions. It is that the eschatological 'time' – the day of judgment – when God will abolish all evil and destroy the demons has not yet come. Jesus' ministry of victory over evil anticipates that time; he can deliver people from the power of the demonic; God's destruction of the evil forces that oppress people has decisively begun (cf. Matt. 12:28); but nevertheless Jesus does not yet abolish the demons or send them back to the abyss (Luke 8:31). Until the end of history evil can be deflected and diminished but not abolished (cf. Matt. 13:24–30).[53]

Thus Jesus, in this story, permits a lesser evil. There is no reason at all to suppose that he sets no value on the life of the pigs or values it only for the sake of human beings. But the destruction of the pigs is preferable to the destruction of a human personality. The principle that human beings are of more value than other animals here operates to the detriment of the latter, in a case, unique within the Gospels, where a choice has to be made.

---

[52] Graham H. Twelftree, *Christ Triumphant: Exorcism Then and Now* (London: Hodder & Stoughton, 1985), p. 66.

[53] Cf. Twelftree, *Christ Triumphant*, pp. 77–82.

Sacrifices and Meat-Eating

We have seen that Jesus' attitude to animals belongs wholly within the Old Testament and Jewish tradition. In this tradition it was permitted to kill certain animals for sacrifice to God in the temple and for food. For Jesus to have rejected either of these practices in principle would have been a significant innovation. Of course, there were innovatory aspects of Jesus' interpretation of the law of Moses, but there is no evidence at all that he innovated in either of these two ways.

With regard to sacrifice, had there been any tradition of words of Jesus rejecting the sacrificial system, then the Gospels, probably all written by and for Christians who had abandoned the practice of sacrifice in the temple, would surely have recorded it. The so-called cleansing of the temple (Mark 12:15–17), which has sometimes been interpreted as a symbolic rejection of the system of sacrificial worship, would certainly not have been so understood by Jesus' contemporaries. Jesus objected to the way the priestly aristocracy who ran the temple were exploiting the sacrificial system as a means of financial profit, thus distorting the real purpose of sacrifices as a vehicle of prayer.[54] Matthew twice attributes to Jesus, in his debates with the Pharisees, a quotation from Hosea 6:6: 'I desire mercy, not sacrifice' (Matt. 9:13; 12:7). In neither context is a reference to sacrifice as such especially relevant. Sacrifice must be taken here as representative of the ritual aspect of Jewish religion, to which the Pharisees are seen to give precedence over the ethical demand of God's law. But the sharp antithesis is not really intended, any more than it is in its original context in Hosea, to mean that sacrifice is not God's will. The meaning is that mere ritual observance is of no value in God's sight. We can be sure that Matthew does not understand Jesus to be rejecting the sacrificial system, because in Matthew 5:23–4 he preserves a saying of Jesus which takes it for granted that his hearers, like almost all Jews, would be following the practice of offering sacrifice in the temple.[55] It seems clear that, despite his criticism of the way the priestly hierarchy ran the temple, Jesus did not go as far as the Qumran sect, who rejected the legitimacy of the worship in the temple (while not rejecting sacrifice in principle). We must also take it as virtually certain that he himself participated in sacrificial worship, both in attending the

---

[54] See Richard Bauckham, 'Jesus' Demonstration in the Temple,' in *Law and Religion* (ed. Barnabas Lindars; Cambridge: James Clarke, 1988), pp. 72–89.

[55] Note also Luke 17:14 (cf. Lev. 14:1–32).

prayers that accompanied the regular sacrifices in the temple, and in offering sacrifices himself (which were not of course only offered in atonement for personal sin, but also for purification from ritual impurity and as offerings of praise and thanksgiving).[56] His attendance at the regular annual festivals in Jerusalem (Luke 2:41–2; John 2:13; 7:1–10; 10:22–3) would have involved this. If the impression the Synoptic Gospels give that the Last Supper was a Passover meal is correct (Mark 14:12–16; Luke 22:14; but contrast John 18:28; 19:14,31), then Jesus ate with his disciples the Passover lamb that had been sacrificed in the temple that afternoon.

Eventually most early Christians came to believe that the sacrificial system, or at any rate sin-offerings, had been rendered redundant by the sacrificial death of Christ (see especially Hebrews), while the principle of the Pauline mission to the Gentiles was that Gentile converts to Christianity were free from all the ritual requirements of the Mosaic law. But there is no suggestion in any of the New Testament writers (not even in Stephen's speech in Acts 7)[57] that God had not really commanded Israel to offer animal sacrifices.[58] However, this does seem to have been the view adopted by the later Jewish Christian sect of the Ebionites (to be distinguished from the mainstream of Jewish Christians, who were known as Nazarenes), doubtless in reaction to the destruction of the temple and the end of the temple cult in 70 CE.[59] Accordingly, in the *Gospel of the Ebionites*, which is based on the three Synoptic Gospels,[60] they attributed to Jesus the saying: 'I came to abolish sacrifices, and if you do not cease from sacrificing the wrath will not cease from you' (*apud* Epiphanius, *Pan.* 30.16.5). In the account of the preparation for the Last Supper, this gospel borrowed from Matthew 26:17 the disciples' question to Jesus, 'Where do you want us

---

[56] For a general account of sacrifices in the time of Jesus, see Ed P. Sanders, *Judaism: Practice and Belief: 63 BCE – 66 CE* (London: SCM Press/Philadelphia: Trinity Press International, 1992), ch. 7.

[57] In context, Stephen's quotation of Amos 5:25–7 (Acts 7:42-3) means that Israel in the wilderness failed to offer the sacrifices to God which they should have offered, but offered sacrifices to idols instead.

[58] According to Acts 21:26, even Paul participated in sacrifices in the temple.

[59] The passages in the Pseudo-Clementine literature that treat the laws in the Pentateuch prescribing sacrifices and other aspects of the temple cult as later additions to the law of Moses, not belonging to the law originally given by God (*Clem. Hom.* 2:44; 3:52), are probably of Ebionite origin.

[60] See G. Howard, 'The Gospel of the Ebionites', in *Aufstieg und Niedergang der römischen Welt*, vol. 2/25/5 (ed. W. Haase; Berlin/New York: De Gruyter, 1988), pp. 4034–53.

to make the preparations for you to eat the Passover?' For Jesus' answer the words of Luke 22:15 ('I have eagerly desired to eat this Passover with you') were used, but turned into a question expecting the answer 'no': 'Have I eagerly desired to eat meat with you this Passover?' (*apud* Epiphanius, *Pan.* 30.22.4). The addition of 'meat' to the words taken from Luke probably indicates not only that the Ebionites could not accept that Jesus would have eaten a sacrificial animal, but also that they thought Jesus was vegetarian. To the latter point we shall return below. But it is clear that these features of the *Gospel of the Ebionites* are late adaptations of the gospel tradition, designed to bring it into line with the particular views of the Ebionite sect and of no historical value.

Just as we can scarcely doubt that Jesus participated in the sacrificial system, so we can scarcely doubt that he also ate meat other than that of sacrificial animals. It is true that meat was a luxury in Jewish Palestine (cf. Sir. 39:26–7).[61] Jesus would not have eaten it regularly. But the meals to which he was invited in the houses of the wealthy (Mark 2:15; Luke 7:36; 11:37; 14:1; 19:5) are likely to have included meat. Jesus does not seem to have disapproved of the employment of those of his disciples who had been fishermen (see especially Luke 5:3–10). In the feeding miracles, he multiplied fish, along with loaves, to provide food for the crowd (Mark 6:38–43; 8:7), while after his resurrection, he not only cooked and served fish for the disciples (John 21:9–13), but also ate fish himself (Luke 24:42–3). Even though the historical value of some of these passages in the Gospels is widely disputed, it is hard to believe that if Jesus had been vegetarian such traditions could have arisen in the early church.

Some Jews in Jesus' time did practise abstention from meat, for two main reasons.[62] One was the need, in a Gentile context, to avoid the

---

[61] See Schochet, *Animal Life*, pp. 15–17.

[62] On Jewish and Christian vegetarianism in New Testament times, see Roger T. Beckwith, 'The Vegetarianism of the Therapeutae, and the Motives for Vegetarianism in Early Jewish and Christian Circles,' *Revue de Qumran* 13 (1988): pp. 407–10 (but he overlooks some evidence: Dan. 10:2; 4 Ezra 9:23–6; 12:51; *T. Reub.* 1:9–10; *T. Jud.* 15:4; Eusebius, *Hist. Eccl.* 2.23.5). He divides his evidence into five categories of vegetarianism, but it can all be included in my two categories, with the exception of his fourth category. This is a single reference in Philo (*Prov.* fragment 2, 69-70), which commends vegetarianism on the grounds that eating meat reduces humans 'to the savagery of wild beasts'. On the more general question of vegetarianism in the ancient world, see David E. Aune, in Hans Dieter Betz ed., *Plutarch's Theological Writings and Early Christian Literature* (SCHNT 3; Leiden: Brill, 1975), pp. 305–8.

defilement which eating Gentile food might incur (Dan. 1:5–16; Tob. 1:10–13; Jdt. 10:5; 12:2). Red meat would not have been correctly slaughtered and drained of blood. Especially there was the probability that Gentile meat had been offered to idols in pagan temples before being sold in the market. This is almost certainly the reason why some Jewish Christians in the church in Rome were vegetarian (Rom. 14:2). But such problems did not occur in Jewish Palestine where Jesus lived.

The second reason for abstention from meat was as an ascetic practice of self-denial. As such, it was relatively unusual. Jews regularly practised fasting, which meant complete abstention from food and drink for short periods. The traditional form of long-term self-denial was the Nazirite vow, which required abstention from alcoholic drink but not from meat (Num. 6:3; Judg. 13:4,7,14). According to Luke 1:15 John the Baptist, like Samson, was a Nazirite from birth, which did not therefore prevent him from making locusts part of his ascetic diet in the wilderness (Mark 1:6). However, because meat was regarded as a luxury, the practice of abstaining from wine and meat was sometimes adopted as a kind of semi-fast that, unlike true fasting, could be maintained over a long period. It was considered a form of mourning (Dan. 10:2; *T. Reub.* 1:10). It might be practised for a few days or weeks (Dan. 10:2; 4 Ezra 9:23–6; 12:51) or, exceptionally, for several years (*T. Reub.* 1:9–10) or a lifetime (*T. Jud.* 15:4). The Therapeutae, a Jewish community who lived a kind of monastic life in Egypt, never drank wine or ate meat (Philo, *Contempl.* 73–4). Apparently, after the destruction of the temple in 70 CE, many Jews abstained permanently from wine and meat, as a form of mourning for the temple (*t. Sot.* 15:11–15). In an account of James the Lord's brother, which is largely legendary but probably does derive from second-century Palestinian Jewish Christian tradition, in which the memory of James was revered, Hegesippus represents him as, in effect, a Nazirite who augmented his vow by abstaining from meat as well as from wine. Since he is also said to have been constantly in prayer for the forgiveness of the Jewish people, his asceticism is probably to be understood as a form of mourning for their sins (*apud* Eusebius, *Hist. Eccl.* 2.23.5–6).

In the *Gospel of the Ebionites*, John the Baptist's diet in the wilderness is said to have been, not locusts (Greek *akris*) and wild honey (as in Matt. 3:4; Mark 1:6), but wild honey that tasted like a cake (Greek *ekris*) in oil (*apud* Epiphanius, *Pan.* 30.13.4). Clearly the change is designed to make the Baptist the kind of ascetic who abstained not only from wine but also from meat. Probably, in representing Jesus also as vegetarian (as we noticed above), this gospel was making Jesus also into this kind of ascetic. Perhaps the Ebionites took the Jewish Christian tradition about the asceticism of James the Lord's brother as the model to which they conformed both John the Baptist and Jesus. It does not necessarily follow that the Ebionites themselves were all lifelong vegetarians.

However, we can be sure that Jesus did not practise this form of asceticism. A reliable gospel tradition strikingly contrasts him with the ascetic figure of John the Baptist:

> Luke 7:33–4 (par. Matt. 11:18–19): For John the Baptist has come eating no bread and drinking no wine; and you say, 'He has a demon'; the Son of Man has come eating and drinking; and you say, 'Look, a glutton and a drunkard, a friend of tax-collectors and sinners!'

Moreover, Jesus' vow of abstention from wine taken at the Last Supper (Mark 14:25) implies that he had not previously abstained from wine, and abstention from meat without abstention from wine is unknown in Jewish or early Christian ascetic practice. When Jesus was asked why his disciples did not follow the normal Jewish practice of regular fasting, he compared his ministry with the festivities of a wedding celebration in which it is inappropriate to fast (Mark 2:18–20). With this view of his ministry, we cannot imagine Jesus adopting a practice that symbolized mourning.

According to Genesis, both meat-eating (Gen. 1:29; 9:3) and wine-drinking (Gen. 9:20–21) began after the Flood. So it is possible that the ascetic practice of abstaining from both was associated with a return to the practice of early humanity, before divine concessions to human corruption. But there is no evidence for this, and it is not easy to relate this notion to the fact that abstention from meat and wine symbolized mourning. Nor is there any evidence of any Jews or early Christians adopting vegetarianism out of a desire to return to the paradisal condition of humanity.[63] We might think this would have been appropriate

---

[63] It is not very clear whether, in Jewish and early Christian eschatology, people in the messianic age are expected to be vegetarian, though it is clear that they will drink wine (*1 Enoch* 10:19; Mark 14:25). But if wild animals are to be once again vegetarian (Isa. 11:6–9; *Sib. Or.* 3:788–95; cf. Gen. 1:30), it would seem that humans must also be, and the abundance of food that is to be provided without human effort (*2 Bar.* 29:5; *1 Enoch* 10:19; Papias, *apud* Irenaeus, *Adv. Haer.* 5.33.5–6) is to be vegetarian. On the other hand, Leviathan and Behemoth are to be slaughtered to provide food (4 Ezra 6:52; *2 Bar.* 29:4).

in Jesus' case (especially in view of Mark 1:13, to be discussed in our next section), but the evidence is entirely against it. We must conclude that Jesus neither adopted vegetarianism for reasons that other Jews had for doing so nor adopted it for innovatory reasons of his own. Of course, it does not follow that there cannot be any kinds of valid Christian arguments for vegetarianism,[64] but an argument that meat-eating is absolutely wrong would clearly contradict the Christian belief in the sinlessness of Jesus. It would also cut Christianity's roots in the Jewish tradition of faith to which Jesus so clearly belonged.

The Messianic Peace with Wild Animals

Mark's account of the forty days Jesus spent in the wilderness following his baptism (Mark 1:13) falls into a different category from most of the material in the Gospels which we have studied so far, and for this reason has been left till last. In the first place, whereas we have so far been concerned for the most part with gospel traditions which we can be fairly sure preserve accurately the teaching of Jesus, it is much more difficult to assess the historical character of Mark 1:13. Even if Jesus did spend a period alone in the wilderness before the commencement of his public ministry, which is likely enough, many scholars would regard the details of Mark's account of this as not so much a historical report, but more in the nature of an early Christian attempt to express the theological significance of Jesus and his messianic mission. So we shall here be content to understand the significance Mark and his readers would have seen in the statement that Jesus 'was with the wild animals', without attempting to decide the historical question. But secondly, Mark 1:13 differs from the other gospel material we have studied in that, whereas other references to animals are incidental, in the sense that they take for granted a well-established Jewish attitude to animals in order to make a point which is not primarily about animals, in Mark 1:13 the evangelist, as we shall see, understands Jesus' mission as designed to make a difference to the human relationship with wild animals.

---

[64] For an argument for vegetarianism which takes account of the fact that Jesus was not a vegetarian, see Andrew Linzey, 'The Bible and Killing for Food', in *Using the Bible Today* (ed. Dan Cohn-Sherbok; London: Bellew Publishing, 1991), pp. 110–20.

Mark 1:13 reads: Jesus 'was in the wilderness forty days, tempted by Satan; and he was with the wild beasts; and the angels waited on him'. The statement that Jesus was with the wild animals[65] is a mere four words of the Greek text, but we should not be misled by its brevity into thinking it insignificant or merely incidental. In Mark's concise account of Jesus in the wilderness no words are wasted. Each of the three clauses has its own significance.

Mark's prologue (1:1–5), in which this verse occurs, presents Jesus as the messianic Son of God embarking on his mission to inaugurate the kingdom of God. Following his anointing with the Spirit at the baptism, the Spirit drives him into the wilderness (v. 12) for a task that evidently must be fulfilled before he can embark on his preaching of the kingdom (v. 14). The wilderness had gathered rich symbolic associations in Jewish tradition, but we should not be distracted by the symbolism it carries in the fuller Matthean and Lukan accounts of the temptation (Matt. 4:1–11; Luke 4:1–13). Nor should we describe Mark 1:13 as Mark's temptation narrative: the testing by Satan is for Mark only the first of three encounters, all important. In Mark 1:13 the wilderness carries its most fundamental biblical and natural significance: it is the non-human sphere. In contrast to the cultivated land, where humans live with their domesticated animals, the wilderness was the world outside human control, uninhabitable by humans, feared as it threatened to encroach on the precarious fertility of the cultivated land and as the haunt of beings hostile to humans.[66] It was the natural home not only of the wild animals but also of the demonic. Hence Jesus goes into the wilderness precisely to encounter the beings of the non-human world: he must establish his messianic relationship to these before he can preach and practise the kingdom of God in the human world. Significantly, none of the three non-human beings he encounters in the wilderness – Satan, the wild animals, the angels – subsequently appear in Mark's narrative of Jesus' activity in the human world.

The order of the non-human beings in Mark 1:13 – Satan, the wild animals, the angels – is not accidental. Satan is the natural enemy of the righteous person and can only be resisted: Jesus in the wilderness wins the fundamental victory over satanic temptation which he can

---

[65] For a much fuller discussion of this text, see Chapter 5 in this volume.

[66] Johannes Pedersen, *Israel: Its Life and Culture* (trans. A. Moller; London: OUP/Copenhagen: Pio/Povl Branner, 1926), pp. 454–60; Williams, *Wilderness*, pp. 12–13.

then carry through against the activity of Satan's minions in the human world later in the Gospel (see especially Mark 3:27). The angels, on the other hand, are the natural friends of the righteous person: they minister to Jesus as they did to Elijah in the wilderness (1 Kgs. 19:5–8) and to Adam and Eve in paradise (*b. Sanh.* 59b). Between Satan and the angels the wild animals are more ambiguous: they are enemies of whom Jesus makes friends. This is the point that we shall shortly establish.

We must first ask: which animals are designated by the word *thēria* ('wild animals') in Mark 1:13? The word usually refers to wild animals in distinction from animals owned by humans, and usually to four-footed animals in distinction from birds, reptiles and fish, though snakes can be called *thēria* (e.g. Acts 28:4–5). However, the word can also have the more limited sense of beasts of prey or animals dangerous to humans. Though sometimes given by the context or an adjective, this sense of dangerous beast of prey seems quite often required by the word *thērion* without further indication of it.

This linguistic phenomenon corresponds to an ancient tendency, at least in the Jewish tradition, to consider wild animals primarily as threats to humanity, either directly threats to human life (e.g. Gen. 37:20,33; Lev. 26:6,22; 2 Kgs. 2:24; 17:25–6; Prov. 28:15; Jer. 5:6; Lam. 3:10–11; Ezek. 5:17; 14:15; 34:25,28; Hos. 13:7–8; Amos 5:19; Rev. 6:8) or, by attacks on flocks and herds, threats to human livelihood (Lev. 26:22; 1 Sam. 17:34–7; Hos. 2:12; Amos 3:12; John 10:12). The sense of wild animals as threatening belongs to the prevalent conceptualization of the world as conflict between the human world (human beings, their animals and their cultivated land) and wild nature. Not many wild animals (as distinct from birds and fish) were hunted for food in Jewish Palestine, and so interest in wild animals tended to be limited to those which were threats to humanity. Seeing these animals purely from the perspective of sporadic human contact with them can produce a distorted and exaggerated view of their enmity to humans, as can be seen in a remarkable passage of Philo of Alexandria (*Praem.* 85–90), who portrays wild animals, meaning the dangerous beasts of prey, as engaged in a continuous war against humans, constantly waiting the opportunity to attack their human victims. Alien and excluded from the human world, wild animals had human fears projected onto them. Of course, ancient peoples who perceived wild animals primarily as a threat did not notice that they themselves were also a threat to wild animals by steadily reducing their habitats as they extended the area of cultivated or deforested land.

The Jewish tradition, in the context of which Mark 1:13 should be read, saw the enmity of the wild animals as a distortion of the created relationship between humans and animals and the result of human sin. In creation God established human dominion over the animals (Gen. 1:26,28; Ps. 8:6–8; Sir. 17:2–4; Wis. 9:2–3), which should have been peaceful and harmonious, but was subsequently disrupted by violence. The Noahic covenant (Gen. 9:1–7) takes account of the violence. But that humans should live in fear of animals should not be the case even by the terms of the Noahic covenant, which promises that animals shall go in fear of humans (Gen. 9:2). In fact, wild animals were perceived as menacing. Jewish literature therefore envisaged two ways in which the true relationship of humans and wild animals might be restored: one individual, one eschatological. In the first place, it could be thought that the truly righteous person should enjoy divine protection from wild animals as from other threats to human life: as Eliphaz told Job: 'At destruction and famine you shall laugh, and shall not fear the wild animals of the earth . . . [They] shall be at peace with you' (Job 5:22–3). In later Jewish literature the idea is that the truly righteous person exercises the human dominion over the animals as it was first intended, as it was given at creation (*b. Sanh.* 38b; *b. Shabb.* 151b; *Gen. Rab.* 8:12).[67]

Secondly, Jewish eschatological expectation included the hope that the righting of all wrongs in the messianic age would bring peace between wild animals and humans. The classic scriptural expression of this hope is Isaiah 11:6–9:[68]

> The wolf shall live with the lamb,
> the leopard shall lie down with the kid,
> the calf and the lion and the fatling together,
> and a little child shall lead them.
> The cow and the bear shall graze,
> their young shall lie down together;
> and the lion shall eat straw like the ox.
> The nursing child shall play over the hole of the asp,
> and the weaned child shall put his hand on the adder's den.
> They will not hurt or destroy on all my holy mountain;
> for the earth shall be full of the knowledge of the LORD,
> as the waters cover the sea.

---

[67] Cf. Cohen, *'Be Fertile'*, pp. 87, 100–1, 103, where additional references are given. See also *T. Naph.* 8:4, 6; *T. Iss.* 7:7; *T. Benj.* 3:4–5; 5:2.

[68] On this passage, see Murray, *Cosmic Covenant*, pp. 103–10.

This has often been misunderstood by modern readers as a picture simply of peace between animals. In fact, it depicts peace between the human world, with its domesticated animals (lamb, kid, calf, bullock, cow), and the wild animals (wolf, leopard, lion, bear, poisonous snakes) that were normally perceived as threats both to human livelihood (dependent on domestic animals) and to human life. Peace between all animals is certainly implied, both in the fact that the bear and the lion become vegetarian (11:7) and the snakes harmless (11:8), and also in the cessation of all harm and destruction (11:9), which must mean also that humans are to be vegetarian. The picture is of a restoration of paradise ('my holy mountain' is Eden, as in Ezek. 28:13–14) and the original vegetarianism of all living creatures (Gen. 1:29–30), but it is presented from the perspective of ancient people's sense of threat from dangerous wild animals. That threat is to be removed, the enmity between humans and wild animals healed. Later Jewish literature, down to the New Testament period, continued the same expectation, primarily inspired by Isaiah 11:6–9 (see Isa. 65:25; Sib. Or. 3:788–95; Philo. *Praem.* 87–90; 2 *Bar.* 73:6). In such passages, the dominant notion is that the original, paradisal situation, in which humans and wild animals lived in peace and harmony, will be restored in the messianic age.

We need not limit the wild animals (*thēria*) of Mark 1:13 to the somewhat dangerous animals that might be encountered in the wilderness of Judea: bears, leopards, wolves, poisonous snakes (cobras, desert vipers and others), scorpions. The word does not prohibit well-informed readers from thinking also of other animals: hyenas, jackals, caracals (the desert lynx), desert foxes, Fennec foxes, wild boars, wild asses (the onager and the Syrian wild ass), antelopes (the desert oryx and the addax), gazelles, wild goats (the Nubian ibex), porcupines, hares, Syrian hyraxes, and so on.[69] But both the word usage and the habits of thought that went with it would be likely to bring especially the dangerous animals to mind.

Mark's simple but effective phrase indicates Jesus' peaceable presence with them. The expression 'to be with someone' (Greek *einai*

---

[69] For this (not exhaustive) list of animals to be found in such areas of Palestine, I am indebted to Henry Baker Tristram, *The Natural History of the Bible* (London: SPCK, 1911); Friedrich Simon Bodenheimer, *Animal Life in Palestine* (Jerusalem: L. Mayer, 1935); George Cansdale, *Animals of Bible Lands* (Exeter: Paternoster, 1970). Some Old Testament passages are informative as to the animals generally associated with the desert: Deut. 8:15; Job 24:5; 39:6–8; Isa. 13:21–2; 32:14; 34:11–15; Jer. 2:24; 5:6; 10:22; Zeph. 2:14–15; Mal. 1:8.

meta tinos) frequently has the strongly positive sense of close association or friendship or agreement or assistance (e.g. Matt. 12:30; 26:69,71; 28:20; Luke 22:59; John 3:2; 8:29; 15:27; 16:32; 17:24; Acts 7:9; 10:38; 18:10; Rom. 15:33), and in Mark's own usage elsewhere in his Gospel, the idea of close, friendly association predominates (3:14; 5:18; 14:67; cf. 4:36). Mark 1:13 depicts Jesus enjoying the peaceable harmony with wild animals which had been God's original intention for humanity but which is usually disrupted by the threat of violence.

Apart from the context, we might class Jesus, in terms of the Jewish traditions we have outlined, simply as the individual righteous person who is at peace with the wild animals. But Jesus in Mark's prologue is no mere individual. Just as he resists Satan, not as merely an individual righteous person, but as the messianic Son of God on behalf of and for the sake of others, so he establishes, representatively, the messianic peace with wild animals. He does so only representatively, in his own person, and so the objection that a restoration of paradise should not be located in the wilderness is beside the point. More to the point is that all the wild animals of Isaiah 11 would be most easily encountered in the wilderness. Jesus does not restore the paradisal state as such, but he sets the messianic precedent for it.

If Mark's phrase ('with the wild animals'), indicating a friendly companionship with the animals, would certainly evoke, for his original readers, the Jewish expectation of the age of messianic salvation, it also contrasts with some aspects of the way the restoration of the proper human relationship to wild animals was sometimes portrayed in the Jewish literature. There the animals are portrayed as fearing humans (a reversal of the present situation of human fear of the animals and no doubt thought to be the proper attitude of respect for their human rulers: *T. Naph.* 8:4; *T. Benj.* 5:2; Philo, *Praem.* 89; cf. Sir. 17:4; *Ap. Mos.* 10:3; *Gen. Rab.* 34:12) and the expectation is that they will serve humans (*2 Bar.* 73:6). In other words, they too will become domestic animals. The human dominion over them is conceived as domination for human benefit. Such ideas of the ideal human relationship to the wild animals as one of lordship over subjects or domestic servants did continue in Christianity, but they are very notably absent from Mark 1:13. Mark says nothing of that sort at all. Jesus does not terrorize or dominate the wild animals, he does not domesticate or even make pets of them. He is simply 'with them'.

The context to which Mark 1:13 originally spoke was one in which wild animals threatened humanity and their wilderness threatened to encroach on the human world. The messianic peace with wild animals promised, by healing the alienation and enmity between humans and animals, to liberate humans from that threat. Christians who read Mark 1:13 today do so in a very different context, one in which it is now clearly we who threaten the survival of wild animals, encroach on their habitat, threaten to turn their wilderness into a wasteland they cannot inhabit. To make the point one need only notice how many of the animals Jesus could have encountered in the Judean wilderness have become extinct in Palestine during the past century: the bear, the onager, the desert oryx, the addax, the ostrich and no doubt others. Others, such as the leopard and the gazelle, would not have survived without modern conservation measures. But Mark's image of Jesus' peaceable companionship with the animals in the wilderness can survive this reversal of situation. Its pregnant simplicity gains a new power for modern Christians in a world of ecological destruction. For us Jesus' companionable presence with the wild animals affirms their independent value for themselves and for God. He does not adopt them into the human world, but lets them be themselves in peace, leaving them their wilderness, affirming them as creatures who share the world with us in the community of God's creation. Mark's image of Jesus with the animals provides a christological warrant for and a biblical symbol of the human possibility of living fraternally with other living creatures, a possibility given by God in creation and given back in messianic redemption. Like all aspects of Jesus' inauguration of the kingdom of God, its fullness will be realized only in the eschatological future, but it can be significantly anticipated in the present.

Jesus and the Wild Animals in the Wilderness (Mark 1:13)

The Hermeneutical Context

Modern New Testament scholarship is historically situated. It inevitably approaches the texts with concerns that derive from its cultural context, both Christian and secular. Such concerns can be heuristically useful, but they can also limit and distort our perceptions of the texts. In the present context of ecological crisis, in which it has become urgently necessary that Christian thinking recover a sense of human beings' place within God's creation, as fellow-creatures with other creatures in the community of creation, new concerns are slowly bringing neglected aspects of the texts to light. At the same time it is becoming painfully obvious that much modern interpretation of the New Testament has been consciously and unconsciously influenced by the prevalent ideology of the modern West which for two centuries or so has understood human history as emancipation from nature. This modern ideology imagined human beings as the omnipotent subjects of their own history, and history as a process of liberation from nature, so that, freed from a limited place within the given constraints of the natural world, human beings may freely transform nature into a human world of their own devising. This rejection of human embeddedness in nature and of the mutual interrelations between human history and the rest of nature, in favour of an assumed independence of and supremacy over nature, is, of course, the ideological root of the present ecological crisis. Biblical theology has not escaped its influence, which appears in the strong tendency to set history against nature and salvation against creation. The assertion of salvation-history and/or eschatology as the key concepts of biblical theology has at least tacitly endorsed the modern understanding of history as emancipation from nature. References to nature in the New Testament, especially the Gospels, have been persistently understood from the perspective of modern urban people, themselves alienated from nature, for whom literary references to nature can only be symbols or picturesque illustrations of a human world unrelated to nature. But once the prevalent modern ideology is questioned, as it must be today, we are freed to read the New Testament differently. We can recognize that, in continuity with the Old Testament tradition, it assumes that humans live in mutuality with the rest of God's creation, that salvation-history and eschatology do not lift humans out of nature but heal precisely their distinctive relationship with the rest of nature.

However, to recognize that a concern with the human relationship to the rest of creation is a genuine aspect of the texts must not mean that we read into the texts our own particular ecological concerns, which arise from our own specific situation at a highly critical juncture in the history of creation on this planet. Before the texts can be relevant to our situation we must place them in the very different context of concern with the human relationship to nature to which they originally spoke. This task takes us into a whole area of historical scholarship – the study of ancient perceptions of the human relationship to nature and of the way such perceptions corresponded to ecological realities – that has been almost as neglected as the specifically biblical aspect of it. The present chapter is a preliminary contribution to the task: an ecological reading of one, very brief but significant, New Testament text. The attempt will be made both to understand the text in its original context, especially against the background of early Jewish perceptions of the relation between humans and wild animals, and then also to indicate its new relevance today, when re-contextualized in our own situation of ecological destruction.

Our text is a mere four words of Mark's Gospel: Jesus 'was with the wild animals' (*ēn meta tōn thēriōn*). But the brevity of the statement should not mislead us into thinking it incidental. In Mark's concise account of Jesus in the wilderness (1:13) no words are wasted. In these four words, Mark takes up the question of the human relationship to wild animals and gives it a key place in the christological programme which the prologue to his Gospel is designed to set out. Dealing with the human relationship with wild animals evidently belongs to Jesus' identity and mission as the messianic Son of God. Our text provides us with a christological image, unique to Mark's Gospel, sadly neglected in the Christian tradition, but, once its background is understood, of considerable symbolic resonance and ripe for contemporary retrieval. It is one of the biblical resources for developing a Christology whose concern for the relationship of humanity to God will not exclude, but include humanity's relationship to the rest of God's creatures.

Exegetical Options

On the significance of Mark's statement that Jesus was with the wild animals, broadly three lines of interpretation have been proposed:[1]

1. The wild animals are simply part of the setting in the wilderness, mentioned in order to stress the solitude: Jesus' lack of human companionship.[2] However, it is very doubtful that the animals would appear in this role in so concise an account, where otherwise every feature is charged with theological significance.
2. The animals are to be associated with the demonic and seen as allies of Satan in his attack on Jesus. The scene is understood as a kind of holy war, with Satan and the wild animals ranged on one side, and Jesus and the angels on the other.[3] However, several important points can be made against this interpretation. First, the text is quite explicit about the role of the angels.[4] They do not belong to the armies of heaven, protecting Jesus or fighting with him against evil. They are ministering angels, present to provide for Jesus' needs (*diēkonoun auton*), almost certainly to provide him with food.

    Secondly, the animals are not portrayed as antagonistic to Jesus, as Satan is. If Mark intended to line them up with Satan against Jesus and the angels, he has expressed himself very badly. *Einai meta tinos* can refer to mere physical proximity (Matt. 5:25; John

---

[1] E. Fascher, 'Jesus und die Tiere', *TLZ* 90 (1965): pp. 561–70, provides an overview of interpretations (in German literature only) up to 1961.

[2] E.g. W. Foerster in *TDNT* 3.134; other references in U. Holzmeister, '"Jesus lebte mit den wilden Tieren": Mk 1,13', in *Vom Wort des Lebens: Festschrift für Max Meinertz* (ed. Nikolaus Adler; Münster: Aschendorff, 1951), pp. 85–6; Erich Grässer, 'ΚΑΙ ΗΝ ΜΕΤΑ ΤΩΝ ΘΗΡΙΩΝ (Mk 1,13b): Ansätze einer theologischen Tierschutzethik', in *Studien zum Text und zur Ethik des Neuen Testaments: Festschrift zum 80. Geburtstag von Heinrich Greeren* (ed. Wolfgang Schrage; Berlin/New York: De Gruyter, 1986), pp. 144–157.

[3] Ernest Best, *Mark: The Gospel as Story* (Edinburgh: T&T CLark, 1983), p. 57; other references in Grässer, 'ΚΑΙ ΗΝ ΜΕΤΑ ΤΩΝ ΘΗΡΙΩΝ', p. 149 n. 27.

[4] Grässer, 'ΚΑΙ ΗΝ ΜΕΤΑ ΤΩΝ ΘΗΡΙΩΝ', p. 149.

9:40; 12:17; 20:24,26), but it frequently has a strongly positive sense of close association in friendship or agreement or assistance (Matt. 12:30; 26:69,71; 28:20; Luke 22:59; John 3:2; 8:29; 15:27; 16:32; 17:24; Acts 7:9; 10:38; 18:10; 15:33; Ignatius, *Phld.* 3:2; cf. the positive but less strong sense in John 3:26; 13:33; 14:9; 16:4; 17:12). In Mark's usage elsewhere the idea of close, friendly association predominates (3:14; 5:18; 14:67; cf. 4:36). Thus in Mark 1:13 the phrase *ēn meta tōn thēriōn*, in the absence of any other indication of the kind of relationship envisaged, may convey a more or less strongly positive sense of association,[5] but it certainly does not express hostile confrontation.[6]

Thirdly, there is no good evidence that in Jewish thinking the wild animals were regarded as demonic or as allies of Satan. The evidence usually cited for this does not in fact demonstrate it. There are indeed passages in which dangerous animals are used as metaphors of Satan or demons (Luke 10:19; 1 Pet. 5:8; *Jos. Asen.* 12:9–10; cf. Ps. 91:13), just as they appear, in the Psalms for example, as metaphors for human enemies (e.g. Pss. 10:9; 17:12; 22:12–13,16,21; 58:4–6; 118:12; 140:3). This is a natural metaphorical usage which tells us nothing about the significance of actual animals in a narrative such as Mark 1:13. It no more means that such actual animals are demonic than the fact that, for example, the lion is used as a symbol of the Messiah (Rev. 5:5) means that actual lions are allies of the Messiah. There are also passages in which desolate places are portrayed as inhabited both by wild animals of the desert and by demons (Isa. 13:21–2; 34:13–15; Rev. 18:2). This shows that places uninhabitable by humans were associated both with wild animals and with evil spirits, and so helps to explain why Jesus encounters both Satan and the wild animals in the desert. The desert is a realm of threat to humans, and its inhabitants, whether animal or demonic, seem alien and threatening to humans. But

---

[5] So Holzmeister, 'Jesus lebte mit den wilden Tieren', p. 86 (quoting Wohlenberg); Antonio Vargas-Machuca, 'La tentación de Jesús según Mc. 1,12-13: Hecho real o relato de tipo haggádico?,' *EstEcl* 48 (1973): p. 172; Grässer, 'ΚΑΙ ΗΝ ΜΕΤΑ ΤΩΝ ΘΗΡΙΩΝ', p. 149. But by not recognizing that the expression can express mere physical proximity, they put the point too strongly.

[6] *Einai meta tinos* can express the physical proximity of someone known from other information to be hostile (Matt. 5:25; John 9:40), but it cannot itself convey hostility. Therefore, if it is the hostile confrontation between Jesus and the animals that matters to Mark, he has oddly failed to express it, while using a phrase that instead could readily suggest peaceable and friendly association.

again this does not make the animals themselves demonic or allies of Satan.

Finally, wild animals frequently appear in the Old Testament and later Jewish literature as inimical to humans and threatening human life and livelihood. Of special interest here are a series of closely related passages in the *Testaments of the Twelve Patriarchs* (*T. Naph.* 8:4,6; *T. Iss.* 7:7; *T. Benj.* 3:4–5; 5:2), which will be quoted and discussed more fully in section III below. In these passages wild animals are mentioned in parallel with Satan or demons as threats to humanity. But this does not make them demonic. It merely shows that wild animals were perceived as menacing to human beings, as the demons are also in different ways. The animals and the demons appear as different kinds of non-human enemies of humanity. This evidence is relevant to Mark 1:13a – which, as we shall see, does need to be read against the background of the common Jewish view of wild animals as threats to humanity – but it does not prove that Mark portrays Jesus in conflict with the wild animals, as he is with Satan.

3. According to the third line of interpretation, Jesus is portrayed at peace with the wild animals as the paradisal state of humans and animals was supposed to be in Jewish thought. By means of this motif Mark represents Jesus as the eschatological Adam who, having resisted Satan, instead of succumbing to temptation as Adam did, then restores paradise: he is at peace with the animals and the angels serve him.[7] This is the interpretation that has been argued most fully and persuasively in recent discussion,[8] and probably now commands the support of a majority of exegetes.[9] I shall broadly

---

[7] For older literature taking this view, see Vargas-Machuca, 'La tentación de Jesús', pp. 170 n. 33, 173–4 n. 45.

[8] See especially J. Jeremias in *TDNT* 1.141; W.A. Schultze, 'Der Heilige und die wilden Tiere: Zur Exegese von Mc 1 13b,' *ZNW* 46 (1955): pp. 280–3; André Feuillet, 'L'épisode de la Tentation d'après l'Evangile selon Saint Marc (I,12-13)', *EstBib* 19 (1960): pp. 49–73; Vargas-Machuca, 'La tentación de Jesús'; Grässer, 'ΚΑΙ ΗΝ ΜΕΤΑ ΤΩΝ ΘΗΡΙΩΝ'. H.-G. Leder, 'Sünderfallerzählung und Versuchungsgeschichte: Zur Interpretation von Mc 1 12f.,' *ZNW* 54 (1963): pp. 188–216, rejects the idea of an Adam typology, but accepts a reference to the Old Testament expectation of peace with the wild animals in the messianic age.

[9] Among recent commentaries on Mark, see Rudolf Pesch, *Das Markusevangelium*, vol. 1 (HTKNT 2/1; Freiburg/Basel/Vienna: Herder, 1976), pp. 95–6; Joachim Gnilka, *Das Evangelium nach Markus*, vol. 1 (EKK 2/1; Zurich: Benziger/Neukirchen-Vluyn: Neukirchener, 1978), pp. 57–8; Walter Schmithals, *Das Evangelium nach Markus*, vol. 1 (2nd edn; Gütersloh: Mohn/Würzburg: Echter, 1986), pp. 92–3; Robert A. Guelich, *Mark 1–8:26* (WBC 34A; Dallas, Texas: Word, 1989), pp. 38–9.

agree with it, but I shall shift the emphasis that most of its advocates have given. They generally fail to give the motif of Jesus' being with the wild animals any independent significance of its own, but tend to see it either as making a christological point – that Jesus is the new Adam – purely for its own sake or as just a way of expressing Jesus' victory over evil and inauguration of the kingdom. That Mark or his tradition should have been genuinely interested in affirming that the kingdom of God inaugurated by Jesus includes peace with wild animals seems not to occur to them.[10] It needs to be asked whether they are projecting their own lack of interest in the human relationship with non-human creatures back onto Mark.

Friends and Enemies

The four words of Mark 1:13 in which we are interested form part of Mark's prologue (1:1–15), which introduces Jesus as the messianic Son of God embarking on his mission to inaugurate the kingdom of God. Following his anointing with the Spirit at the baptism, the Spirit drives Jesus into the wilderness (v. 12) for a task that evidently must be fulfilled before he can embark on his preaching of the kingdom (v. 14). Of Jesus' period in the wilderness Mark recounts:

> He was in the wilderness for forty days, being tempted by Satan.
> And he was with the wild animals (*ēn meta tōn thēriōn*).
> And the angels ministered to him. (1:13, my translation)

The wilderness, of course, had gathered rich symbolic associations in Jewish tradition,[11] but we should not be distracted by the symbolism it carries in the fuller Matthean and Lukan accounts of the temptation. Nor should we describe Mark 1:13 as Mark's temptation narrative, as is still commonly done.[12] The testing by Satan is for Mark only the first of three encounters, all important. So the wilderness as the place of Israel's testing, after the exodus, which is certainly significant in the Matthean and Lukan temptation narratives, is probably not determinative of the

---

[10] Grässer, 'ΚΑΙ ΗΝ ΜΕΤΑ ΤΩΝ ΘΗΡΙΩΝ' is an exception.

[11] See Ulrich Mauser, *Christ in the Wilderness: The Wilderness Theme in the Second Gospel and its Basis in the Biblical Tradition* (SBT; London: SCM Press, 1963), chs 2–4; Williams, *Wilderness*, pp. 12–20.

[12] E.g. Jack D. Kingsbury, *The Christology of Mark's Gospel* (Philadelphia: Fortress, 1983), pp. 68–9; Guelich, Mark 1–8:26, p. 36.

significance of the wilderness here, while the period of forty days is more likely to echo the period in which Elijah was fed by an angel in the wilderness (1 Kgs. 19:4–8) than the forty years of Israel's wanderings in the wilderness.[13]

In Mark 1:13 the wilderness carries its most fundamental biblical and natural significance: it is the non-human sphere. In contrast to the cultivated land, where humans live with their domesticated animals, the wilderness was the world outside human control, uninhabitable by humans, feared as it threatened to encroach on the precarious fertility of the cultivated land and as the haunt of beings hostile to humans. It was the natural home not only of the wild animals but also of the demonic.[14] Hence Jesus goes into the wilderness precisely to encounter the beings of the non-human world. He must establish his messianic relationship to these before he can preach and practise the kingdom of God in the human world. Significantly, none of the three kinds of non-human being he encounters in the wilderness – Satan, the wild animals, the angels – subsequently appear in Mark's narrative of Jesus' activity in the human world.

The order of the non-human beings in Mark 1:13 – Satan, the wild animals, the angels – is not accidental. Satan is the natural enemy of the righteous person and can only be resisted: Jesus in the wilderness wins the fundamental victory over satanic temptation which he can then carry through against the activity of Satan's minions in the human world later in the Gospel (cf. especially 3:27).[15] The angels, on the other hand, are the natural friends of the righteous person: they minister to Jesus as they did to Elijah in the wilderness (1 Kgs. 19:5–8) and to Adam and Eve in paradise (*b. Sanh.* 59b).[16] Between Satan and the angels the wild animals are more ambiguous: they are enemies of whom Jesus makes friends. This is the point I shall shortly establish.

---

[13] The forty days Moses spent on Mount Sinai (Exod. 24:18) and the forty days Adam spent fasting and standing in the river (*L.A.E.* 6:1–3) are scarcely relevant. Feuillet, 'L'épisode', attempts to link all the motifs in Mark 1:13 with Israel's wanderings in the wilderness, while also accepting the themes of the new Adam and the restoration of paradise.

[14] Pedersen, *Israel*, pp. 454–60; Williams, *Wilderness*, pp. 12–13.

[15] For this interpretation of 3:27, see Ernest Best, *The Temptation and the Passion: The Markan Soteriology* (SNTSMS 2; Cambridge: CUP, 1965), p. 15.

[16] The reference to *L.A.E.* 4, given by Joachim Jeremias in *TDNT* 1.141 n.6, and repeated mechanically by many others, is not relevant. *L.A.E.* 4:2 says that Adam and Eve in paradise ate the food of angels, not that angels fed them.

We must first ask: what animals are Mark's *thēria*? The word usually refers to wild animals in distinction from animals owned by humans, and usually to four-footed animals in distinction from birds, reptiles and fish (so Gen. 6:20; 7:20; Ps. 148:10; Hos. 2:18; 4:3 LXX; *1 Enoch* 7:5; *Ap. Mos.* 29:13; Jas. 3:7; *Barn.* 6:18), though snakes can be called *thēria* (Gen. 3:2 LXX; Acts 28:4–5; Hermas, *Sim.* 9:26:1, 7; cf. Josephus, *Ant.* 17.117). However, the word can also have the more limited sense of beasts of prey or animals dangerous to humans. Though sometimes given by the context or an adjective (cf. Gen. 37:20,32; Lev. 26:22; Job 5:22–3; Hos. 13:8 LXX; Tit. 1:12; Josephus, *Ant.* 17:120), this sense of dangerous beast of prey seems sometimes required by the word *thērion* without further indication of it (e.g. Josephus, *Ant.* 2.35; Acts 11:6; Ignatius, *Eph.* 7:1; *Rom.* 4:1–2; 5:2; *Smyrn.* 4:2; Philostratus, *Vit. Apoll.* 4:38).

This linguistic phenomenon corresponds to an ancient tendency, at least in the Jewish tradition, to consider wild animals primarily as threats to humanity, either directly threats to human life (Gen. 37:20,33; Lev. 26:6,22; 2 Kgs. 2:24; 17:25–6; Prov. 28:15; Jer. 5:6; Lam. 3:10–11; Ezek. 5:17; 14:15; 34:25,28; 13:7–8; Amos 5:19; *Pss. Sol.* 13:3; *T. Ab.* A 19:14–15; Rev. 6:8) or, by attacks on flocks and herds and crops, threats to human livelihood (Lev. 26:22; 1 Sam. 17:34–7; Hos. 2:12; Amos 3:12; John 10:12). The sense of wild animals as threatening belongs to the prevalent conceptualization of the world as conflict between the human world (human beings, their animals and their cultivated land) and wild nature. Not many wild animals (as distinct from birds and fish) were hunted for food in Jewish Palestine, and so interest in wild animals tended to be limited to those that were threats to humanity. Seeing these animals purely from the perspective of sporadic human contact with them can produce a distorted and exaggerated view of their enmity to humans, as can be seen in a remarkable passage of Philo of Alexandria (*Praem.* 85–90), who portrays wild animals (*thēria*), meaning the dangerous beasts of prey, as engaged in a continuous war against humans, constantly waiting the opportunity to attack their human victims. That Philo, living in Egypt, thinks this is true of the Indian elephant is only mildly surprising, but that he considers the Egyptian hippopotamus to be a man-eater[17] suggests a

---

[17] Cf. *Historia Monachorum in Aegypto* 4.3, where the hippopotamus is a threat – but to farmers' crops, not to human life. See also Friedrich Simon Bodenheimer, *Animal and Man in Bible Lands* (Collection de Travaux de l'Academie Internationale d'Histoire des Sciences 10; Leiden: Brill, 1960), pp. 51–2.

degree of paranoia. Alien and excluded from the human world, wild animals had human fears projected onto them. It is also worth noting that the staging of conflicts between people and wild animals in the Roman amphitheatres, in which of course the animals were provoked into antagonism, would have heightened first-century people's sense of the enmity of wild animals. Of course, ancient peoples who perceived wild animals primarily as a threat did not notice that they themselves were also a threat to wild animals by steadily reducing their habitats as they extended the area of cultivated or deforested land.

We need not limit the *thēria* of Mark 1:13 to the somewhat dangerous animals that might be encountered in the wilderness of Judaea:[18] leopards, bears, wolves, poisonous snakes (cobras, desert vipers and others), scorpions. The word does not prohibit well-informed readers from thinking also of other animals: hyenas, jackals, caracals (the desert lynx), desert foxes, Fennec foxes, wild boars, wild asses (the onager and the Syrian wild ass), antelopes (the desert oryx and the addax), gazelles, wild goats (the Nubian ibex), porcupines, hares, Syrian hyraxes, spiny-mice, gerbils, sand-rats, jirds.[19] But both the word usage and the habits of thought that went with it would be likely to bring especially the dangerous animals to mind. Mark portrays Jesus in peaceable companionship with animals that were habitually perceived as inimical and threatening to humans. For clues to the meaning of this portrayal, we must turn now to the way in which the Jewish religious tradition understood the enmity between humans and wild animals and the ways in which it envisaged a healing of this enmity.

The Wild Animals in Jewish Tradition

The Jewish tradition, against which Mark 1:13 should be read, saw the enmity of wild animals as a distortion of the created relationship of humans and wild animals and the result of human sin. In creation

---

[18] Mark does not, of course, specify the area geographically, beyond implying that it was accessible from the Jordan.

[19] For this (not exhaustive) list of animals to be found in such areas of Palestine, I am indebted to Tristram, *Natural History*; Bodenheimer, *Animal Life*; Cansdale, *Animals*. Some Old Testament passages are informative as to the animals generally associated with the desert: Deut. 8:15; Job 24:5; 39:6–8; Isa. 13:21–2; 32:14; 34:11–15; Jer. 2:24; 5:6; 10:22; Zeph. 2:14–15; Mal. 1:8.

God established human dominion over the animals (Gen. 1:26,28; Ps. 8:6–8; Sir. 17:2–4; Wis. 9:2-3; *Jub.* 1:14; *2 Enoch* 58:3; Philo, *Opif.* 83–8, 148; *2 Bar.* 14:18; 4 Ezra 6:54),[20] which should have been peaceful and harmonious, but was subsequently disrupted by violence (cf. *Ap. Mos.* 10–11). The Noahic covenant took account of this violence. As a result of the Noahic covenant, human dominion now involves permission to kill animals for food (Gen. 9:3; Josephus, *Ant.* 1.102), whereas according to Genesis (followed by many later Jewish writers) both humanity and the wild animals alike were originally vegetarian (Gen. 1:29–30). The Noahic covenant also introduces the fear of humans by animals (Gen. 9:2), presumably in order to protect humanity, now that violence has disrupted the originally peaceable relationship of humans and animals. But many later Jewish writers, not distinguishing the original institution of human dominion from its reformulation in the Noahic covenant, took the animals' fear of humans to be intrinsic to the human dominion as such (Sir. 17:4; *Ap. Mos.* 10:3; *Gen. Rab.* 34:12; cf. *T. Naph.* 8:4; *T. Benj.* 5:2). The animals are conceived as properly servants of their human rulers. Their fear of humans is the proper attitude of awe and respect owed by obedient subjects to their king (cf. Philo, *Praem.* 89; *Opif.* 148).

However, the situation in which wild animals were commonly perceived as menacing and humans went in fear of them was not even in accordance with the terms of the Noahic covenant, which promised that animals should go in fear of humans. This situation was sometimes understood as a reversal of the human dominion over the animals, resulting from human sin. Instead of humans ruling the animals, the animals rule humans (cf. *T. Naph.* 8:6). When, according to the *Apocalypse of Moses*, Seth is attacked by a wild animal and Eve demands to know why the animal is no longer afraid to attack the image of God, to which it was subjected in Eden (10:1–3), the animal points out that the situation is Eve's fault, 'since the rule of the beasts (*hē archē tōn thēriōn*) has happened because of you' (11:1).[21]

In the face of this situation, Jewish literature envisaged two ways in which the true relationship of humans and animals might be restored: one individual, one eschatological. In the first place, it could be

---

[20] Several of these passages (Sirach, Wisdom, Philo, 2 Baruch, 4 Ezra) are discussed by John R. Levison, *Portraits of Adam in Early Judaism: From Sirach to 2 Baruch* (JSPSup 1; Sheffield: JSOT Press, 1988), pp. 36–7, 55–6, 66–73, 119–20, 131–2.

[21] Daniel A. Bertrand, *La Vie Grecque d'Adam et d'Eve* (Recherches Intertestamentaires 1; Paris: Maisonneuve, 1987), p. 118, takes this to mean that Eve's own rebellion set a precedent for the animals.

thought that the truly righteous person should enjoy the relationship to animals that God originally intended for humanity. The earliest expression of this idea is found in Job 5:22–3, where Eliphas argues that the righteous person be protected from all natural threats to human life, including that from wild animals:

> At destruction and famine you shall laugh,
> and shall not fear the wild animals of the earth.
> For you shall be in league with the stones of the field,
> and the wild animals shall be at peace with you.[22]

This passage notably does not refer to the idea of human dominion over the animals, and certainly not to the way this dominion was often interpreted in later Jewish literature, as requiring the fear, submission and service of wild animals to humanity. Instead, it portrays a covenant of peace, a pact, between the righteous person and all God's creatures, even the stones of the field.[23]

In the rest of the passage of the *Apocalypse of Moses* to which we have already referred, 'the rule of the beasts' proves not to be an entirely accurate statement of the situation after the fall. Seth commands the animal to have regard for the image of God in him, and the animal accordingly flees from him (12:1–2). Evidently, Seth is a righteous person, who can therefore still exercise, to some degree at least, the human dominion over the animals. Here it is accepted that, as a result of the fall, the animals are hostile to humanity (11:2), but the righteous person is at least protected from them.

Later the rabbis taught that the righteous person will rule the animals, but the unrighteous will be ruled by the animals (*Gen. Rab.* 8:12; *b. Sanh.* 38b; *b. Shabb.* 151b).[24] The same contrast appears in a series of passages in the *Testaments of the Twelve Patriarchs*,[25] in which the patriarchs warn their descendants that if they are wicked they will be subject to the wild

---

[22] Biblical quotations in this section are from the NRSV.

[23] The reference to stones is usually thought to be problematic, but it may well mean what the extant text says, implying that the stones will not frustrate agriculture: cf. Murray, *Cosmic Covenant*, p. 198 n. 14.

[24] Cf. Cohen, '*Be Fertile*', pp. 87, 100–1, 103, where additional references are given.

[25] The general scholarly opinion that the *Testaments of the Twelve Patriarchs* is an originally Jewish work, which has received some Christian editing, is challenged by the argument of Hollander and De Jonge, *Testaments*, pp. 82–5, that the Testaments as we have them are a Christian work, whose Jewish sources cannot be reconstructed. But it is in any case probable that the passages quoted here preserve Jewish traditions.

animals, but if they are righteous they will exercise dominion over the animals, i.e. they will subdue the animals and the animals will fear them:

> If you achieve the good, my children, men and angels will bless you,
> and God will be glorified through you among the Gentiles.
> The devil will flee from you;
> wild animals (*ta thēria*) will be afraid of you,
> and the Lord will love you,[26]
> and the angels will stand by you . . .
> The one who does not do good, men and angels will curse,
> and God will be dishonoured among the Gentiles because of him.
> The devil will inhabit him as his own instrument.
> Every wild animal will dominate (*pan thērion katakurieusei*) him,
> and the Lord will hate him. (*T. Naph.* 8:4, 6)

> You do these as well, my children,
> and every spirit of Beliar will flee from you,
> and no act of human evil will have power over (*kurieusetai*) you.
> Every wild creature you shall subdue (*panta agrion thēra
>   katadoulōsesthe*),
> as long as you have the God of heaven with you,
> and walk with all mankind in sincerity of heart. (*T. Iss.* 7:7)

> For the person who fears God and loves his neighbor cannot be plagued by the spirit of Beliar since he is sheltered by the fear of God. Neither man's schemes nor those of animals (*thēriōn*) can prevail over (*kurieuthēnai*) him, for he is aided in living by this: by the love which he has toward his neighbour. (*T. Benj.* 3:4–5)

> If you continue to do good, even the unclean spirits will flee from you and wild animals (*ta thēria*) will fear you. (*T. Benj.* 5:2)[27]

The idea of reversal of dominion is evident in these passages, where the use of *katakurieuō* and *katadouloō* echoes Genesis 1:26,28. (The

---

[26] This line is omitted in some manuscripts, but the parallel with the last line of v. 6 shows that it is most probably original: cf. Hollander and De Jonge, *Testaments*, p. 318.

[27] Translations from Howard C. Kee, 'Testaments of the Twelve Patriarchs,' in *The Old Testament Pseudepigrapha*, vol. 1 (ed. James H. Charlesworth; London: Darton, Longman & Todd, 1983), pp. 813–14, 804, 825–6. For the idea that Beliar (Satan) will flee from the righteous person, see also *T. Dan.* 5:1; *T. Sim.* 3:5; Jas 4:7; Hermas, *Mand.* 12:4:7.

LXX uses *archō* for the dominion [*rdh*] over the animals [Gen. 1:26,28; cf. also Barn. 6:18] and *katakurieuō* for the subduing [*kbš*] of the earth [Gen. 1:28; 9:1,7; cf. also *Barn.* 6:17], but at least in Genesis 9:1,7, where the Septuagint differs from the Masoretic Text in referring to the subduing of the earth,[28] it is clear that in context this includes the dominion over the animals. *Katakurieuō* is used for dominion over the animals in Sir. 17:4 LXX, and for dominion over all creatures in Hermas, *Mand.* 12:4:2.)[29]

Of particular interest in these passages from the *Testaments of the Twelve* is the way that the devil and angels are correlated with the wild animals, just as they are in Mark 1:13. However, it is unlikely that there is a direct literary relationship between the *Testaments of the Twelve* and Mark 1:13,[30] since in the *Testaments of the Twelve* the relationships of the wicked and the righteous to other beings are not limited to their relationships to the devil, the wild animals and angels, but also include their relationships to God and to other humans. This also shows that in these passages the wild animals are not represented specifically as the agents or allies of the devil, but simply as one category of living being, who behave differently toward the righteous and the wicked, as do also God, the angels, the devil and other humans. In *Testament of Naphtali* 8:4,6, the complete set of five relationships appear; in *Testament of Issachar* 7:7 and *Testament of Benjamin* 3:4–5, the reference is to evil spirit(s), humans and wild animals; in *Testament of Benjamin* 5:2, only evil spirits and wild animals appear. The general point is that the righteous and the wicked enjoy different kinds of relationship (beneficial for the righteous, detrimental for the wicked) to other living beings, who are comprehensively specified in *Testament of Naphtali* 8:4,6, and selectively instanced in the other passages. In Mark 1:13, however, it is not Jesus' relationships with all other living beings which are depicted, but his relationships with precisely the three kinds of living being he could encounter in the wilderness, rather than in the human world. In a general sense the

---

[28] On this difference, see Cohen, '*Be Fertile*', pp. 26–7.

[29] In this passage the human dominion over all creatures seems to provide the basis not only for mastering (*katakurieuō*) the commandments given by the Shepherd, but also for dominating (*katakurieuō*) the devil (12:4:7; 12:6:2,4; cf. 5:1:1; 7:2; 9:10; 12:2:5). Since this is connected with the notion that the devil will flee from the righteous person (12:4:7), there may be some connexion, via common tradition, between Hermas and the *Testaments of the Twelve*.

[30] Murray, *Cosmic Covenant*, p. 128 (following H.A. Kelly) suggests that *T. Naph.* 8 is dependent on Mark 1:13.

passages in the *Testaments of the Twelve* enable us to see that Mark 1:13 depicts relationships with other beings which characterize a righteous person, but in its selection of three such relationships it must have a more specific purpose in view.

For a clue to this more specific purpose, we must turn to the second way in which Jewish literature envisaged that the originally intended relationship of humans and wild animals might be restored. This is the eschatological expectation that the righting of all wrongs in the messianic age of the future would bring peace between wild animals and humans. For example, Hosea's promise of the renewal of God's covenant with his people,[31] when their punishment is over, includes a covenant God makes with the animals for his people's sake: 'I will make for you a covenant on that day with the wild animals, the birds of the air, and the creeping things of the ground; and I will abolish the bow, the sword, and war from the land; and I will make you lie down in safety' (Hos. 2:18).

Here protection from wild animals is linked with protection from war, as it is in Leviticus 26:6; Ezekiel 34:25–9 (cf. 14:15–18). Since birds and creeping things (insects and reptiles) are mentioned, the thought is not primarily or exclusively of the threat to human life from dangerous wild animals, but of the threat to human livelihood from all animals which consume or destroy the produce or the domestic animals of humans (cf. Hos. 2:12; Lev. 26:22). The covenant with the animals is therefore not unconnected with the promise of plenty that is characteristic of such prophecies of an ideal time to come (Hos. 2:22; Lev. 26:4–5; Ezek. 34:26–7,29; Zech. 8:12).

The classic scriptural expression of the hope of peace between humans and wild animals is, of course, Isaiah 11:6–9:

> The wolf shall live with the lamb,
> the leopard shall lie down with the kid,
> the calf and the lion and the fatling together,
> and a little child shall lead them.
> The cow and the bear shall graze,
> their young shall lie down together;
> and the lion shall eat straw like the ox.
> The nursing child shall play over the hole of the asp,
> and the weaned child shall put its hand on the adder's den.

---

[31] Murray, *Cosmic Covenant*, pp. 27–32, discusses the whole passage (Hos. 2:2–23), arguing that it turns on the 'cosmic covenant' of 2:18.

They will not hurt or destroy on all my holy mountain;
for the earth shall be full of the knowledge of the LORD,
as the waters cover the sea.

It is important to notice that this passage belongs in the context of the account of the messianic king and his righteous rule (11:1–5).[32] It has often been misunderstood by modern readers as depicting simply peace between animals, as well as between animals and humans. In fact, it depicts peace between the human world, with its domesticated animals (lamb, kid, calf, bullock, cow), and the wild animals (wolf, leopard, lion, bear, poisonous snakes) that were normally perceived as threats both to human livelihood (dependent on the domestic animals) and to human life. Human children, rather than adults, appear for the same reason that the domestic animals are represented mainly by their young: children (cf. Lev. 26:22; 2 Kgs. 2:23–4) and young animals (cf. 1 Sam. 17:34–5) were especially vulnerable to wild predators. That the expectation is controlled by the prevalent perception of enmity between the human world and the dangerous wild animals is shown by the fact that there is no mention of peace between the predatory wild animals and the wild animals (such as gazelles or antelope) that they usually hunt and kill, but only of peace between the predatory wild animals and the domestic animals which they sometimes attack.[33] Of course, the former is also implied, both in the fact that the bear and the lion become vegetarian (Isa. 11:7) and the snakes harmless (11:8),

---

[32] Murray, *Cosmic Covenant*, pp. 103–5.

[33] So the Isaianic vision is closer than Murray, *Cosmic Covenant*, p. 108, allows to the account of the mythical ideal land of Dilmun in the Sumerian poem *Enki and Ninhursaga*:

> In Dilmun . . .
> no lion kills,
> no wolf carries off a lamb.
> Unknown is a dog harassing kids,
> unknown is a hog devouring grain.
> (If) a widow spreads malt on the roof
> no bird of the skies comes foraging,
> no pigeon gorges itself (?)

(quoted in Murray, *Cosmic Covenant*, p. 108). Cf. also Virgil, *Eclog.* 4.21–5; 5.60–1; Horace, *Epod.* 16.33. Henri Jeanmaire, *Le Messianisme de Vergil* (Paris: J. Vrin, 1930), pp. 194–5, points out the parallel between the Sumerian poem and Virgil's fourth Eclogue, in order to suggest that the idea of peace between the animals in a terrestrial paradise had a wide currency, with ancient origins. For the wild animals of Isa. 11:6–7 as threats to farm animals, see Cansdale, *Animals*, pp. 108, 112, 118, 119; Bodenheimer, *Animal and Man*, p. 42.

and also in the cessation of all harm and destruction (11:9), which must mean also that humans are to be vegetarian. The picture is of a restoration of paradise ('my holy mountain' is Eden, as in Ezek. 28:13–14) and the original vegetarianism of all living creatures (Gen. 1:29–30), but it is presented from the perspective of ancient people's sense of threat from dangerous wild animals.[34] That threat is to be removed, the enmity between humans and wild animals healed. The emphasis is on peaceable relationships (as in Job 5:22–3) rather than the human dominion over the animals, but there is at least a hint of the latter (strong enough to be taken up, as we shall see, in later Jewish literature) in Isaiah 11:6. It seems that the wild animals are to become domestic animals, herded by a child along with the animals which humans now keep for their own purposes. But, since they are evidently not to be killed for food, we should not take the point too literally. When the writer wishes to envisage peace between humans and wild animals, he thinks naturally of the peaceable relationship already existing between humans and their domestic animals (leaving aside the slaughter of animals for food) and extends it to include the wild animals too.

In a later passage in the book of Isaiah, depicting the new heavens and the new earth (65:17), 11:6–9 is taken up in an abbreviated form:

> The wolf and the lamb shall feed together,
> the lion shall eat straw like the ox;
> but the serpent – its food shall be dust!
> They shall not hurt or destroy
> on all my holy mountain, says the LORD. (Isa. 65:25)

Here an explicit allusion to Genesis (3:14) has been introduced, presumably implying that although the original harmony of humans and animals will be restored, the serpent which was responsible for first disrupting that harmony will continue to serve its punishment.

---

[34] Therefore I do not accept the neat distinction suggested by Murray, *Cosmic Covenant*, p. 34: 'The Bible contains, in fact, two models for thinking about humans and animals: one paradisal, the other this-worldly and realistic. The first way uses the picture of peace with and between wild animals as a metaphor for cosmic and social peace; the second way sees peace from them as a practical aspect of desired shalom.' He does not recognize that the second model includes peace between wild animals and domestic animals, and so gives more emphasis than is justified to the first model in his interpretation of Isa. 11:6–9 (*Cosmic Covenant*, pp. 105–9).

Isaiah 11:6–9 continued to inspire post-biblical Jewish expectations of the messianic age. In book 3 of the *Sibylline Oracles* it is very faithfully paraphrased:

> Wolves and lambs will eat grass together in the mountains.
> Leopards will feed together with kids.
> Roving bears will spend the night together with calves.
> The flesh-eating lion will eat husks at the manger
> like an ox, and mere infant children will lead them
> with ropes. For he [God] will make the beasts on earth harmless.
> Serpents and asps will sleep with babies
> and will not harm them, for the hand of God will be upon them.
>
> (Sib. Or. 3:788–95)[35]

Philo takes up the hope in very much his own way.[36] Having spoken, in the passage to which we have already referred, of the continuous war in which all wild animals are engaged against humans, he expresses the hope that it will come to an end:

---

[35] Translation from J.J. Collins, 'Sibylline Oracles', in *The Old Testament Pseudepigrapha*, vol. 1, p. 379. Lactantius, *Div. Inst.* 7.24.12, quoting this passage, was the first to suggest that it was Virgil's source for his picture of paradise in *Eclog.* 4.21–5 ('the herds shall not fear the great lions . . . The serpent, too, shall perish'). J.B. Mayor, 'Source of the Fourth Eclogue,' in *Virgil's Messianic Eclogue: Its Meaning, Occasion, and Sources* (Joseph Bickersteth Mayor, William Warde Fowler and Robert Seymour Conway; London: J. Murray, 1907), pp. 87–140, examined the parallels between the fourth *Eclogue* and both Isaiah and the Sibylline Oracle, concluding that Virgil knew either Isaiah or a source which reproduced Isaiah more fully than the Sibylline Oracle. Since Mayor wrote, the possibility that Virgil knew either Isaiah or the third Sibylline has often been discounted (see Jérôme Carcopino, *Virgile et le Mystère de la IVᵉ Eglogue* [Paris: L'Artisan du Livre, 1930], pp. 69–70; H.J. Rose, *The Eclogues of Vergil* [Berkeley/Los Angeles: University of California Press, 1942], p. 194), but the only parallel to the idea of peace between animals in Greek or Roman literature seems to be Horace, *Epod.* 16.33, while Carcopino's supposition of Pythagorean influence on both Virgil and Horace is vague. In view of Virgil's own reference to the Cumaean Sibyl (*Eclog.* 4.4), it remains possible that he knew a Jewish Sibylline text and accepted it (as it was intended to be accepted by pagans) as a genuine Sibylline oracle.

[36] That Philo has Isaiah 11 in mind is suggested by the fact that he not only refers to the wolf and the lamb (*Praem.* 87), which was a virtually proverbial image (Matt. 10:16; Luke 10:3; Acts 20:29), but also to all the other wild animals that appear in Isaiah 11: bears, lions, leopards, poisonous snakes, while adding some more exotic examples (*Praem.* 89–90).

This war no mortal can quell; that is done only by the Uncreated, when He judges that there are some worthy of salvation, men of peaceful disposition who cherish brotherly affection and good fellowship . . . Would that this good gift might shine upon our life and that we might be able to see that day when savage creatures become tame and gentle. But a very necessary preliminary to this is that the wild beasts within the soul shall be tamed . . . For is it not foolish to suppose that we shall escape the mischief which the brutes outside us can do if we are always working up those within us to dire savagery? Therefore we need not give up hope that when the wild beasts within us are fully tamed the animals too will become tame and gentle. When that time comes I believe that bears and lions and panthers and the Indian animals, elephants and tigers, and all others whose vigour and power are invincible, will change their life of solitariness and isolation for one of companionship, and gradually in imitation of the gregarious creatures show themselves tame when brought face to face with mankind. They will no longer as heretofore be roused to ferocity by the sight, but will be awe-struck into respectful fear of him as their natural lord and master, while others will grow gentle in emulation of the docility and affection for the master shown for instance by the little Maltese dogs, who express their fondness with the tails which they so cheerily wag. Then too the tribes of scorpions and serpents and the other reptiles will have no use for their venom. The Egyptian river too carries man-eating creatures called crocodiles and hippopotamuses in close proximity to the inhabitants of the country, so too the seas have multitudinous species of very formidable animals. Among all these the man of worth will move sacrosanct and inviolate because God has respected virtue and given it the privilege that none should imagine mischief against it (*Praem.* 87–90).[37]

Several points are of special interest in this passage. In the first place, it seems that Philo brings together the idea that the truly righteous person will enjoy peace with wild animals and the eschatological expectation of a time when the wild animals will cease to be a threat to humans. At first he seems to be speaking in terms of the former idea, but it then becomes clear that he does envisage a time when there will be a sufficiently widespread change of heart in human beings to bring about a general peace with the animals. Secondly, like Isaiah 11, he expects the wild animals to become like domestic animals. Thirdly, it is

---

[37] Translation from Francis Henry Colson, *Philo*, vol. 8 (LCL; London: Heinemann/Cambridge, Massachussetts: Harvard University Press, 1939), pp. 365, 367.

clear that what he envisages is a restoration of the human dominion over the animals given at creation.

The restoration of human dominion is also the theme of the adaptation of Isaiah 11:6–9 in 2 *Baruch* 73:6. In the context of an account of how all the evils of life in the present age will be abolished in the messianic age to come, this verse predicts:

> And the wild beasts will come from the wood and serve men,
> and the asps and the dragons will come out of their holes to
>   subject themselves to a child.[38]

Since the following verse predicts that women will no longer suffer pain in childbirth (cf. Gen 3:16), it is clear that a restoration of paradisal conditions is envisaged.

These conditions include the restoration of human dominion over the animals, which involves not only that the wild animals become tame like domestic animals, but also that they serve humanity like domestic animals. The author has found this notion in Isaiah 11:6, and deduced that, if the animals subject themselves to the child in that verse, then the reference to the child again in verse 8 must have the same sense.

Finally, Papias of Hierapolis quotes, as words of Jesus transmitted by John the Elder, a prophecy of the paradisal age of the future which is closely dependent on Jewish apocalyptic tradition. Following an account of the extraordinary fruitfulness of the earth (cf. 2 *Bar.* 29:5; 1 *Enoch* 10:19),[39] the prophecy continues: 'all the animals feeding on these fruits produced by the soil will in turn become peaceful and harmonious toward one another, and fully subject to man (*subiecta hominibus cum omni subiectione*), (*apud* Irenaeus, *Adv. Haer.* 5.33.3).[40]

Here Isaiah 11:6–9 is interpreted in a way similar to 2 *Baruch* 73:6, as implying the subjection of animals to humanity, but the link with the paradisal fruitfulness of the earth is novel. Presumably the idea is not only that all the wild animals will be vegetarian, but also that there will no longer be any competition between animals or between animals and humans for limited resources. Vegetarian abundance will

---

[38] Translation from Albertus Frederik Johannes Klijn, '2 (Syriac Apocalypse of) Baruch,' in *The Old Testament Pseudepigrapha*, vol. 1, p. 645.

[39] For other parallels, see Jean-Daniel Dubois, 'Remarques sur le Fragment de Papias cité par Irénée,' *RHPR* 71 (1991): pp. 6–8.

[40] Translation from Joseph Barber Lightfoot, John Reginald Harmer and Michael W. Holmes, *The Apostolic Fathers* (2nd edn; Leicester: Apollos, 1990), p. 322.

guarantee both peace between animals and also the restoration of human dominion in its original form, so that the animals willingly obey their human rulers.

Inaugurating the Messianic Peace

If we ignored the context of Mark 1:13, we might classify Jesus, in terms of the Jewish traditions we have examined, simply as the individual righteous person who is at peace with the wild animals. But Jesus in Mark's prologue is no mere individual. He is the messianic Son of God. When he resists Satan in the wilderness, he does so, not as merely an individual righteous person, but as the messianic Son of God on behalf of and for the sake of others. Similarly it is the messianic peace with wild animals that Jesus establishes. He establishes it only representatively, in his own person, and so the objection that a restoration of paradise should not be located in the wilderness is beside the point. More to the point is that all the wild animals of Isaiah 11, with the exception of the lion (unless the forests of the Jordan valley may be included in Mark's wilderness), would be most easily encountered in the wilderness. Jesus does not restore the paradisal state as such, but he sets the messianic precedent for it.

Whether, in that case, Mark 1:13 should be said to embody a new Adam Christology is more doubtful. Proponents of the view that Mark 1:13 refers to the paradisal state of peace with the wild animals, eschatologically restored, have usually linked this idea with that of Jesus as the new or eschatological Adam, who resists the devil, whereas Adam and Eve succumbed, and who restores the peaceful relationship with other creatures which Adam and Eve disrupted. Such an implication cannot be ruled out, but there seems to be no other trace of a new Adam Christology in Mark. So it may be more relevant to recall that Isaiah 11:6–9, the classic vision of the messianic peace with wild animals, is connected with Isaiah 11:1–5, the classic prophecy of the Davidic Messiah. The peace with wild animals belongs to this Messiah's righteous reign. Mark's account of Jesus' baptism (1:9–11), in which he is anointed with the Spirit (Isa. 11:2) and addressed as God's Son (Ps. 2:7), identifies him as this Davidic Messiah,[41] who therefore inaugurates the messianic age not only by overcoming Satan, but also by establishing the messianic peace with wild animals.

---

[41] Kingsbury, *Christology*, pp. 60–8.

Against the background of the Jewish eschatological expectation, the latter has a real significance in its own right. It is not simply a symbol of Jesus' victory over Satan or of his inauguration of the age of eschatological salvation.[42] Peace with wild animals is actually one aspect of eschatological salvation. There is no reason to doubt that first-century people, who were well aware that they shared the world with wild animals, would be interested in this aspect of salvation for its own sake.

Mark's simple phrase *ēn meta tōn thēriōn* indicating a peaceable and friendly companionship with the animals, contrasts with the way the restoration of the proper human relationship to wild animals is often portrayed in the Jewish literature. The animals are not said to fear him, submit to him or serve him. The concept of human dominion over the animals as domination for human benefit is entirely absent. The animals are treated neither as subjects nor as domestic servants. In its image of peaceable companionship Mark 1:13 is closest, among the passages we have discussed, to Job 5:22–3 and Isaiah 11:6–9. Jesus does not terrorize or dominate the wild animals, he does not domesticate or even make pets of them. He is simply 'with them'. But the real beauty of that phrase in Mark 1:13 will only appear fully when we recontextualize the image in our own context and our very different perception of the human relationship to wild animals.

The context to which Mark 1:13 originally spoke was one in which wild animals threatened humanity and their wilderness threatened to encroach on the human world. The messianic peace with wild animals promised, by healing the alienation and enmity between humans and animals, to liberate humans from that threat. But our context is one in which it is now clearly we who threaten the survival of wild animals, encroach on their habitat, threaten to turn their wilderness into a wasteland they cannot inhabit. To make the point one need only notice how many of the animals Jesus could have encountered in the Judaean wilderness have become extinct in Palestine this century: the bear, the onager, the desert oryx, the addax, the ostrich and no doubt others. Others, such as the leopard and the gazelle, would not have survived without modern conservation measures. Mark's image of Jesus' peaceable companionship with the animals in the wilderness survives this reversal of situation and its pregnant simplicity gains a new power. For us Jesus' companionable presence with the wild animals affirms their independent value for themselves and for God. He

---

[42] Contra, e.g. Vargas-Machuca, 'La tentación de Jesús'.

does not adopt them into the human world, but lets them be themselves in peace, leaving them their wilderness, affirming them as creatures who share the world with us in the community of God's creation.

Most of the Christian tradition in the modern period, understanding the God-given human dominion over the animals as permission to treat them with regard to nothing other than their usefulness to humans, has encouraged and colluded with modern western society's spoliation of the earth, which is currently exterminating whole species daily. In this situation we urgently need to retrieve another perspective, which the Christian tradition has occasionally glimpsed, most famously and clearly in the life of Francis of Assisi.[43] This is the possibility of living fraternally (I use the word because of Francis's sense of all creatures as sisters and brothers) with wild creatures, and experiencing thereby the grace of otherness which God gives us in the diversity of the animal creation and which is missed when animals are reduced merely to usefulness or threat. Mark's image of Jesus with the wild animals can be retrieved as the christological warrant for and symbol of this possibility, given in creation, given back in messianic redemption. It is a symbol. It does not constitute an ethic of animal rights. But since it is precisely the modern demythologizing of nature that has turned it into a mere object of human use and exploitation, our need is very much for religious symbols of the human relationship to nature.

---

[43] See Chapter 2 of this volume.

6.

Reading the Sermon on the Mount in an Age of Ecological Catastrophe

Introduction

From one point of view, at least, the ecological catastrophe we are living through is a matter of limits and excess: on the one hand, the limits of the earth's resources and the limits to which humans can tamper with the earth's ecosystem with impunity, and, on the other hand, the excess of consumption and expansion that has come to define the project of modern western, but increasingly globalized, civilization. George Monbiot recently wrote that 'we inhabit the brief historical interlude between ecological constraint and ecological catastrophe'.[1] Whereas for most of history humans have lived within considerable ecological constraints, the modern attempt to abolish such constraints can only lead to catastrophe. One might add that, whereas many human societies of the past have collapsed precisely through exceeding the resources of their ecological base and thus destroying it, as Jared Diamond has shown,[2] we now face a situation in which it is the ecological base of all human civilized life on the planet that is in course of destruction through human excess.

The notion of limits fits badly with our notions of technological progress (including now, notably, bioengineering), with our economics of unlimited growth, and with our lifestyle of consumption to excess that depends on and feeds both the technology and the

---

[1] George Monbiot, *Heat: How to Stop the Planet Burning* (London: Penguin, 2007), p. xxi.

[2] Jared Diamond, *Collapse: How Societies Choose to Fail or Succeed* (London: Allen Lane, 2005); cf. also Ronald Wright, *A Short History of Progress* (Edinburgh: Canongate, 2005).

economics. We are unlikely to be able to embrace the notion of limits in the way that seems necessary unless we have a view of the world and the place of humans in it that incorporates limits and enables us to see them as an entirely good aspect of the world and our life in it. In my view the Christian view of the world as the creation of the good Creator who provides abundantly for all his creatures offers such a vision. It entails envisaging the creation as a community of creatures in which we belong as fellow-creatures with others. Modern Christian thinking on this topic has been good at envisaging humans as stewards or guardians or in some such role, exercising responsibility over creation, and I do not wish to deny the value such a perspective has had.[3] But I think we also need to recover a stronger sense of our own creatureliness as participants in the community of creation, constrained by it and dependent on it.[4]

So can the Sermon on the Mount help us? I shall restrict myself in this chapter to Matthew 6:25–34, with some reference to its wider context in the Sermon.[5] This is not the only part of the Sermon that is of relevance to the issue,[6] but restricting myself to this passage will enable me to incorporate some detailed exegesis, which may be the most useful contribution a biblical scholar can make to the field of Christian ethics.

---

[3] See now especially R.J. Berry (ed.), *Environmental Stewardship: Critical Perspectives – Past and Present* (London: T&T Clark [Continuum], 2006).

[4] I have argued this in Chapter 2 in this volume.

[5] For my study of Matt. 6:25–34, besides the commentaries, I am indebted especially to Olsthoorn, *Jewish Background*; Luise Schottroff and Wolfgang Stegemann, *Jesus and the Hope of the Poor* (trans. Matthew J. O'Connell; Maryknoll, New York: Orbis, 1986), pp. 39–45; Thomas E. Schmidt, *Hostility to Wealth in the Synoptic Gospel* (JSNTSup 15; Sheffield: Sheffield Academic Press, 1987), pp. 124–30; Leske, 'Matthew 6.25–34', pp. 15–27; Robert C. Tannehill, *The Sword of His Mouth: Forceful and Imaginative Language in Synoptic Sayings* (Semeia Supplements 1; Philadelphia: Fortress/ Missoula, Montana: SBL, 1975), pp. 60–7; Grant Macaskill, *Revealed Wisdom and Inaugurated Eschatology in Ancient Judaism and Early Christianity* (JSJSup 115; Leiden: Brill, 1007), pp. 187–94; Juan José Bartolomé, 'Los Pájaros y los Lirios: Una Aproximación a la Cuestion Ecologica desde Mt 6,25–34', *EstBib* 49 (1991): pp. 165–90.

[6] For the synoptic teaching of Jesus generally, with a focus on Luke, see Thorsten Moritz, 'New Testament Voices for an Addicted Society', in *Christ and Consumerism: Critical Reflections on the Spirit of Our Age* (ed. Craig Bartholomew and Thorsten Moritz; Carlisle: Paternoster, 2000), pp. 54–80.

Structure of Matthew 6:25–34

The genre of this text, like much of Jesus' teaching, is that of wisdom instruction, incorporating appeals to observation and common sense as well as to truths of faith. The main part of the text, vv. 25–33, is a carefully composed passage. The negative admonition, 'Do not worry . . .' is stated, followed by accumulating reasons for heeding it, before being repeated in v. 31, with further reasons in v. 32. The corresponding positive admonition is then added, as a climax to the passage, in v. 33.

At the heart of the passage are the two extended sections inviting hearers to observe, respectively, the birds and the wild flowers. These passages are formulated in close parallel. One concerns food, the other clothing. The first refers to an example from the animal creation, the other to an example from the vegetable creation, the first belonging to the sky, the second to the earth: 'the birds of the air' and 'the lilies of the fields'. It may be that each is meant to be seen as a relatively insignificant member of their class: the small birds and the ephemeral wild flowers, whose transience is highlighted. What the birds do not do (sow or reap or gather into barns) is probably to be seen as characteristically male activity, while what the lilies do not do (toil or spin) is the characteristically female work of making clothes. Both examples are concluded with the 'how much more' argument, common in Jesus' teaching as in that of the rabbis. The argument is that if God provides for these, how much more for you. The point is made more expansively in the case of the lilies, perhaps reflecting the accumulating force of the arguments for not worrying, prior to the repetition of the admonition not to worry itself.

Structurally v. 34 stands rather apart from the rest of the text, but its character as a proverbial saying or perhaps two proverbial sayings[7] (and this is by no means the only occasion on which Jesus' teaching makes use of a probably already existing proverb)[8] justifies its being appended to the main passage as a more or less independent unit. It has, as we shall see, an important function in relating this passage to its wider context in the Sermon.

---

[7] Similar aphoristic sayings are adduced by William David Davies and Dale C. Allison, *A Critical and Exegetical Commentary on the Gospel according to Saint Matthew* (Edinburgh: T&T Clark, 1988), pp. 662–3.

[8] Gustaf Dalman, *Jesus-Joshua: Studies in the Gospels* (trans. Paul P. Levertoff; SPCK, 1929), pp. 223–36.

Audience and Context

It has often been supposed that the passage, either on the lips of Jesus or in Q tradition from which Matthew drew it, addressed itinerant disciples who travelled with or like Jesus, preaching the kingdom and provided by others with their basic needs of food and clothing. This raises a question not unlike that to be found in the history of reception as to whether this teaching is a counsel of perfection, for those, mainly in the religious orders, who can follow it, but not required of ordinary believers.[9] Much depends on whether we should suppose that the implied hearers, like the birds and the lilies, do not work to support themselves. As we shall see, I think that conclusion is unlikely. But, particularly in the Matthean context of the Sermon, it would be hard to maintain this reading. Even though Jesus addresses the Sermon to his disciples, with the crowds as auditors (5:1; 7:28), it would be hard to read the whole Sermon as addressed only to itinerant preachers or wandering charismatics.

To be oppressed by anxiety about meeting one's very basic needs of food and clothing, one did not have to be an itinerant preacher who had left home and possessions voluntarily. A large proportion of ordinary people would have been in this situation. The smallholder or the tenant farmer had only a modest sufficiency for living. It could take only a bad harvest and consequent debt, along with the often unscrupulous practices of large landowners keen to extend their property, for such people to lose the access to the land that was their only means of support. Even more vulnerable were the day labourers, like those in the parable of the labourers in the vineyard (Matt. 20:1–16), who were paid for their labour only one day at a time and could never depend on finding work at times when the agricultural seasons required less labour than others, such as harvest. Only beggars lived a more economically insecure existence than the day labourers. Paradoxically perhaps, slaves had a good deal more economic security, at least while strong and healthy. Incapacitating illness or accident could, of course, be catastrophic for any of these people who had little opportunity to save. (At the same time it is worth remembering that, in a much less individualistic society than our own, family and community could often be relied on for support in trouble.)

---

[9] According to Ulrich Luz, *Matthew 1 – 7: A Commentary* (trans. Wilhelm C. Linss; Edinburgh: T&T Clark, 1990), p. 410, Rupert of Deutz (early thirteenth century) was the first to interpret it as a counsel of perfection in this sense.

Thus our passage would have addressed the anxiety about basic livelihood that many ordinary people must have felt. Disciples who left home to accompany Jesus may not have been putting themselves in so much more insecure a position than many others who struggled to make a living. At the other end of the social scale, the wealthy were a tiny percentage of the whole population. Unless specifically addressed, as in the Lukan woes (Luke 6:24–5), we should not expect the teaching of Jesus ordinarily to have them in view. Most people, while not being destitute, not the day labourers and the beggars who are the subject of the first beatitude (Matt. 5:3), enjoyed only a modest sufficiency that we, unlike they, would regard as poverty. In reading the teaching of Jesus on material possessions we must take very seriously this economic situation so very unfamiliar to us in the affluent West, though it is, of course, very familiar in much of the global South.

To such people Jesus addresses the recommendation not to store up treasures on earth, in Matthew 6:19, shortly before our passage. Even for the moderately prosperous peasant, this would be a hard saying. But note that the theme of anxiety already appears here: 'Do not store up for yourselves treasures on earth, where moth and rust consume and where thieves break in and steal.' The rich too have their anxieties, as was stereotypically recognized in the ancient world.[10] With wealth come constant worries about losing it. The accumulation of wealth does not, typically, free people from concern about material things because, as Jesus puts it, the treasure is where the heart is (Matt. 6:21).

A similar point is made in the saying about the impossibility of serving two masters (Matt. 6:24), which is the saying immediately presupposed by the opening words of our passage: 'Therefore I tell you . . .' (6:25). Implicitly it raises the question: how is it possible to avoid serving Mammon? How can the pursuit of material possessions not rule one's life? Especially for those who have little, for whom securing the necessary minimum of a livelihood is a daily struggle – how can their lives fail to be dominated by striving for material things, so that everything else in their lives is subordinated to that? It is that question to which our passage gives the radical answer: You must replace anxiety about basic material needs, natural as it is, with something that is in its way even more natural: radical trust in the Creator who provides for the needs of all his living creatures.

---

[10] Schottroff and Stegemann, *Jesus*, p. 40.

God Feeds the Birds of the Air

The most weighty considerations that Jesus, as it were, puts into the balance in order to outweigh anxiety are the two examples from the natural world: the birds and the wild flowers. The two terms with which Jesus invites his hearers to attend to these examples – 'look at' (*emblepō*) and 'observe' (*katamanthanō*) – are virtually technical terms as used by a teacher inviting his hearers to attend carefully to some aspect of the natural world with the expectation of learning from it.[11] They show that Jesus is not merely using two picturesque illustrations of his point, but seriously invites his readers to learn from what they can observe in the natural world. However, this is not natural theology in the usual modern sense. It is through the lens of the creation theology of the Hebrew Bible that Jesus invites his hearers to consider the natural world. The birds and the wild flowers are a deterrent to anxiety only if they are seen as creatures of the Creator who cares for them.

This is not the only place in the Sermon on the Mount where Jesus draws on creation theology (cf. 5:45). Creation theology is not as alien to the eschatological message of Jesus as some scholars suppose. In our particular case Jesus, in pointing to the example of the birds God feeds, alludes to a familiar theme of biblical creation theology: the Creator's provision of food for all his living creatures. Jesus and his hearers would have been familiar with this theme especially from the psalms, well known to any devout Jew of that time. The following passages are relevant:

> He *gives* to the animals *their food*,
> and to *the young ravens* when they cry. (Ps. 147:9)

> You make springs gush forth in the valleys . . .
> giving drink to every wild animal . . .
> You cause the grass to grow for the cattle,
> and plants for people to use . . .
> The young lions roar for their prey,
> seeking their food from God . . .
> These all look to you
> *to give them their food* in due season;
> when you *give to them*, they gather it up;
> when you open your hand, they are filled with good things.
> (Ps. 104:10–11,14,21,27–8)

---

[11] *emblepō*: Sir. 33:15 (LXX); *katamanthanō*: Job 35:4 (LXX); *1 Enoch* 3:1.

Can you hunt the prey for the lion,
or satisfy the appetite of the young lions,
when they crouch in their dens,
or lie in wait in their covert?
Who *provides for the raven* its prey,
when its young ones cry to God,
and wander about for lack of food? (Job 38:39–41)

The eyes of all look to you,
and *you give them their food* in due season.
You open your hand,
satisfying the desire of every living thing. (Ps. 145:15–16)

These passages show how God is envisaged as himself directly pro-viding food for his creatures: the lions seek their food from God, the young ravens cry to God, all creatures (including humans) look up to God to provide for them, and God opens his hand to provide them with food. The writers are, of course, speaking of the ordinary, natu-ral ways in which animals and birds get their food, but they see these as very directly the Creator's provision for his creatures. Jesus speaks in the same way. In the texts above I have italicized the references to God feeding his creatures in general and to God feeding specifically the birds to show how relatively often the example Jesus uses occurs. In the Lukan version of the saying the reference is not to 'the birds of the air' (as in Matthew) but to 'the ravens' (Luke 12:24), which turns the general dependence on the Old Testament into a specific allusion to Job 38:41 or Psalm 147:9. Ravens were a favourite case presumably because their raucous cry sounds as though they are calling to God to feed them.

In the great creation psalm, Psalm 104, notable for its depiction of human beings as one species among others in the community of cre-ation for which the Creator cares, humans are included in the living creatures who all look to God for food (Ps. 104:27–8). The same words are echoed in Psalm 145:15, where the context shows that the psalmist's real concern at that point is God's care for humans who turn to him in need: God's provision for humans is assured by citing his provision for all living creatures. A later Jewish work, the *Psalms of Solomon*, echoes some of these passages, again drawing the lesson that, since God provides for all his living creatures, he can be trusted to provide for humans, including those who have the least material resources and whose livelihood is very insecure:

For if I am hungry, I will cry out to you, O God,
and you will give me (something).
You feed the birds and the fish
as you send rain in the wilderness that grass may sprout
to provide pasture in the wilderness for every living thing,
and if they are hungry, they will lift their eyes up to you.
You feed kings and rulers and peoples, O God,
and who is the hope of the poor and needy, if not you, Lord?

(*Pss. Sol.* 5:8–11)[12]

I cite this passage to show that there is nothing original about the way Jesus uses the example of the birds. Where his saying does depart from extant precedents is in calling attention to the fact that the birds 'neither sow nor reap nor gather into barns'.

What is the function of this information about the birds? Interpretations have varied. One view is that it contributes to the 'how much more' argument. Jesus contrasts the birds who do not work with people who do. If God feeds even the idle birds, how much more will he provide for people who work hard for their living! We should note, however, that the birds are not said not to work. The saying does not deny the rather obvious fact that birds expend a lot of energy and effort in finding their food. It only says that they do not then have to process their food in the way that humans do.

Secondly, the more recently popular view is that Jesus compares the birds who do not work with disciples who do not work either. Jesus' disciples or early Christian wandering charismatics who did not engage in economically productive labour are assured that God will provide for them just as he does for the birds. I have already suggested that, at least in its context in the Sermon on the Mount, it is unlikely that our passage is addressed only to itinerant preachers.

In my view it is unlikely that either of these alternatives is the point. Rather the point is that, because the birds do not have to labour to process their food from nature, their dependence on the Creator's provision is the more immediate and obvious. True, they have to find it, but they eat it just as they find it. Humans, on the other hand, preoccupied with the daily toil of supplying their basic needs, may easily suppose that it is up to them to provide themselves with food. This is the root of the anxiety about material needs that Jesus is showing to be unnecessary. The way in which humans get their food by farming

---

[12] Translation from Wright, 'Psalms', p. 657.

allows them to focus on their own efforts and to neglect the fact that more fundamentally they are dependent on the divine provision, the resources of creation without which no one could sow, reap or gather into barns. The birds, in their more immediate and obvious dependence on the Creator, remind us that ultimately we ourselves are no less dependent on the Creator.

God Clothes the Wild Flowers

This example seems to be a more original variation on the Old Testament theme that God provides for his creatures. Except when he clothes Adam and Eve after the fall (Gen. 3:21), God is never said in the Hebrew Bible to clothe any of his creatures. It is more natural to think that creatures other than humans do not wear and do not need clothes. But here in the Sermon on the Mount Jesus wishes to treat in parallel the two forms of basic material need which humans have: food and clothing.

The saying may depend on a conventional view that natural beauty exceeds even the magnificence of kings. Diogenes Laertius (1.51) tells this story of the famously wealthy King Croesus and the Athenian wise man Solon: 'Croesus in magnificent array sat himself down on his throne and asked Solon if he had ever seen anything more beautiful. "Yes," was the reply, "cocks and pheasants and peacocks; for they shine in nature's colours, which are ten thousand times more beautiful."'[13]

Such a story illustrates how Jesus can take it for granted that his hearers will agree with his aesthetic judgment that the wild flowers are more beautiful than Solomon in all his glory. In its own way his saying makes the contrast in as extreme a form as Solon does, by selecting the wild flowers whose beauty is so very transient. This serves the point very well: if God takes the trouble to give such beauty to creatures that live so briefly, how much more will he provide clothing for his human creatures!

There is no implication that this clothing will equal the splendour of Solomon's. There may even be an implied critique of Solomon for foolishly attempting to rival the created beauty of nature. Was this not part of the accumulation of treasure on earth that the disillusioned Solomon of Ecclesiastes saw to have been vanity (Eccl. 2:4–11)?

---

[13] Quoted in John Nolland, *The Gospel of Matthew* (NIGTC; Grand Rapids: Eerdmans; Bletchley: Paternoster, 2005), p. 312, n. 411.

Living within the Community of Creation

We should note that, unlike the exhortation to the lazy to consider the ant in Proverbs 6:6–11 and similar sayings in Hellenistic popular philosophy,[14] Jesus does not present the birds and the wild flowers as ethical examples for humans to imitate. They are not examples of how to behave, but of God's generous provision for his creatures. This means that the creation theology is absolutely necessary to the point being made: that Jesus' hearers do not need to worry about their basic needs for survival. They can take away this lesson only by understanding themselves to belong to the community of God's creatures along with the birds and the wild flowers. The examples from nature are thus not mere illustrations that can be dispensed with as soon as the lesson is learned. They are integral to the way the world must be seen if Jesus' disciples are to live without oppressive anxiety.

The following verse (6:32) reinforces this. The reference to the Gentiles is not an appeal to Jewish contempt for other peoples. The point is that the Gentiles are those who do not know the Creator and cannot see the world as his creation. So of course they occupy themselves with trying to secure for themselves the necessities of life. The disciples who know that their heavenly Father is the generous Creator who provides for all his creatures need not do so. They may exercise the radical trust in God that Jesus recommends, and, in doing so, they are freed to concern themselves with God's 'kingdom' and his 'righteousness'. For present purposes we can bypass the exegetical discussion of the meaning of these words here. It is sufficient to say only that they stand for God's good purpose for his creation. The kind of eschatology they evoke is not in tension with the creation theology of the passage because the kingdom is the eschatological renewal of creation. In order to enter into and pursue the vision of God's purpose for fulfilling his rule over his creation the disciples must understand the world as God's creation and live in it accordingly.

The Faith of the Day Labourer

Verse 34, as a proverbial saying, puts the message of the passage into a handy, takeaway form, which is at the same time the most extreme

---

[14] Craig S. Keener, *A Commentary on the Gospel of Matthew* (Grand Rapids: Eerdmans, 1999), pp. 234–5.

expression of the message. It addresses most appropriately the day labourer, for it was the day labourer whose economic circumstances gave really serious reason for oppressive anxiety about basic needs for even the very next day. To appreciate the force of the saying we must be realistic about the fact that many of Jesus' hearers really did live as close as that to having nothing to support themselves, while some of Jesus' disciples voluntarily put themselves into precisely the same position (Matt. 19:29). Jesus recommends to all his hearers the radical trust in the generous Creator that is necessary for the day labourer or the beggar to live without anxiety. Within the Sermon on the Mount, this proverb also serves to create a link with the Lord's Prayer. To pray daily for one's daily bread (Matt. 6:11) – and, of course, bread did not keep long, it was baked daily – is to rely day by day on God's day-by-day provision. It is a prayer that, faithfully prayed, erodes the anxiety that sustains the service of Mammon.

This exegesis of the passage has brought us face to face with the same hyperbolic extremity that characterizes Jesus' teaching throughout the Sermon.

Is it Impractical?

When we recognize the rootedness of Jesus' teaching in the creation theology of the Hebrew Bible, we can see that, by contrast with how this passage has often been understood, the divine provision of material needs of which Jesus speaks cannot be a special providential provision for disciples who live by faith. It is God the Creator's provision for all his creatures. It is the resources of the earth that God provides for all to live from. Jesus' point is that when people recognize this provision, when they see that in the end they are dependent not so much on their own efforts to provide for themselves but on what the Creator gives them in the form of the resources of the natural world, then they can trust God instead of worrying.

But is this hopelessly unrealistic? An important consideration is that, just as Jesus here presupposes the ordinary agricultural means by which food reaches people, so he can presuppose the provisions of the Torah that are intended to supply the basic needs of the poor who do not have economic resources of their own. Such institutions as the triennial tithe (Deut. 14:28–9; 26:12–15) and the requirement that farmers should leave some of the harvest for the poor to glean (Lev. 19:9–10) can be taken into account along with the ordinary generous almsgiving of which Jesus himself speaks in the Sermon (Matt. 6:2–4).

Both hard work and community sharing are the channels by which the Creator's provision supplies the needs of all.

Yet birds do die of starvation and natural catastrophes deprive whole communities of resources. At this point it is helpful to remember something about the nature of wisdom instruction that applies also to Jesus' teaching. Typically wisdom makes one point at a time. It does not try to say everything at once, and it tends not to dilute the force of one point by introducing qualifications or compromise into its statement of that point. The need for qualifications may well appear only when one point is placed alongside another. In this and other ways, wisdom requires wisdom in those who seek to apply it. The sheer extremity that is so distinctive of Jesus' own brand of wisdom makes these points even more relevant in its case.

If Jesus' teaching on material possessions is extreme, so is our consumerist society's addiction to excess. How might we come anywhere near to allowing one to speak to the other?

Approaches to Contemporary Appropriation

1. We must 're-enter God's creation'.[15] We are creatures of God alongside other creatures in the community of creation. The modern project, as an ideology of progress that supposedly liberates us from nature and gives us godlike power over it, has been an exercise in forgetting our creatureliness. It has been a kind of secular eschatology that substitutes a human-made utopia for the givenness of the created order. But the kingdom of God is the renewal of creation. We can seek the kingdom of God only by first understanding the world as God's creation and finding our place within it.

2. To re-enter God's creation is to experience the resources of the earth as given to us by God. If already in Jesus' time the processes by which people make a living out of the resources of nature could foster an illusion of independence, how much more is this the case today when a long and complex series of processes separates most of what we buy and use from its origins in nature. In reality we are utterly dependent on the earth, even at our most creative. In order to live within limits we must regain a sense of this dependence and renounce our alienation from the natural world.

---

[15] I borrow this phrase from Edward P. Echlin, 'Let's re-enter God's creation now'. *Month* 252 (1991): pp. 359–64.

3. Along with recognizing the givenness of nature's bounty, we must recognize also the limits that being recipients of this bounty entails. There is more than enough for all, but not enough for some to squander and consume like there's no tomorrow. It is not true that humans are the species that transcends all limits, but it is true that humans have much more scope than other creatures for attempting to do so. We can store up treasures until the earth is depleted; we can compete with other species and render them extinct; we can continue to transform nature into a human-made world to the point where there is no wilderness left; and we can resist the order of nature to the point where it will take its revenge. But, as Bill McKibben says: 'Should we so choose, we could exercise our reason to do what no other animal can do: we could limit ourselves voluntarily, *choose* to remain God's creatures instead of making ourselves gods.'[16]

4. Like the definition of poverty, the determination of limits can hardly be done in an absolute way, and we are so far gone in excess that we have much to do in accommodating the very notion of limits. But useful attempts can be made – and must be made – as, for example, Michael Northcott, addressing the key issue of carbon emissions, does when he adopts a distinction between 'livelihood emissions' and 'luxury emissions'.[17]

5. Jesus recommends freedom from anxiety about the basic material needs of life on the basis of trust in God the good and generous Creator. This recommendation requires that, in order to follow it, we make a distinction between such basic needs and unnecessary excess, and so the notion of limits is integral. Moreover, Jesus' recommendation presupposes not an individualistic spirituality but a context of generous community sharing. Finally, it presupposes our place in a community of creation in which the birds and the wild flowers are fellow-creatures. We can hardly expect to combine it with complicity in the reckless extinction of species and destruction of habitat that are the price of our addiction to excess.

---

[16] Bill McKibben, *The End of Nature* (London: Penguin, 1990), p. 198 (italics original).
[17] Michael S. Northcott, *A Moral Climate: The Ethics of Global Warming* (London: Darton, Longman & Todd, 2007), pp. 56–7, following Henry Shue.

A Parable from Kierkegaard

The gospel passage on the birds and the lilies was a great favourite of Søren Kierkegaard's, and it inspired the following parable of his. (I have abbreviated and rewritten it a little.)[18]

Once upon a time there was a lily that grew in an out-of-the-way place by a little brook, and lived in happy companionship with some nettles and a few other little wild flowers that grew nearby. The lily, as the Gospel says, was more beautifully arrayed even than Solomon in all his glory. Moreover, she was carefree and happy all the day long.

But one day there came a little bird to visit the lily. He came day after day and chattered to the lily. He talked fast and loose, true and false, of how in other places there were great numbers of lilies far more magnificent than she; there was also a joy, a perfume, a splendour of colours, a song of the birds, which surpassed all description. He told her that the crown imperial was the most beautiful of all lilies, and was an object of envy to all others. Usually he ended his stories by telling the lily how insignificant she was by comparison with such glory.

And so the lily began to worry; and the more she listened to the bird, the more worried she became. No longer did she sleep soundly at night. No longer did she wake up happy in the morning. She felt herself imprisoned and bound. 'Why, O why,' she said to herself, 'was I not put in another place and in different circumstances? Why was I not made a crown imperial?'

At last she felt she could assuage her worry only by trying to achieve her new-found ambition. She confided in the bird and they made a plan. The bird agreed to take the lily to the place where those magnificent lilies bloomed. The bird was to help replant her there, to see whether, by the change of place and the new surroundings, the lily might not succeed in becoming a magnificent lily or even perhaps a crown imperial, envied by all the others. So the bird set to work. With his beak he pecked away the soil from the lily's root, so that she might be free. Then he took the lily under his wing and flew. For a moment or two the lily enjoyed her liberation, no longer rooted in one place, no longer having to get on with stinging nettles and weeds, free as the bird in the air. Alas, before they reached the place where the crown imperials grew, the lily withered and died. Needless to say, this was not one of those lilies the Lord recommended we consider.

---

[18] I am following the translation in T.H. Croxall, *Meditations from Kierkegaard* (trans. and ed. T.H. Croxall: London: James Nisbet, 1955), pp. 89–91.

7.

Joining Creation's Praise of God

A Biblical and Christian Tradition

It was often the habit of the man of God [the Saxon saint Benno of
Meissen, d. 1106] to go about the fields in meditation and prayer: and
once as he passed by a certain marsh, a talkative frog was croaking in
its slimy waters: and lest it should disturb his contemplation, he bade it
to be a Seraphian, inasmuch as all frogs in Seraphus are mute. But when
he had gone on a little way, he called to mind the saying in Daniel: '*O
ye whales and all that move in the waters, bless ye the Lord. O all ye beasts and
cattle, bless ye the Lord.*' And fearing lest the singing of the frogs might
perchance be more agreeable to God than his own praying, he again
issued his command to them, that they should praise God in their
accustomed fashion: and soon the air and the fields were vehement
with their conversation.[1]

The words in Daniel that Benno recalled are from two verses of the
Benedicite, familiar to all medieval clergy and religious from its frequent liturgical use. It is the canticle that begins

Bless the Lord, all you works of the Lord;
sing praise to him and highly exalt him for ever,[2]

and continues through thirty verses which each call on one category
of God's creatures to praise him. The last seven of these verses are
addressed to humans, but all the others to non-human creatures from

---

[1] Waddell, *Beasts*, pp. 71–2. The story can also be found in Bell, *Wholly Animals*, pp.
25–6.

[2] Biblical quotations in this chapter are all from NRSV.

the angels, through the heavenly bodies, the elements of the weather, the mountains, the plants, the waters, to all the living creatures of water, air and earth. The canticle occurs in one of the so-called Greek additions to the book of Daniel (3:52–90), where it is placed on the lips of the three Jews Hananiah, Mishael and Azariah (Shadrach, Meshach and Abednego) as they walk unharmed in the flames of Nebuchad-nezzar's fiery furnace. As part of the Greek versions of Daniel, the canticle belongs to the canonical Scriptures of the Orthodox and Roman Catholic churches, but since it is not in the Hebrew and Aramaic version of Daniel it is not part of the canon for Jews or Protestant Christians. At the Reformation it joined the books Protestants called the Apocrypha, where in English versions it used, rather oddly, to be called 'the Song of the Three Children'. But it did not cease to be known. In the Church of England, for example, it was given a prominent place among the canticles used in liturgy.

Lynn White recognized that it did not fit his thesis of the dominant and disastrous anthropocentrism of the Judeo-Christian tradition, which he insisted had its roots in the Old Testament. He therefore hypothesized that it was composed by an Alexandrian Jew 'who felt that there were spiritual values in Greek animism that should be rec-onciled with the rigid monotheism of his ancestral tradition. The result smelt a bit of heresy, so both the rabbis and the more rigorous Reformers rejected it.'[3]

This is quite wrong. The rabbinic canonical principle that only texts extant in Hebrew or Aramaic could be canonical meant that the Greek additions to Daniel were complete non-starters for inclusion in the Jewish Scriptures,[4] quite irrespective of their content, while the prin-ciple of the Reformers that it was Israel who defined the Old Testament for Christians had the same effect. The *Benedicite* has never 'smelt a bit of heresy'. We do not know where or when it was written, but we can certainly exclude the influence of 'Greek animism', because it is really nothing more than an elaborate expansion of Psalm 148, where just the same range of God's creatures is exhorted to praise God, though fewer specific examples are given. The *Benedicite* makes no theological statement not already made in Psalm 148. There is no question that Psalm 148 belongs integrally to the Israelite/Jewish

---

[3] White, 'Continuing the Conversation', p. 62.

[4] The Song of the Three has often been supposed to have had a Hebrew or Aramaic original and to have formed part of an edition of the book of Daniel in Hebrew/Aramaic before its translation into Greek. This may well be the case. My point is that the edition of the book of Daniel known to the rabbis did not include it.

religious tradition of monotheistic worship, while it is worth noting that this psalm also became especially prominent in Christian liturgical tradition, being one of the psalms invariably used daily in one of the (western) monastic offices (lauds).

The theme of creation's praise of God has certainly become much less familiar to Christians in the modern period than it was in earlier times. When modern Christians encounter it in Psalm 148 or in other biblical expressions of this theme (Isa. 42:10; Pss. 69:34; 96:11–12; 98:7–8; 103:22; 150:6; Phil. 2:10; Rev. 5:13; and cf. Ps. 19:1–4) they are apt not to take it seriously. They may take it to reflect some kind of pre-scientific 'animism' (so Lynn White) or pan-psychism that attributes rational consciousness to all things. Or they may take it to be a mere poetic fancy. Both reactions miss the significance of this biblical theme. The passages about creation's praise are, of course, metaphorical: they attribute to non-human creatures the human practice of praising God in human language. But the reality to which they point is that all creatures bring glory to God simply by being themselves and fulfilling their God-given roles in God's creation. A lily does not need to do anything specific in order to praise God; still less need it be conscious of anything. Simply by being and growing it praises God: 'Creation's praise is not an extra, an addition to what it is, but the shining of its being, the overflowing significance it has in pointing to its Creator simply by being itself.'[5]

This is the implication of one of the passages in Psalm 148 which give a reason for creation's praise:

> Let them praise the name of the LORD,
> for he commanded and they were created.
> He established them for ever and ever;
> he set a law that cannot pass away. (Ps. 148:5–6)[6]

As Terence Fretheim comments, the creatures' praise is 'praise for being what they are'.[7] And they praise by being what they are, what God has made them, and by doing what they do, what God has created them to do.[8] When St Benno identified the frogs' croaking as their

---

[5] Daniel W. Hardy and David F. Ford, *Jubilate: Theology in Praise* (London: Darton, Longman & Todd, 1984), p. 82.

[6] For this last line I give the translation in NRSV footnote.

[7] Terence E. Fretheim, 'Nature's Praise of God in the Psalms', *Ex Auditu* 3 (1987), p. 23.

[8] But those passages in which the creatures praise God for his salvific activities require further explanation.

praise of God, he slipped into a harmless and not uncommon anthropomorphism (we shall come across it again in Francis of Assisi) that is nevertheless not to be found in the biblical passages about creation's praise. Frogs praise God by their jumping, their feeding, their mating, and whatever else belongs to being a frog, just as much as by their croaking. It is distinctively human to bring praise to conscious expression in voice, but the creatures remind us that this distinctively human form of praise is worthless unless, like them, we live our whole lives to God's glory.

I suspect the major reasons why the theme of creation's praise has fallen out of most modern Christians' consciousness are urban people's isolation from nature, which deprives them of a sense of participation in nature, and the modern instrumentalizing of nature, for which it becomes simply material for human use. But these reasons also suggest how valuable it could be to recover a living sense of human participation in creation's praise of God. It is the strongest antidote to anthropocentrism in the biblical and Christian tradition. Certainly an appropriate interpretation of the Genesis motif of human dominion over other creatures (Gen. 1:28) should avoid the anthropocentric and instrumentalist interpretation this motif acquired in the modern period.[9] Humanity is entrusted with the care of the creatures for God's sake, to whom they belong, and their own sake. But all interpretations of this motif necessarily invoke a hierarchical relationship between humans and other creatures, recognizing our God-given power over and therefore responsibility for them. Yet for this element of hierarchy to be properly understood, not to say exercised, it must be combined with a lively sense that we too are creatures of God alongside our fellow-creatures. Just as the king of Israel was not to exalt himself over his brothers and sisters (Deut. 17:20), so the human dominion over other creatures is not the domination of superiors over inferiors but the responsibility of some creatures for their brother and sister creatures.

This sense of fellow-creatureliness is most appropriately realized when humans join in the whole creation's praise of God. In this common attribution of glory to the one Creator there is no hierarchy or anthropocentricity. Here all creatures, including ourselves, are simply fellow-creatures expressing the theocentricity of the created world, each in our own created way, differently but in complementarity. In the worship of God there can be no hierarchy among the creatures, as Psalm 148 itself makes clear:

---

[9] For the history of interpretation, see Chapter 2 in this volume.

Let them praise the name of the LORD,
for his name alone is exalted;
his glory is above earth and heaven. (Ps. 148:13)

God's name alone is exalted: there is no place in worship for the exaltation of any creature over another.

Moreover, to recognize creation's praise is to abandon an instrumental view of nature. All creatures exist for God's glory, and we learn to see the non-human creatures in that way, to glimpse their value for God that has nothing to do with their usefulness to us, as we learn to join them in their own glorification of God.

Humans Are Not the Priests of Creation

If we are to recover the true value of joining in creation's praise, we must avoid a move that assimilates this theme to the hierarchical model of humanity mediating between God and the rest of creation. Such a move has proved irresistible in some parts of the Christian tradition, especially where the hierarchical model has been understood in a benevolent rather than dominating or exploitative way. We find it seductively expressed in the poetry of George Herbert:

> Of all the creatures both in sea and land
> Only to Man thou hast made known thy ways,
> And put the pen alone into his hand,
> And made him Secretary of thy praise.
> Beasts fain would sing; birds ditty to their notes;
> Trees would be runing on their native lute[10]
> To thy renown: but all their hands and throats
> Are brought to Man, while they are lame and mute.
> Man is the world's high Priest: he doth present
> The sacrifice for all; while they below[11]
> Unto the service mutter an assent,
> Such as springs use that fall, and winds that blow.[12]

---

[10] Herbert means that if they could the beasts, birds and trees would put their praise of God into words.

[11] Hierarchical subordination is here explicit.

[12] George Herbert, 'Providence', in *George Herbert: The Country Parson, The Temple* (ed. J.N. Wall, Classics of Western Spirituality; New York/Mahwah: Paulist, 1981), p. 238.

I do not know what the antecedents to Herbert's idea of humanity as creation's priest were, but it reappears in contemporary Orthodox writing on ecological themes,[13] where it is connected with the eucharistic offering of bread and wine to God. Through this offering to God of what belongs to him, according to John Zizoulias, 'creation is brought into relation to God and not only is it treated with the reverence that befits what belongs to God, but it is also liberated from its natural limitations and is transformed into a bearer of life.'[14]

This eucharistic relationship to creation is then treated as a kind of model for all of the human relationship with creation. Humanity's priesthood is exercised in human creativity that brings creation to a fulfilment it could not have otherwise. Creation needs the mediation of humanity in order to be truly itself and to be in relationship to God. Though in a way less open to technological misinterpretation, Philip Sherrard makes the same point: '[M]an – when he is truly human – is also and above all a priest – the priest of God: he who offers the world to God in his praise and worship and who simultaneously bestows divine love and beauty upon the world.'[15]

Of this arrogant assertion that only through human mediation can the rest of creation be itself in relation to God there is not a trace in the Scriptures. This Orthodox sacerdotal universe is not the world of the Old Testament where the creatures have their own relationships with God quite apart from humanity and fulfil their God-given existence without human interference (e.g. Ps. 104; Job 38 – 39). When the psalmist calls on the creatures to praise God, this is a rhetorical device that clearly does not mean that they wait until humans summon them before uttering their praise. Contrary to Herbert's idea, there is no indication in the biblical passages about creation's praise of God that the other creatures are mute and need humanity to voice their praise. All the creatures praise God in their own distinctive ways, and humanity is merely added to the list (Ps. 148:11–12) after all the others. In a striking use of this biblical theme, Jesus himself claimed that, if human praise of God failed, even inanimate nature would be able make up for the loss (Luke 19:40). Moreover, Herbert's notion that humanity alone is qualified to voice creation's praise neglects the

---

[13] For this theme in Philip Sherrard and Paulos Gregorios, with trenchant critique of its anthropocentrism, see Northcott, *Environment*, pp. 132–4.

[14] John D. Zizioulas, 'Preserving God's Creation: Lecture 3', *King's Theological Review* 13/1 (1990), p. 5.

[15] Philip Sherrard, *The Rape of Man and Nature* (Ipswich: Golgonooza Press, 1987), p. 40.

place of the angels (Ps. 148:2): if creation needs priests to voice God's praise, why should not the angels, those who exist to praise God in his presence without ceasing, not be better than humans in that role?

This is in fact a valuable clue, for in the biblical world picture there are indeed priests who praise God representatively on behalf of all the creatures, offering praise without ceasing in God's heavenly presence. They are the four 'living creatures' of Revelation 4:6b–8.[16] One of these is indeed humanoid, but the faces of the others resemble those of the lion, the ox and the eagle (probably understood as the dominant species in the categories of wild animals, domestic animals, and birds respectively). There is no anthropocentrism in heaven.

Or, if we turn from biblical pictures to empirical and scientific knowledge, what sense could we make of the idea that all the creatures need us in order to glorify God? Did those extraordinary creatures that live in the deepest depths of the oceans, only very recently even seen by humans (and undoubtedly there are many such species still unknown), not glorify God in the way that he made them to do until some humans discovered them? What about the millions of species that lived on earth before humans ever appeared?

The whole idea is dangerously close to (in Zizioulas virtually identical to) the notion that other creatures have not fulfilled their God-given purpose until humans have interfered with them and integrated them into some human idea of what we would like creation to be like. We should have learned from the fact that far too much human 'creativity' has in fact disabled the creatures from being themselves and destroyed their own distinctive ways of praising their Creator. To recognize that creation praises God very well without us will help us, for example, at last to leave a few wildernesses alone, valuing as God does the way they glorify God in themselves. In place of the arrogance of the cosmic priest we need to learn the humility of a St Benno who recognized that God might delight more in the croaks of the frog than in his own praise of God.

In the Bible, the horizontal model of fellow-creatureliness in the praise of God exists in counterpoise to the vertical model of human dominion over other creatures. We should not assimilate either to the other. Just as this rules out a sort of deep ecology in which humans abdicate responsibility for the distinctive powers they have been given by God, so it also rules out the model of human priesthood which deprives the creatures of their own God-given ways of being themselves to the glory of God.

---

[16] See Chapter 8 in this volume.

Antiphonal Praise

In fact, it is much more obvious that other creatures can help us to worship God than that we can help other creatures to. In the order of praise in Psalm 148 and the *Benedicite* all other creatures are called to worship before humans are then called to join them. The creatures help us to worship primarily by their otherness that draws us out of our self-absorption into a world that exists not for us but for God's glory. This is what happens to Job in chapters 38 – 39, when the Lord speaking out of the whirlwind displays his whole creation to Job, from the immensity of the stellar universe to the sheer stupidity of the ostrich and the soaring otherness of the eagle. It is not just the moments of breathtaking beauty that help us to worship God, but the endlessly remarkable quiddity of other creatures, their being themselves in all the strangeness, intricacy and difference that God has given to each. This being themselves *is* their glorification of God, the way they continuously give back to God the glory the Creator has given them, and so for believers in God to attend to their quiddity is also to recognize the greater glory of the Creator who surpasses them. Otherwise put, sharing something of God's primal delight in his creation (Gen. 1:31) enables us also to delight in God himself.

The otherness of the creatures in their own integrity is thus essential to our joining their praise of God. The more we praise God with the other creatures, the more we shall want to resist the relentless trend towards a total humanizing of the world in which the rest of creation will have become no more than the material from which we have fashioned a world of our own creation. In such a world we shall see only ourselves and only such of the glory of God as we human creatures can reflect. Instead of, as George Herbert imagined, giving voice to the mute creatures, we shall have silenced their song. It is, of course, intrinsic to our God-given humanity to make human things out of the created world around us, such as the bread and the wine of the eucharistic offering. But it is not our vocation to absorb the whole created world into our own human life in this way, as the modern Orthodox interpretation of the eucharistic offering mentioned above would suggest, as though all creatures were given by God for us to make them into such as bread and wine.

If other creatures help us to praise God, do we in any sense return the compliment? Is there a way in which we can think not in hierarchical but in reciprocal terms of our own distinctive contribution to creation's praise? At the present juncture of our history with creation it is probably most important to emphasize that we need, much more than we have done, to allow creation's praise by letting it be. But we may also consider the role of the ways in which we give other creatures a place in our human life that preserves in some degree and form their otherness. In our gardens and our pets, for example, and in all the arts, creaturely otherness is reduced to a human context, but in ways that are for us real encounters with the otherness of the creatures in their diversity and integrity. This is the case when the creatures are not instrumentalized into the material of our lives and creations, but are respected and loved in their otherness. Art that does this and in so doing glorifies God is a human participation in the glorification of God by the creatures. It emphatically does not take the creatures' own praise onto some higher plane, but gives it a place within our own praise in addition to its entirely adequate place apart from us. In some sense we are then not only adding our own praise to that of the other creatures but also repeating in our humanly distinctive ways the praise of the other creatures themselves.[17] It would be worth careful thought about what distinguishes art of which this is true from art that, while it may glorify God in a human way, does not echo the praise of other creatures.

Francis of Assisi

I offer two signal exemplars of a Christian spirituality that attends to the praise of the other creatures in order to join their praise of God. The first is Francis of Assisi, who made this motif very much his own but owed it to the biblical and liturgical tradition we have discussed. In his own works he echoes the main biblical texts about creation's praise of God: the *Benedicite* (Dan. 3:52–90); Psalms 69:34; 96:11–12; 103:22; 148; 150:6; Revelation 5:13.[18] The famous *Canticle of the Creatures* seems indebted to Psalm 148 and the *Benedicite* in its catalogue of creatures,[19] but it should probably not be understood as referring to the creation's own praise of God but rather to humanity's

---

[17] In this sense we might agree with Hardy and Ford, *Jubilate*, pp. 81–2, that humanity is the poet of creation, but not, as they add, the priest.

[18] The allusions are in the *Exhortation to the Praise of God* (Ps. 69:35; Dan. 3:78; Ps. 103:22; 150:6; Dan. 3:80); the *Second Letter to the Faithful* 61 (Rev. 5:13); the *Praises to be Said at All the Hours* (Dan. 3:57; Ps. 69:35; Rev. 5:13); the *Office of the Passion* 7:4 (Ps. 96:10–11); the *Canticle of the Creatures* (Ps. 148; *Benedicite*).

[19] Sorrell, *St. Francis*, pp. 99, 102–5.

praise of God for the creatures.[20] More significant for our present interest are his liturgical compositions, which often consist of a collage of texts carefully selected from Scripture, especially the Psalms. One of these, the *Praises to be Said at All the Hours*,[21] was to be used by the friars before each hour of the office. This outpouring of praise to the Trinity is based largely on the heavenly liturgy depicted in Revelation 4 – 5, and like that liturgy it culminates in the praise of God by every creature in the cosmos. Calls to all the creatures to praise alternate with a refrain ('Let us praise and glorify him forever') based on that in the *Benedicite*. The *Exhortation to the Praise of God*[22] calls on all the creatures, including both general references and specific references to rivers and birds, to praise God. In these liturgies of creation, as in their biblical sources, there is no hierarchy, not even an order of importance in calls to praise. The impression is of a vast and harmonious chorus of praise going up from all creatures, animate and inanimate, with humans interspersed among the others.

It was typical of Francis to put biblical passages into practice in a way that might seem naively literal, but really constituted a particularly potent expression of a biblical theme. In this case, Francis translated the liturgical practice of calling on all the creatures to praise God into a practice of actually addressing the creatures in person. This began with the famous sermon to the birds, which initiated a regular practice: 'From that day on, he carefully exhorted all birds, all animals, all reptiles, and also insensible creatures, to praise and love their Creator, because daily, invoking the name of the Savior, he observed their obedience in his own experience.'[23]

The reference to 'the name of the Savior' is significant, because it relates creation and salvation in a way that is rarely explicit in Francis's thought about creation's praise of God but is surely often implicit. Since salvation entails the restoration of creation to its proper harmony and order in relation to God, the praise of the creatures is directed to Christ as Saviour as well as to God as Creator. This is what occurs at the end of the great cosmic liturgy in Revelation 4 – 5, which Francis evidently knew well: when the slaughtered Lamb is enthroned in heaven, every creature in the cosmos joins in the doxology addressed to God and the Lamb. This eschatological goal of all

---

[20] Sorrell, *St. Francis*, pp. 118–22.
[21] Regis J. Armstrong, Hellmann and Short, *Francis of Assisi*, p. 161.
[22] Regis J. Armstrong, Hellmann and Short, *Francis of Assisi*, vol. 1, p. 138.
[23] Thomas of Celano, *First Life of St Francis*, 58, translated in Regis J. Armstrong, Hellmann and Short, *Francis of Assisi*, vol. 1, p. 234.

worship Francis anticipated whenever he invoked the name of Jesus and called on creatures to praise their Creator.

We should also mention Francis's habit of singing along with cicadas or birds in what he understood as their praise of their Creator.[24] In this way he translated the sentiments of the *Benedicite* into a real human solidarity with the rest of creation understood as a theocentric community existing for the praise and service of God. There is no trace in Francis of the idea that the creatures need humans to voice their praise of God for them. On the contrary, the cicadas and the birds are already singing to God's glory; Francis joins their song.

Christopher Smart

The eighteenth-century English poet Christopher Smart belongs, like George Herbert, to the Anglican tradition of spiritual poetry, but by comparison with Herbert has been grossly neglected. His eighteenth-century style is less appealing today than Herbert's, but he has much more to say to our present interest because he was, as it were, a specialist in praise. Edward Hirsch speaks of his 'dedication to a poetry of absolute praise'.[25] Smart came to see it as his vocation to be 'the Reviver of ADORATION amongst ENGLISH-MEN'.[26] This was certainly no pose. Throughout his difficult and disappointed life, praise and thanksgiving to God welled up constantly, and were clearly fed by, among other sources, his delight in everything around him in the natural world. He was also deeply familiar with the biblical sources on creation's praise of God. It is notable that, in his complete rendering of all the Psalms into English verse, there are only seven psalms for which he offers two alternative versions, and three of these are the psalms in which the worship of God by the non-human creation is most prominent (98; 103; 148; the others are 23; 100; 117; 149).[27] But probably his finest expression of the theme is in stanzas 51–71 of his

---

[24] Thomas of Celano, *First Life of St Francis*, 58, in Habig, *St. Francis*, pp. 499–500 (cicada); Moorman, *A New Fioretti* 57, in Habig, *St. Francis*, pp. 1881–2 (nightingale).

[25] Edward Hirsch, *How to Read a Poem* (Durham, North Carolina: Duke University Center for Documentary Studies, 1999), p. 77.

[26] *Jubilate Agno* B332, in K. Williamson ed., *The Poetical Works of Christopher Smart*, vol. 1, *Jubilate Agno* (Oxford: Clarendon Press, 1980), p. 63.

[27] Marcus Walsh ed., *The Poetical Works of Christopher Smart*, vol. 3. *A Translation of the Psalms of David* (Oxford: Clarendon Press, 1987).

'A Song to David,' where he was not constrained by a biblical text he was rendering but could compose freely. What is notable in these verses is the way some special characteristic or characteristics of each creature is concisely evoked, to convey the sense that each worships in its own distinctive way precisely by being the creature God has made it to be and doing what God intended for it. For example:

> Rich almonds colour to the prime
> For ADORATION; tendrils climb,
>   And fruit-trees pledge their gems;
> And Ivis[28] with her gorgeous vest
> Builds for her eggs her cunning nest,
>   And bell-flowers bow their stems (53).[29]

A series of verses find the praise of God varyingly sung by the changing seasons. For example, this is the onset of winter:

> The cheerful holly, pensive yew,
> And holy thorn, their trim renew;
>   The squirrel hoards his nuts;
> All creatures batten o'er their stores,
> And careful nature all her doors
>   For ADORATION shuts (63).[30]

Probably the best-known instance of this theme in Smart's poetry is in his Christmas hymn ('Where is this stupendous stranger'), and two lines are worth quoting because they show how Smart related the praise of the creatures to the redemptive work of Christ as well as to creation:

> Spinks and ouzles[31] sing sublimely,
> 'We too have a Saviour born'.[32]

Smart develops this theme also in his hymns for Epiphany and the Presentation.[33]

---

[28] Humming-bird.

[29] Marcus Walsh and Karina Williamson eds, *The Poetical Works of Christopher Smart*, vol. 2: *Religious Poetry 1763–1771* (Oxford: Clarendon Press, 1983), p. 139.

[30] Walsh and Williamson, *Poetical Works of Christopher Smart*, p. 142.

[31] Finches and blackbirds.

[32] Walsh and Williamson, *Poetical Works of Christopher Smart*, p. 89.

[33] Walsh and Williamson, *Poetical Works of Christopher Smart*, pp. 37–9, 41–3.

And His Cat Jeoffry

The *Jubilate Agno* is an extraordinary work, quite unlike Smart's compositions for publication, which he wrote in a period when he was living in a private asylum in Bethnal Green. It seems to have been a kind of personal discipline of praise, written at the rate of one to six short verses each day. In the scheme of the work the verses are paired, each pair consisting of a verse beginning 'Let . . .' and a verse beginning 'For . . .' The first is a summons to praise, the second a reason for praise. (In many cases we have only the 'Let . . .' verse or only the 'For . . .' verse.) This is not the place to discuss many features of the poem, which is full of esoteric learning and personal references. But the design of the 'Let . . .' verses relates to our interest here. In each case Smart calls on a person (either a biblical person, in many cases a very obscure one, or a contemporary English person) to praise God along with one of the non-human creatures, about which Smart often provides some apt comment or learned information. Here is a series of three examples for which we have both the 'Let . . .' verses and 'For . . .' verses, and where the connexion between the two is readily understood:

> LET PETER rejoice with the MOON FISH who keeps up the life of the
> waters by night.
> *FOR I pray the Lord JESUS that cured the LUNATICK to be merciful to*
> *all my brethren and sisters in these houses.*
> Let Andrew rejoice with the Whale, who is array'd in beauteous blue
> and is a combination of bulk and activity.
> *For they work me with their harping-irons, which is a barbarous*
> *instrument, because I am more unguarded that others.*
> Let James rejoice with the Skuttle-fish, who foils his foe by the effusion
> of his ink.
> *For the blessing of God hath been on my epistles, which I have written*
> *for the benefit of others* (B123–5).[34]

Eccentric and bizarre as much of the material is, we should see it as the genuinely devotional work of a learned man who wished to join his praise of God with that of the biblical worshippers and that of all God's prodigally varied creatures. The ingenuity of the verses is offered to God in exultant praise, along with the personal circumstances, even the most tragic.

---

[34] Williamson, *Poetical Works*, pp. 31–2.

This long poem is the context for Smart's well-known lines about
his cat Jeoffry, consisting entirely of 'For . . .' verses for which we lack
the corresponding 'Let . . .' verses (they may never have been written).
The lines begin:

> For I will consider my Cat Jeoffry.
> For he is the servant of the Living God duly and daily serving him.
> For at the first glance of the glory of God in the East he worships in his
> way.
> For this is done by wreathing his body seven times round with elegant
> quickness.
> For then he leaps up to catch the musk, which is the blessing of God on
> his prayer (B6959).[35]

There is lovingly close observation and much humour in the whole
description, but we should not miss the fact that Smart is entirely serious in supposing that his cat worships God 'in his own way'. This is
how he speaks elsewhere of other creatures. The mountain and the
rock 'also have their ways/In spirit God to praise' (from Smart's version of Ps. 98).[36] 'Come with all your modes of praising' he calls to the
lambs, kids, colts and other young animals in his hymn for
Epiphany.[37] Each creature praises God in doing as God has created it
to do. Admittedly, in Jeoffry's case the notion seems to be pressed to
the point of supposing that he is conscious of God:

> For he purrs in thankfulness, when God tells him he's a good Cat
> (B726).
> For he knows that God is his Saviour (B 737).[38]

Smart indulges his fancy here in a passage that is undoubtedly playful as well as serious, but throughout he is engaged in thankfulness to
God for God's creature and recognition that the closely observed features of this much-loved creature bring glory to God.

---

[35] Williamson, *Poetical Works*, p. 87.
[36] Walsh, *Poetical Works*, p. 237.
[37] Walsh and Williamson, *Poetical Works of Christopher Smart*, p. 38.
[38] Williamson, *Poetical Works*, p. 88.

Nature Divine or Sacred?

In a recent, sensitive and enthusiastic discussion of Smart's verses on his cat Jeoffry and of Smart's poetry more generally,[39] Edward Hirsch nevertheless somewhat distorts Smart's religious perception in a way that it is quite instructive to notice. There are two mistakes, one of which paves the way for the other. First, Hirsch thinks that what Smart perceives is the divinity in things: '[I]n Smart's world . . . everything is infused with divinity. Everything is charged with a deeply animating force. The world shines out with radiant particularity. This is what Gerard Manley Hopkins means by indwelling.[40] . . . [Smart] was writing from the far side of daily life where the world appears mysterious and unfamiliar, where everything trembles with divine presence.[41]

This is not quite wrong, but it is misleading. The reflection of God the Creator in his creation is a kind of divine immanence. But Smart does not perceive God as an animating force within things. Rather he sees the creatures precisely *as creatures*, that is, as pointing beyond themselves to the God who made them and surpasses them. He does not so much find divinity in them as join the Godward movement of their praise. But Hirsch's first mistake, which may not in itself seem too serious, enables his second, which is serious. The theme of his discussion is 'the poetry of praise', and the theme slides imperceptibly from Smart's praise of God to speaking as though Smart is praising the creatures, and thereby classifying his work with poetry that praises not God but everything in the world ('I look for things/to praise on the riverbanks, and I praise them').[42] True, in Hirsch's general sense Smart's work does belong with poetry that is enraptured by the world, poetry that is 'a way of falling in love with the world again'.[43] But Smart's distinctive religious vision is lost here in the interests of making his work appealing to non-religious people who do not wish to join with him in praising the Creator. Smart's own vision is theocentric in a much more than immanentist sense. He does not praise the creatures in the specific sense in which he praises God. Rather he appreciates the quiddity of the creatures as glorifying the God who

---

[39] Hirsch, *How to Read*, pp. 66–80.
[40] Hirsch, *How to Read*, p. 70.
[41] Hirsch, *How to Read*, p. 72.
[42] William Meredith quoted in Hirsch, *How to Read*, p. 79.
[43] Hirsch, *How to Read*, p. 79.

made them. His adoration is not directed at the creatures themselves, but finds in the creatures fellow-worshippers with whom he is the better able to adore God.

In the heyday of the modern scientific-technological project the biblical and Christian tradition was credited with having de-divinized the natural world and so enabled scientific study and technological use of it. More recently, in Green and New Age circles, the same tradition is often condemned for the same reason. Such judgments pose a false alternative between, on the one hand, a pantheistic or animistic vision of nature as divine (and to be worshipped) and, on the other hand, a modern scientific and secular view of nature as mere object of human use. The biblical and Christian vision of the whole creation's worship of God illuminates another possibility, which is the truly Christian one. In the biblical and Christian tradition, nature is certainly de-divinized but it is not de-sacralized. The creatures are not divine, but they belong to God, are valued by God and point to God. Adequately perceived, they do not let our attention rest purely in themselves, but take us up into the movement of glorification of God that is their own existence. To deny them divinity as such is not to depreciate them but to let them be truly themselves in all the variety of their endlessly specific ways of being and doing. They are not to be discarded in a religious move to a God who can be known only through leaving the world aside. On the contrary, it is attention to the quiddity of each that continually assists our praise of the God who gives them themselves and surpasses them and us. We need to learn the habit of joining creation's praise of God if we are to discover an adequately Christian ecological spirituality for today.

8.

Creation's Praise of God in the Book of Revelation

That all creation worships God is a biblical theme that has not been given the attention it deserves, at least in the modern period, and despite the burgeoning interest in ecological aspects of the Bible.[1] But it has a distinctive significance for delineating a biblical perspective on the non-human creation.[2] To recognize that all creatures praise God is to enter an appreciative vision of creation in which a purely instrumental view of nature has to be left aside. It is to see that all creation exists for God's glory, not for human use. All creatures have their own value for God and praise God simply by being what he has made them to be and doing what he has made them to do. To recognize that all creatures praise God is also to recognize ourselves as fellow-creatures with others. A living sense of participation with other creatures in the worship that all creatures owe and give to God is the strongest antidote to Christian anthropocentrism. When humans join their fellow-creatures in giving glory to their common Creator there is no hierarchy or anthropocentricity. In this respect all creatures, ourselves included, are simply fellow-creatures expressing the theocentricity of the world, each in their own created way, differently but in complementarity.

The theme of all creation's praise of God is prominent most especially in the Psalms (65:12–13; 69:34; 96:11–12; 98:7–8; 103:22; 148; 150:6;

---

[1] Exceptions include: Fretheim, 'Nature's Praise', pp. 16–30; Howard N. Wallace, '*Jubilate Deo omnis terra*: God and Earth in Psalm 65', in *The Earth Story in the Psalms and the Prophets* (ed. Norman C. Habel; The Earth Bible 4; Sheffield: Sheffield Academic Press/Cleveland: Pilgrim Press, 2001), pp. 51–64; John Eaton, *The Circle of Creation: Animals in the Light of the Bible* (London: SCM Press, 1995), pp. 94–103.

[2] See Chapter 7 in this volume.

cf. Isa. 42:10). If the theme as such has been neglected, this is even more true of its occurrence in the book of Revelation. All commentators recognize it in 5:13 but they are not inclined to dwell on it. For some, the main issue seems to be whether the worship of all creatures implies the voluntary acknowledgment of God by all or includes the forced submission of God's opponents.[3] That this is the main issue suggests that such commentators are really interested only in humans or in humans and angels.[4] But for an adequate appreciation of the theme of all creation's worship in Revelation, we need to attend not only to the praise of God sung by the whole cosmos in 5:13, but also to the worship unceasingly given to God by the four living creatures around the throne (4:6b–8). That this is related to the worship of all creation is more controversial and we shall have to discuss the matter in considerable detail.

The Four Living Creatures in Revelation 4

In the first part of the prophet John's vision of the heavenly throne-room (Rev. 4) he sees the divine sovereignty as it is in heaven, where God's rule is perfectly accomplished. On earth, on the other hand, as the rest of the book makes clear, it is contested and must be established in the eschatological future. What is true in heaven must become true on earth. In this vision of heaven John sees the sovereignty of the God who created all things, depicted not so much directly, through a sight of the Enthroned One himself, but through what happens around his throne: the worship of those who surround the throne and sing his praises unceasingly. These figures are the twenty-four elders and the four living creatures, the former making an outer circle, the latter an inner circle, around the divine throne.

One key to understanding this vision is to recognize that the imagery involves both political and cultic elements. The setting is the

---

[3] George B. Caird, *The Revelation of St John the Divine* (BNTC; London; A&C Black, 1966), pp. 77; Mathias Rissi, *The Future of the World* (SBT 2/23; London: SCM Press, 1972), p. 81; Gregory C. Beale, *The Book of Revelation* (NIGTC; Grand Rapids: Eerdmans/Carlisle: Paternoster, 1999), p. 365; Wes Howard-Brook and Anthony Gwyther, *Unveiling Empire: Reading Revelation Then and Now* (Bible and Liberation Series; Maryknoll, New York: Orbis, 1999), p. 209; Stephen S. Smalley, *The Revelation to John* (London: SPCK, 2005), p. 140.

[4] Rissi, *Future*, p. 11, says, explicitly and remarkably, that 'John is not interested in any cosmological speculation, for the "cosmos" in his view is *the world of man*' (italics original).

throne-room from which God rules the universe, but it is also the heavenly sanctuary in which he is worshipped, the heavenly proto-type of the earthly temple in Jerusalem. The identity and significance of the twenty-four elders has been much discussed, and we cannot enter the discussion here. But in my view they are best understood as the angelic beings who form the divine council and exercise political authority in the heavenly world on God's behalf. They are engaged in constant obeisance to God, getting down from their thrones and lay-ing their crowns before the throne of God (4:10), thus making clear that God is the source of all power and authority and that their own authority is entirely derivative from his. For our present purpose the key point is to distinguish their significance as heavenly rulers from that of the four living creatures who are heavenly priests. Their exis-tence is wholly taken up in worship. Closer than any to the throne of God, they are the central worshippers of the whole creation, and, as priests, they worship representatively, on behalf of the whole animate creation, human and non-human, as their forms (4:7) indicate.[5] It is this understanding of the function and significance of the living crea-tures that we must now demonstrate through a detailed study.

The Four Living Creatures in the Context of Jewish Traditions

Like much else in Revelation, the account of the four living creatures is exegetical.[6] It is based on the extraordinary descriptions in the prophet Ezekiel (1:5–25; 3:12–13; 10:1–22) of four living creatures (*ḥayyōt*) who bear the firmament on which the throne of God stands and who, along with the wheels that are also described, transport it from place to place. In Ezekiel 10, though not in chapter 1, they are identified with the cherubim who formed a throne for God in the holy of holies of the temple. These mysterious descriptions were the object of considerable interest among Jewish exegetes and visionaries, and

---

5 This paragraph summarizes my somewhat fuller account in Richard Bauckham, *The Theology of the Book of Revelation* (Cambridge: CUP, 1993), pp. 33–4.

6 Carol A. Newsom, 'Merkabah Exegesis in the Qumran Sabbath Shirot', *JJS* 38 (1987): pp. 11–30, here p. 18, judges, using Michael Fishbane's categories, that the relationship of Rev. 4:2b–8 to Ezekiel 1 is 'better described as one of borrowing and allusion than as exegetical appropriation'. I think this probably underestimates the extent to which exegesis lies behind at least the account of the living creatures in Rev. 4:6b–8.

by the time of the book of Revelation there were traditions of interpretation of them to which Revelation is indebted.

In two main respects Revelation 4:6b–8 coheres with early Jewish exegetical traditions about the *ḥayyōt*. The first is what David Halperin calls the hymnic tradition of exegesis.[7] To modern scholars and ordinary readers alike the function of the *ḥayyōt* in Ezekiel seems to be to carry the throne of God, but to most Jewish interpreters, both in the late Second Temple period and later, their main function appears rather to have been that of worshipping God in continuous hymnody. These interpreters understood the sound of the wings of the creatures (Ezek. 1:24–5) to be not merely a deafening noise, but hymnic praise of God. The wings were understood to be organs of song. This interpretation found strong support in the text of Ezekiel 3:12–13. Here modern scholars[8] usually amend the Masoretic text of verse 12 to read: 'as the glory of the LORD rose (*b^erûm*) from its place, I heard behind me the sound of loud rumbling' (NRSV), which the following verse identifies as the sound of the wings of the living creatures and of the wheels. But the unamended text of verse 12 can be translated: 'I heard behind me a voice of a great rushing, [saying,] Blessed (*bârûk*) be the glory of the LORD from his place' (AV). This is how the Septuagint translates the verse, evidently following a text identical with our Masoretic text. If verse 12 is read in that way, then, in the light of verse 13, it appears that the wings of the living creatures give voice to a benediction: 'Blessed be the glory of the LORD from his place.' According to the same reading of verses 12–13 the wheels also sing this benediction, and this is no doubt the main source of the common Jewish understanding of the wheels as animate beings (the *'ofannîm*), another order of heavenly beings engaged in the continuous worship of God, like the living creatures.[9] In these interpretations the Lord's 'place' is understood to be the heavenly sanctuary in which he is continuously worshipped by the heavenly creatures.

---

[7] David J. Halperin, *The Faces of the Chariot: Early Jewish Responses to Ezekiel's Vision* (TSAJ 16; Tübingen: Mohr Siebeck, 1988), pp. 46, 51, 54, 59–61, etc.

[8] See, e.g. William H. Brownlee, *Ezekiel 1–19* (WBC 28; Waco: Word Books, 1986), p. 36; Daniel I. Block, *The Book of Ezekiel Chapters 1–24* (NICOT; Grand Rapids: Eerdmans, 1997), pp. 134–5. Block argues that there must have been a very early copyist's mistake, 'prior to the adoption of the square Aramaic script', since it was in the archaic cursive script that M could easily have been mistaken for K. Both Halperin, *Faces*, pp. 44–5, and Newsom, 'Merkabah Exegesis', p. 22 n. 28, suggest that the alteration was intentional, designed to make the passage resemble Isa. 6:2–3.

[9] Halperin, *Faces*, pp. 44–5. Halperin also, less conclusively, finds the hymnic tradition in the LXX of Ezek. 1:7; 43:2: *Faces*, pp. 57–60.

This interpretation of Ezekiel 3:12–13 is found in the Songs of the Sabbath Sacrifice (4Q/11Q ShirShabb) from Qumran (where the *ḥayyōt* are identified with the cherubim):

> The [cheru]bim fall before Him and they b[l]ess when they raise themselves. A voice of quiet of God [is heard] and tumult of chanting; at the rising of their wings, a voice of [quie]t of God. They are blessing a structure of a throne-chariot above the firmament of the cherubim [and] they chant [the effulge]nce of the firmament of light << from >> beneath His glorious seat (11Q17 vii 709 + 4Q405 ii 21–2: 7–9)[10]

This hymnic interpretation of Ezekiel's *ḥayyōt* is also found in the Targum to Ezekiel 1:24–5; 3:12–13 and 43:2.[11] It is also presupposed in many texts that portray the *ḥayyōt* or cherubim[12] worshipping along with other heavenly beings, such as the seraphim, the *'ofannîm* and others (*1 Enoch* 14:18[?]; 61:10–11; *2 Enoch* 19:6; *Apoc. Ab.* 18; *T. Adam* 4:8; *Apost. Const.* 7.35.3; 8.12.27; b. *Ḥag.* 13b).[13]

The second way in which Revelation's description of the *ḥayyōt* coheres with other Jewish interpretations is in the identification of the *ḥayyōt* or cherubim with the seraphim of Isaiah's vision (Isa. 6:2–3). Some Jewish exegetes did not conflate the cherubim and the seraphim but treated them as two different orders of angelic beings (*1 Enoch* 61:10; 71:7; *2 Enoch* 19:6;[14] 21:1; *T. Adam* 4:8; *Apost. Const.* 7.35.3; 8.12.27). Others, however, identified the two (*Apoc. Ab.* 18; b. *Ḥag.* 13b; *Lev. Rab.* 27:3).

---

[10] Translation from James R. Davila, *Liturgical Works* (Eerdmans Commentaries on the Dead Sea Scrolls; Grand Rapids: Eerdmans, 2000), p. 147. Carol A. Newsom, *Songs of the Sabbath Sacrifice? A Critical Edition* (Harvard Semitic Studies 27; Atlanta, Georgia: Scholars Press, 1985), pp. 313–314; *eadem*, 'Merkabah Exegesis,' pp. 20–24, argues that the passage is based on reading Ezekiel 3:12–13 in relationship to 1 Kgs. 19:12.

[11] Halperin, *Faces*, pp. 121–3.

[12] The identification of the *ḥayyōt* and the cherubim, as in Ezekiel 10, seems to be assumed by most Jewish literature prior to the Hekhalot literature: Halperin, *Faces*, p. 43; Saul M. Olyan, *A Thousand Thousands Served Him: Exegesis and the Naming of Angels in Ancient Judaism* (TSAJ 36; Tübingen: Mohr Siebeck, 1993), pp. 33–4.

[13] Whether or not some of these texts are early Christian, in this respect they continue a Jewish tradition of exegesis.

[14] The text of recension J should here be preferred to that of recension A.

Comparison with the Apocalypse of Abraham

The account of the *ḥayyōt* that corresponds most closely to Revelation's is in the *Apocalypse of Abraham*, which probably dates from around the same time (although we have it only in an Old Slavonic translation from the Greek). Abraham, taken up into heaven, sees the divine throne:

> And as the fire rose up, soaring higher, I saw under the fire a throne [made] of fire and the many-eyed Wheels,[15] and they are reciting the song. And under the throne [I saw] four singing fiery Living Creatures. [4]And their appearance was the same, each one of them had four faces. [5]<And> this was the aspect of their faces: of a lion, of a man, of an ox, of an eagle. Four heads <were on their bodies, so that the four Living Creatures had sixteen faces>, [6]and each one had six wings: from their shoulders, <and from their sides,> and from their loins. [7]With the wings which were from their shoulders they covered their faces, and with the wings from their loins they clothed their feet, and with their middle wings they stretch out straight flying.
> [8]And as they were finishing singing, they looked at one another and threatened one another. [9]And it came to pass when the angel who was with me[16] saw that they were threatening one another, he left me and went running to them. [10]And he turned the face of each Living Creature from the face which was opposite to it so that they could not see each other's threatening faces. [11]And he taught them the song of peace [saying] that everything belonged to the Eternal One.
> [12]While I was still standing and watching, I saw behind the Living Creatures a chariot with fiery Wheels. Each Wheel was full of eyes round about. [13]And above the Wheels there was the throne that I had seen. And it was covered with fire and the fire encircled it round about, and an indescribable light surrounded the fiery people. [14]And I heard the sound of their *qedusha* like the voice of a single man (18:3–14).[17]

Although the account of the living creatures in this passage from the *Apocalypse of Abraham* is considerably longer and more detailed than

---

[15] Alexander Kulik, *Retroverting Slavonic Pseudepigrapha: Toward the Original of the Apocalypse of Abraham* (SBL Text-Critical Studies 3; Atlanta: SBL, 2004), p. 39, justifies this translation in line with a postulated Greek *Vorlage*.

[16] The angel Yahoel.

[17] Translation from Kulik, *Retroverting Slavonic Pseudepigrapha*, p. 24. The brackets < > enclose words not in the oldest manuscript (Codex Sylvester).

that in Revelation, we can identify the following common elements (beyond those that are simply taken from Ezekiel in both cases):

1. The *ḥayyōt* sing the praises of God. Both texts thus belong to the 'hymnic tradition' of interpreting Ezekiel.
2. The *ḥayyōt* have six wings each, like the seraphim of Isaiah 6:2 (and unlike the *ḥayyōt* of Ezekiel which have four).
3. The *ḥayyōt* sing the *trisagion* or *qedushah* from Isaiah 6:3.[18] This third correspondence assumes that Kulik's interpretation of Apocalypse of Abraham 18:14 (embodied in his translation, above; and see also 16:3) is correct.[19]

At the same time we may notice two significant differences:

1. In the *Apocalypse of Abraham* the *ḥayyōt* and the wheels are distinct, as they are in Ezekiel, though the *Apocalypse of Abraham* shares with other Jewish readings of Ezekiel the view that the wheels are animate creatures who sing the praises of God along with the *ḥayyōt*. In the Apocalypse of Abraham, therefore, the many eyes belong to the wheels (18:3,12), but in Revelation they belong to the *ḥayyōt* (4:6,8).
2. In the *Apocalypse of Abraham* each of the four *ḥayyōt* has four faces and looks just like the other three. (It may be that there is some textual confusion and that verse 12b originally meant that each creature had four heads and each head four faces, so that each creature had sixteen faces, making a total of sixty-four faces altogether. This interpretation of Ezekiel is found in the Targum [1:6].)[20] In Revelation, however, each creature is different: one like a lion, one like an

---

[18] On the *trisagion* or *qedushah* in Jewish and Christian literature, see David E. Aune, *Revelation 1–5* (WBC 52A; Dallas: Word Books, 1997), pp. 302–7; Dave Murray Rankin, 'The Inaugural Throne-Room Vision of the Book of Revelation: Its background, content and context' (Ph.D. thesis, University of St Andrews, 2002), pp. 58–9.

[19] It is how the text of 16:3 was understood in two manuscripts (B, K) which substitute a more explicit reference: 'saying, "Holy, holy, holy"' (R. Rubinkiewicz, 'Apocalypse of Abraham', in *The Old Testament Pseudepigrapha*, vol. 1 [ed. James H. Charlesworth; London: Darton, Longman & Todd, 1983]: pp. 689–705, here p. 696 n. 16c).

[20] Halperin, *Faces*, pp. 123–4. This view is also preserved in the Gnostic work, *On the Origin of the World* (CG II,5) 105:5–9. In some Hekhalot literature, each creature has sixty-four faces: Halperin, *Faces*, pp. 368–92. See also Ithamar Gruenwald, *Apocalyptic and Merkavah Mysticism* (AGAJU 14; Leiden: Brill, 1980), pp. 56–7 n. 93.

ox, one with a human face, and one like an eagle (4:7).[21] This is a remarkable simplification and alteration of Ezekiel's description, and again it seems to be unique to Revelation as far as early Jewish literature goes, though something like it appears in a few later rabbinic midrashim.[22]

The *Apocalypse of Abraham*'s account of the *ḥayyōt* has one unique feature that is worth our attention. Only here in Jewish and Christian literature do we find the notion that the *ḥayyōt* are antagonistic towards each other and have to be pacified. This is represented as one of the special tasks given to the angel Yahoel (10:16). According to 18:10–11 he does this by turning the threatening faces of the creatures away from each other and teaching them 'the song of peace'. Probably the meaning is that he teaches them to sing the *qedushah* in harmony (18:14). This peculiar feature of the *ayyōt* in the *Apocalypse of Abraham* has generally been found puzzling and elicited a number of different attempts at explanation.[23] At least part of the explanation must surely be that it constitutes an ingenious attempt to solve an exegetical difficulty in Job 25:2: 'he makes peace in his high heaven.' How could there be conflict for God to pacify in the very height of heaven, in the heavenly throne-room where only God and the worshipping angels are to be found? The question is answered by observing that the faces of the living creatures resemble earthly creatures – the lion, the ox, the human and the eagle – that are naturally aggressive and may well threaten each other. In that case, the pacification of the heavenly creatures may provide a kind of heavenly precedent for the eschatological pacification of the earthly creatures whom they resemble (cf. Isa. 11:6–9). If there is anything in this line of thought, it may be significant that it entails thinking of the *ḥayyōt* as in some sense representing the earthly creatures they resemble, a thought that I shall argue is also implied in Revelation 4.

---

[21] Probably no significance can be attached to the order in which the earthly creatures are listed. It varies widely in the various texts dependent on Ezekiel: see Rankin, 'The Inaugural Throne-Room Vision', p. 54.

[22] Halperin, *Faces*, pp. 164–7, 177.

[23] See G.H. Box and J.I. Landsman, *The Apocalypse of Abraham* (London: SPCK, 1918), pp. 62–3, 87; Halperin, *Faces*, p. 108; Gruenwald, *Apocalyptic*, p. 54; Martha Himmelfarb, *Ascent to Heaven in Jewish and Christian Apocalypses* (New York: OUP, 1993), pp. 64, 137 n. 64.

Detailed Exegesis of Revelation 4:6b–8

The position of the living creatures in relation to the throne

In verse 6b the living creatures are said to be 'in the midst of the throne and around the throne' (*en mes tou thronou kai kukl tou thronou*). The two phrases appear to contradict each other, and the problem has been much discussed. Halperin comments: 'This self-contradictory statement . . . seems to reflect a tension between the hymnic tradition on the one hand, and Ezekiel 10's identification of the *ḥayyōt* with the cherubim on the other. As cherubim, the *ḥayyōt* ought to be part of God's seat (Exodus 25:18–19); as angels in the hymnic tradition they ought to surround it, singing praises.'[24]

That Revelation combines these two aspects of the living creatures is surely correct, but it is less clear that it need have been perceived as a tension. Even in the holy of holies of the earthly temple, the two cherubim were represented as bearing up the throne on which God rests above them (1 Sam. 4:4; 2 Sam. 6:2; 2 Kgs. 19:15; cf. Pss. 80:1; 99:1),[25] which is also the picture in Ezekiel 9 – 10. In the passage quoted above from the Songs of the Sabbath Sacrifice, the cherubim sing their praises from underneath the firmament on which the throne stands (cf. Ezek. 10:1; 2 *Bar*. 51:11), but this position seems not to prevent them prostrating themselves before God, as they do also in Revelation (5:8; 19:4). Robert Hall is probably right to argue that 'in the midst of the throne' (*en mesō tou thronou*) in Revelation 4:6 means, not 'in the centre of the throne', but 'in the space taken up by the throne'.[26] The living creatures are positioned within the area of the throne on all four sides of it.[27] Thus the account of them in Revelation

---

[24] Halperin, *Faces*, pp. 91–2.

[25] The 'mercy seat' itself is never called a throne.

[26] Robert G. Hall, 'Living Creatures in the Midst of the Throne: Another Look at Revelation 4.6', *NTS* 36 (1990): pp. 609–13, here pp. 612–13.

[27] It is also possible that the two phrases are a deliberate combination of the location of the seraphim in Isaiah (6:2 LXX: *kuklō autou*: 'around him' [the Lord] or 'it' [the throne]) and that of the living creatures in Ezekiel (1:5: *en tō mesō*, though this means 'in the midst of the cloud' or 'of the fire', since the throne has not yet been mentioned). Thus Revelation introduces the living creatures with the words that introduce them in Ezekiel and with the words that introduce the seraphim in Isaiah (LXX only). On the allusion to Ezek. 1:5, see Beale, *Revelation*, p. 331, citing J.M. Vogelgesang. Jan Fekkes, *Isaiah and Prophetic Traditions in the Book of Revelation* (JSNTSup 93; Sheffield: Sheffield Academic Press, 1994), pp. 143–9, has a good discussion of the way Rev. 4:8 combines elements from Ezekiel and Isaiah, but he does not discuss 4:6b.

begins by acknowledging their close physical connexion with the throne, but then focuses on their role of offering praise to God, as the central worshippers in his heavenly throne-room.

The eyes and the wings of the living creatures

Given the brevity of Revelation's description of the *ḥayyōt*, it is remarkable how much emphasis is placed on their eyes, which Revelation uniquely attributes to the *ḥayyōt*, rather than to the wheels. (This seems to reflect a reading of the difficult verse Ezekiel 10:12 as describing the cherubim, not merely the wheels, as full of eyes.)[28] According to Revelation, the living creatures are 'full of eyes, in front and behind' (4:6b: *gemonta ophthalmōn emprosthen kai opisthen*) and 'full of eyes all around and inside' (4:8a: *kuklothen kai esōthen gemousin ophthalmōn*). (Perhaps 'inside' means that there are eyes underneath the wings.)[29] The language echoes Ezekiel (1:18; 10:12) but is more elaborate. Why should there be so much emphasis on this feature?

Commentators have offered various suggestions as to the significance of the many eyes, taking them to symbolize such attributes as 'intellectual penetration',[30] 'unlimited intelligence',[31] alertness and knowledge,[32] 'omniscience' (the divine omniscience reflected in his agents),[33] 'all-seeing power',[34] 'wakefulness',[35] 'vigilance'.[36] It is also pointed out that in the ancient world divine and heavenly beings were sometimes depicted or described as having many eyes,[37] or that 'eyes' could mean stars, indicating that the living creatures are actually constellations.[38] The difficulty with many of these suggestions is that they

---

[28] Block, *Ezekiel*, p. 324, considers this the most natural reading of the verse.

[29] Smalley, *Revelation*, p. 122.

[30] William Hendriksen, *More than Conquerors* (London: Inter-Varsity Press, 1962), p. 87.

[31] Isbon T. Beckwith, *The Apocalypse of John* (Grand Rapids: Baker 1967 [reprint of 1919 edition]), p. 500.

[32] Smalley, *Revelation*, p. 121.

[33] Beale, *Revelation*, p. 330.

[34] Howard-Brook and Gwyther, *Unveiling Empire*, p. 204.

[35] John Sweet, *Revelation* (SCM Pelican Commentary; London: SCM Press, 1979), p. 120; cf. Jürgen Roloff, *The Revelation of John: A Continental Commentary* (trans. John E. Alsup; Minneapolis: Fortress, 1993), p. 71: 'watchfulness in the service of God'.

[36] Henry Barclay Swete, *The Apocalypse of St John* (2nd edn; London: Macmillan, 1907), p. 71 ('the secret vigilance of nature'); Josephine Massyngberde Ford, *Revelation* (AB 38; NY: Doubleday 1975), p. 75.

[37] Aune, *Revelation*, p. 298.

[38] Bruce J. Malina, *On the Genre and Message of Revelation: Star Visions and Sky Journeys* (Peabody, Massachusetts: Hendrickson, 1995), pp. 98–9. This astrological

seem to have little to do with what the creatures do in this account in Revelation. Unlike the seven eyes of the Lamb (5:6) they are not sent out into all the earth to see or to understand it. They are creatures of heaven devoted unceasingly to the worship of God (4:8).

This makes John Sweet's suggestion that the eyes indicate their wakefulness[39] attractive. A passage from the Parables of Enoch may provide a good parallel:

> Those who sleep not bless you,
>   and they stand in the presence of your glory;
> And they bless and praise and exalt, saying,
>   'Holy, holy, holy is the Lord of Spirits,
>   he fills the earth with spirits.'
> And there my eyes saw all who sleep not;
>   they stand in his presence,
> and they bless and say,
>   'Blessed are you, and blessed is the name of the Lord forever
>   and ever.'
>
> (*1 Enoch* 39:12–13)[40]

Here the heavenly beings who do not sleep sing a version of the *qedushah*, like Isaiah's seraphim and Revelation's living creatures. They are mentioned again in *1 Enoch* 40:2;[41] 61:12; 71:7.[42] However, there is a difficulty in associating the many eyes of Revelation's living creatures with this constant wakefulness of those who sing the *qedushah*. Simply in order to stay constantly awake for the sake of worshipping God, it would not be necessary for the creatures to have many eyes, merely that

---

interpretation of the living creatures as signs of the zodiac, though still maintained by Malina and others (Austin Farrer, *The Revelation of St. John the Divine* [Oxford: Clarendon, 1964], pp. 91–2; Charles Homer Giblin, *The Book of Revelation* [Good News Studies 34; Collegeville, Minnesota: Liturgical Press, 1991], pp. 72–3), is adequately refuted by the observation that no zodiacal constellation was ever described as an eagle (Beale, *Revelation*, p. 329).

[39] Sweet, *Revelation*, p. 120. The same view is taken by Roloff, *Revelation*, p. 72.

[40] Translation from George W.E. Nickelsburg and James C. VanderKam, *1 Enoch: A New Translation* (Minneapolis: Fortress, 2004), pp. 53–4.

[41] Here they are distinguished from the four archangels.

[42] Here they are apparently the same as the seraphim, cherubim and '*ofannim*. Matthew Black, *The Book of Enoch or 1 Enoch* (SVTP 7; Leiden: Brill, 1985), pp. 106, 198, identifies them with the 'watchers' (Aramaic '*îrîn*: Dan. 4:14,20; *1 Enoch* 1:5; 20:1; *Jub.* 4:15; 8:3; 10:5), but these are surely angels who from heaven watch over the world, not angels engaged in the constant praise of God.

the eyes they have never close. Argos, the many-eyed watchman of the Greek gods, cited as a parallel by Sweet, needed his eyes in order to be watchful and alert for whatever might come along. That is not a function Revelation attributes to the living creatures. So, while Enoch's angels who do not sleep are a good parallel to the ceaseless worship, day and night, by Revelation's living creatures (4:8b),[43] it is not so clear that the parallel explains the latter's many eyes.

So it may be best to understand the eyes as an instance of the common depiction, in ancient religious art, of heavenly beings with many eyes,[44] and to take the characteristic as simply indicating the vast superiority of the living creatures to any earthly creatures, restricted as the latter are to two eyes only. This has the advantage that we can apply the same understanding to the wings. In Isaiah the wings of the seraphim are given specific functions (6:2), while something similar is implied in the case of the living creatures in Ezekiel (1:11,23–5), but no specific function is indicated in Revelation. However, wings commonly, in ancient religious art, indicated celestial beings, especially in the case of hybrid beings like Revelation's living creatures.[45] Again, the six wings (chosen by John in preference to the four wings of Ezekiel's *ḥayyōt*) indicate heavenly superiority to the winged creatures of earth. This emphasis on heavenly superiority is important precisely because the rest of the description of the living creatures (4:7) explains that they do also resemble earthly creatures.

The likenesses of the living creatures

As we have already noted, Revelation is unique in early Jewish literature in assigning one likeness only to each of the four living creatures. The resulting picture is very different from Ezekiel's. Ezekiel's *ḥayyōt* have a humanoid body, with calf's feet, wings, human hands, and four faces each. Each creature has a face resembling a human, a

---

[43] Note also that in *Lad. Jac.* 2:15, the seraphim (described exclusively in terms drawn from Isa. 6:2–3) sing without ceasing.

[44] Aune, *Revelation*, p. 298.

[45] See, for example, Othmar Keel and Christoph Uehlinger, *Gods, Goddesses and Images of God in Ancient Israel* (trans. Thomas H. Trapp; Minneapolis: Fortress, 1998), pp. 195–7, 251–9; Aune, *Revelation*, p. 301. On such winged creatures and their relationship to figures in Jewish apocalyptic literature, see also James H. Charlesworth, 'Folk Traditions in Jewish Apocalyptic Literature', in *Mysteries and Revelations: Apocalyptic Studies since the Uppsala Colloquium* (ed. John J. Collins and James H. Charlesworth; JSPSup 9; Sheffield: Sheffield Academic Press, 1991), pp. 91–113, here pp. 103–13.

face resembling a lion, a face resembling an ox, and a face resembling an eagle (1:5–11). Thus each creature is thoroughly hybrid (like many to be seen in ancient Near Eastern religious art) and bears no particular resemblance to any one sort of earthly creature.[46] In Revelation, on the other hand, each living creature bears an overall resemblance to one of the four earthly creatures mentioned: 'the first living creature like a lion, the second living creature like an ox, the third living creature with a face like a human face, and the fourth living creature like a flying eagle' (4:7). The phrase 'like a flying eagle' must indicate that this living creature has wings outstretched in flight, following 'the ancient visual convention of depicting the eagle with its wings spread'.[47] The resemblances are therefore by no means purely facial, except perhaps in the case of the third creature, which is said to have a face like that of a human. We are left unclear what the rest of this creature is like. The reason for the difference in this case may well be that Revelation reserves the description 'like a human' for another heavenly being (1:13; 14:14: *homoion huion anthrōpou*), following Daniel.[48] It would not be appropriate for one of the four living creatures to be as human-like as the exalted Christ.

We come to the crucial question for our present purposes: what is the significance of these resemblances to four earthly creatures? One possibility is that they symbolize attributes of the One who sits on the throne. This is a plausible view of Ezekiel's *ḥayyōt*. Keel and Uehlinger see them as, in this respect, comparable with throne-bearing creatures in ancient religious art: 'these hybrid creatures reflect the nature of the figure who is enthroned above them.'[49] Appealing to the characteristics

---

[46] Ezek. 10:14 appears to say that each of cherubim has four identical faces, those of the first cherub resembling the face of a cherub, the faces of the second resembling that of a human, the faces of the third resembling that of a lion, and the faces of the fourth resembling that of an eagle. This contradicts 10:22, which says that the faces were the same as those seen by Ezekiel in his first vision. The contradiction can be resolved if v. 14 is read as attributing these faces to the wheels, rather than the cherubim. LXX omits v. 14, either because of these difficulties or because v. 14 in MT is a late gloss not found in the *Vorlage* of the LXX. It does not seem plausible that Rev. 4:7 is following Ezek. 10:14, since Revelation, like Ezek. 1, includes an ox, not the cherub that is substituted for the ox in Ezek. 10:14.

[47] Aune, *Revelation*, p. 300 (with examples).

[48] Aune, *Revelation*, p. 299.

[49] Keel and Uehlinger, *Gods*, p. 168. I have not been able to see Othmar Keel, *Jahwe-Visionen und Siegelkunst: Eine neue Deutung der Majestätsschilderungen in Jes 6, Ez 1, und 10 und Sach 4* (SBS 84/85; Stuttgart: Katholisches Bibelwerk, 1977), where this is discussed and illustrated at length.

the earthly creatures have in the Hebrew Bible, Daniel Block writes: 'Carrying the divine throne, the four-headed cherubim declare that Yahweh has the strength and majesty of the lion, the swiftness and mobility of the eagle, the procreative power of the bull, and the wisdom and reason of humankind.'[50]

On the other hand, William Brownlee, associating similar qualities with these creatures, thinks that as the faces of the *ḥayyōt* they 'represent all the forces of nature over which the Lord reigns'.[51]

While the view that the living creatures display divine attributes is plausible in Ezekiel's text, this is because their role in Ezekiel is to carry the divine throne. In Revelation, on the other hand, their main function is to worship the one enthroned above them. In this role it is much more appropriate to see them as representatives of creation.[52] The whole context in Revelation 4 depicts God as the Creator revered as such by his creatures in heaven. The living creatures are the pre-eminent creatures engaged in that glorification of their Creator to which all creatures are called. They embody pre-eminently all that is most magnificent in the whole creation.[53]

The question whether the living creatures are representatives of creation has been somewhat confused in the discussion in the commentaries, because the words 'represent' and 'representative' have at least two possible meanings in this context. They could mean that John's literary description of the four living creatures is a symbolic reference to the whole creation,[54] or that he understands the living creatures to be acting as representatives of the whole creation.[55] Parallel to the first possible meaning would be to say that the seven-headed beast in

---

50 Block, *Ezekiel*, p. 96.

51 Brownlee, *Ezekiel 1–19*, p. 11.

52 Among recent commentators, this view is taken, for example, by Beale, *Revelation*, pp. 329–30 (though he unnecessarily thinks they also represent God); Sweet, *Revelation*, p. 120.

53 Cf. Swete, *Apocalypse*, p. 71: the forms of the living creatures 'suggest whatever is noblest, strongest, wisest and swiftest in animate Nature'.

54 Thus, for example, Ford, *Revelation*, p. 80, uses 'represent' as synonymous with 'signify' and 'are symbolic of'. Pablo Richard, *Apocalypse: A People's Commentary on the Book of Revelation* (The Bible and Liberation Series; Maryknoll, New York: Orbis, 1995, p. 66), says that the living creatures 'symbolize the cosmos'.

55 It is often difficult to tell which meaning is intended. This seems to me the case in Swete, *Apocalypse*, pp. 71–2 (this sounds like the first meaning of 'representative', but cf. p. 84, where the comment on 5:13 seems to imply the second); Caird, *Revelation*, p. 64. Roloff, *Revelation*, p. 71, says that the living creatures are angelic beings but may also 'symbolize the reign of God over the whole of creation'.

Revelation 13 'represents' the Roman imperial power: it is a literary symbol for the latter. But parallel to the second meaning would be to say that the high priest enters the presence of God in the temple as the representative of the people.

The position I am proposing is not that the living creatures are merely symbols or personifications of nature. Some scholars have taken this view, but against this Hendrikson rightly objects that when 'the seer wishes to refer to all creatures, he does so in clear language (5:13)'.[56] One could add that the living creatures appear in 5:14 in addition to the whole creation in 5:13: they cannot be simply a symbol for the latter. In my view the living creatures themselves are certainly heavenly creatures, superior to all earthly creatures, as we have noted in connexion with their eyes and wings. But they are representatives of the world of earthly creatures[57] in the sense that they worship on behalf of the latter. They act as the priests of creation, offering continuous praise to God in the heavenly sanctuary on behalf of all creatures.

A Jewish exegetical tradition, found in the Babylonian Talmud (where it occurs in a comment on Exodus 15:21 ascribed to Resh Laqish, a third-century Palestinian rabbi) and in other midrashic sources,[58] explains the four faces of Ezekiel's *ḥayyōt* thus: 'The lion is king of beasts, the ox king of animals, the eagle king of birds; humankind exalts itself over them. God exalts himself over them all' (*b. Ḥag.* 13b).[59]

We do not have sources that take this interpretation back to the late Second Temple period, but it is a rather obvious way of explaining the choice of specifically these four creatures. Scripture itself refers to the lion as the mightiest of wild animals (Prov. 30:30), and it would be easy, on the basis of scriptural references to the ox and the eagle,[60] to see the ox as the greatest among domestic animals and the eagle among birds. In the case of Revelation, where each living creature resembles one

---

[56] Hendrikson, *More than Conquerors*, p. 88. The same point is made by Beckwith, *Apocalypse*, p. 501; Smalley, *Revelation*, p. 120.

[57] Ben Witherington, *Revelation* (NCBC; Cambridge: CUP, 2003), p. 118, calls them 'heavenly archetypes of the whole of the animate creation.'

[58] See the passages quoted from *Midrash Tanḥuma*, from a Genizah fragment and from *Hekhalot Rabbati* in Halperin, *Faces*, pp. 162–3, 177, 400; and the other references given by Halperin, *Faces*, pp. 135-6 (including early Christian writers); and add *Exod. Rab.* 23:13.

[59] Translation from Halperin, *Faces*, p. 131.

[60] See Schochet, *Animal Life*, pp. 39–40.

of the four earthly creatures, such an interpretation would suggest that each living creature represents one major category of the animate creation:[61] the living creature like a lion represents the wild land animals, the one like an ox represents domestic land animals,[62] the one like an eagle represents birds,[63] and the one with a face like a human face represents humans.

A further point in support of this view of the living creatures as representing the earthly creatures is the symbolism of the number four.[64] In Revelation, four is the number of the earth, which, following scriptural precedent,[65] has four corners (7:1; 20:8) and four winds (7:1). The earthly creation can be divided into four sectors: earth, sea, rivers and springs, sky and heavenly bodies (8:7–12; 14:7; 16:2–9). These four sectors are respectively the targets of the first four judgments both in the series of trumpet-blasts (8:7–12) and in the series of bowl-pourings (16:2–9), judgments that should bring earth's inhabitants to acknowledge God as Creator of this fourfold world (14:7). In the first series of judgments, the seal-openings, there is the same pattern of four judgments forming a set (6:1–8), followed by three others. In this case, the pattern does not consist of the four sectors of creation but of the four riders with their plagues that kill a quarter of the inhabitants of the earth (6:8). Each of the four riders is summoned by one of the four living creatures (6:1,3,5,7), who are thus explicitly related to the symbolic function of the number four as indicative of the earthly creation.

---

[61] How natural it was to categorize the non-human animate creation as wild animals, domestic animals, and birds, can be seen from this passage of Tertullian: 'The whole creation prays. Cattle and wild beasts pray, and bend their knees, and in coming forth from their stalls and lairs look up to heaven, their mouth not idle, making the spirit move in their own fashion. Moreover the birds now arising are lifting themselves up to heaven and instead of hands are spreading out the cross of their wings, while saying something that may be supposed to be a prayer' (*Orat.* 29; trans. Ernest Evans, *Tertullian's Tract on the Prayer* [London: SPCK, 1953], p. 41).

[62] A distinction between wild animals and domestic ones is standard: e.g. Gen. 1:24–6; Ps. 8:7; Isa. 11:6–7.

[63] Sea creatures are not represented, but they figure rather little in biblical imagery: Schochet, *Animal Life*, p. 37.

[64] Richard Bauckham, *The Climax of Prophecy: Studies on the Book of Revelation* (Edinburgh: T&T Clark, 1993), pp. 31–2; Giblin, *Revelation*, p. 79. In Ezek. 1, the four living creatures with their four wings and four faces must be related to the four winds or directions of the compass (Block, *Ezekiel*, p. 97 n. 53).

[65] Corners: Isa. 11:12. Winds: Ezek. 37:9; Jer. 49:36; Dan. 7:2; 18:8; 11:4; Zech. 2:10; 6:5; cf. *1 Enoch* 18:2–3.

In conclusion, Revelation 4:6b–8 portrays the four living creatures as the central worshippers in creation, who, as heavenly representatives of the animate creatures of earth, unceasingly give to God the praise that all creation owes him.

The form of the qedushah

Jewish and early Christian visions of the worship of God in heaven often echo the song of the seraphim in Isaiah 6:3, but almost always with some modification or expansion, large or small (*1 Enoch* 39:12; *2 Enoch* 21:1 J; *Lad. Jac.* 2:15-20; *Qu. Ezra* A29; *Apost. Const.* 7.35.3; 8.12.27; *T. Isaac* 6:5, 24; *Tg. Isa.* 6:3; *G.Bart.* 3:2; cf. *1 Clem.* 34:6).[66] But these modifications always retain something equivalent to the meaning of the second line in Isaiah's version ('the whole earth is full of his glory'). Revelation alone does not. Instead it adds a further description of God: 'who was and who is and who is to come' (4:8).[67] The reason must be that in this seer's view, while heaven may be full of the glory of God, the earth is not – or not yet. It is not that John has a negative view of the material world, but that he sees it corrupted and destroyed by forces of evil, human and superhuman, which prevent it from reflecting the glory of God as it was created to do. It is subject to 'those who destroy the earth' (11:18). But his version of the *qedushah* contains the only reference in chapter 4 to the eschatological future: the God the living creatures not only was and is, but is to come. God's future is not just his own future existence, but his coming to his creation in judgment and salvation.[68] The time is coming when the earth will be full of his glory.

This has an important bearing on the way in which we should understand the four living creatures to be representatives of the earthly creation. Their representation has an eschatological direction. They worship on behalf of the creatures whose own worship is now marred by the activity of evil on earth, with a view to the time when those who destroy the earth will be destroyed (11:18),[69] and the renewed creation will fully reflect the glory of God. It is, as we shall see, this eschatologically directed character of the living creatures' representation that creates the link

---

[66] There are also a few instances of simply 'Holy, holy, holy,' perhaps used as a shorthand for the whole hymn (*T. Adam* 1:6; 4:8; *3 Enoch* 1:12; *Exod. Rab.* 15:6).

[67] On this designation of God, see Bauckham, *Theology*, pp. 28–30.

[68] Bauckham, *Theology*, p. 29.

[69] This explains the relationship of the living creatures to judgment in Rev. 6:1,3,5,7; 15:7; 19:4.

between them and the actual worship of God by all creatures themselves in 5:13.

The history of interpretation

Christian interpretation of Revelation 4:6b–8 in the patristic and medieval periods was dominated by Irenaeus' view that the four living creatures symbolize the four evangelists. With their correspondence to the four sectors of the earth or four winds, they indicate the universal nature of the fourfold gospel.[70] While this kind of interpretation does perceive the link between the four living creatures and the fourfoldness of the earth, there is little else to be said for it. But the conception of the living creatures as heavenly representatives of the earthly creatures became the traditional view (alongside the Irenaean view) in the Coptic and Ethiopic churches, where the four living creatures are commemorated on a day in the liturgical year, 4 November.[71] In the Ethiopic *Synaxarium* their significance is explained: 'He with a man's form maketh supplication on behalf of the children of men, he with the lion's form maketh supplication on behalf of the beasts, he with the bull's form maketh supplication on behalf of the cattle, and he with the eagle's form maketh supplication on behalf of the birds.'[72] Though understanding the role of the living creatures as petitionary prayer rather than worship, this interpretation clearly expounds their representative role, corresponding to the four categories of earthly creatures.

---

[70] See especially Kenneth Stevenson, 'Animal Rites: The Four Living Creatures in Patristic Exegesis and Liturgy', in *Studia Patristica XXXIV* (ed. Maurice F. Wiles and Edward J. Yarnold; Leuven: Peeters, 2001), pp. 470–92, here pp. 474–92; also William C. Weinrich ed., *Revelation* (ACCS NT12; Downers Grove, Illinois: InterVarsity Press, 2005), pp. 62–6; Judith Kovacs and Christopher Rowland, *Revelation* (Blackwell's Bible Commentaries; Oxford: Blackwell, 2004), p. 66. In the patristic period there are a few scattered explanations of other kinds: e.g. four aspects of the soul (Origen, Macarius, Ammonas: Stevenson, 'Animal Rites', pp. 475, 486–7, though in all these cases it is Ezekiel's living creatures that are being interpreted), the four elements (Methodius, Novatian, Oecumenius, Andrew of Caesarea: Stevenson, 'Animal Rites', p. 487; Weinrich, *Revelation*, p. 65) and the four virtues (Andrew of Caesarea: Stevenson, 'Animal Rites', p. 487).

[71] Stevenson, 'Animal Rites', pp. 488–9.

[72] Quoted in Stevenson, 'Animal Rites', p. 488.

From the Worship of the Living Creatures to the Worship of the Whole Creation

In Revelation 4 the living creatures, as the central worshippers, lead the worship of heaven in which the twenty-four elders join them (4:9–11), but at this stage of the vision the circle of worship expands no further. In chapter 5, however, the circle expands to the myriads of angels who surround the throne (5:11–12) and then to 'every creature in heaven and on earth and under the earth and in the sea, and all that is in them' (5:13). (The redundant 'and all that is in them' makes the universality inescapable.) What accounts for this further expansion is the enthronement of the Lamb on God's own throne (5:1) and the news that he is worthy to open the sealed book of God's purposes that will bring about his universal eschatological rule (5:2–7). This news starts the expanding circle of worship that begins again with the living creatures and the elders (5:8–10) and then widens, as we have seen, to involve the whole creation. This new circle of worship is initially worship of the Lamb, though when all creatures worship their praise is for both God and the Lamb (5:13). Thus the worship of God in chapter 4 and the worship of the Lamb in chapter 5 finally come together. At this point the living creatures appear again, adding their 'Amen' (5:14a) to the furthest extension of the worship they had begun, both that of God in chapter 4 and that of the Lamb in chapter 5. Finally the elders too join in the obeisance, completing the worship of heaven that now involves all creation.[73]

Thus we can see that, if the living creatures are priestly representatives of all creation, the expanding circle of worship moves from their representative worship, first in chapter 4, then their worship of the enthroned Lamb in chapter 5, to draw in the worship of all those on whose behalf they have worshipped. Their representative role is fulfilled when all the creatures they represent themselves worship. We noticed before the significance of the number four, the number of creation, that links the four living creatures to the earthly creation. We can now observe how the number four is embodied in the account of the worship of all creatures in 5:13–14. They belong to all

---

[73] We should probably see the elders also in a representative role. Whereas the living creatures worship on behalf of all creatures, the elders submit their power to God on behalf of all creaturely power. Their representative role will be fulfilled when all earthly power acknowledges its source in God (repudiating the idolatrous attempt of the beast to deify its own power).

four regions of creation (here described as 'in heaven and on earth and under the earth and in the sea') and their acclamation of God and the Lamb is fourfold ('blessing and honour and glory and might': contrast the sevenfold acclamation by the angels in 5:12 and again in 7:12).74 At this fulfilment of their representative role the representatives are emphatically linked to those they represent by the number four.

It is evidently the enthronement of the slaughtered Lamb that makes the difference. Somehow this leads to the acknowledgment of God's sovereignty by the whole creation, where previously it had been contested. In this respect the scene in chapter 5 is closely parallel to the Pauline christological passage in Philippians 2:5–11. There it is the exaltation of the crucified Christ that is acclaimed by everyone 'in heaven and on earth and under the earth' (2:10). There too this acclamation of Christ's universal rule is linked to the glory of God his Father (2:11), so that the implication is that the universal acknowledgment of the sovereignty of God will come about through the death and exaltation of Jesus. This basic pattern has been developed in a different way in Revelation, but the core story is the same. In both cases the universal worship of Jesus is eschatological, and in Revelation it is portrayed proleptically as an initial indication of the goal to which the whole of the following visionary narrative is directed.

I argued that in chapter 4 the living creatures cannot sing the second line of the song of Isaiah's seraphim ('the whole earth is full of your glory') because at that stage the worship of creation is marred and obscured by the activity of evil in the world. This changes when the victory of the Lamb leads to the new creation of all things and the whole creation is liberated to praise God through reflecting his glory without impediment. What the Lamb has already achieved, according to the hymn of the living creatures and the elders, is the redemption of a people of God drawn from all nations (5:9–10). But this is not the end of his victory. The rest of the book portrays the way in which it is to be extended, through the sacrificial witness of those who follow the Lamb in his way of witness, to all nations and even to the whole creation. In chapter 5 this process is indicated only by the expanding circle of worship. The rest of the book will fill out the picture.75

---

74 Giblin, *Revelation*, p. 79.
75 See Bauckham, *Theology*, ch. 4.

An Ecological Perspective for the Twenty-First Century?

At the outset of this chapter I made some general remarks about the importance of the biblical theme of creation's worship of God for a Christian ecological perspective today. We can now consider the more specific contribution the way this theme is developed in Revelation has to make. I would stress two main points. The first is to notice how non-anthropocentric this theme in Revelation is. The vision in chapters 4 and 5 is, of course, thoroughly theocentric, centred on the throne of God who made all things and for whose glory all things exist. In a now otherwise rather dated treatment, Henry Barclay Swete made a comment on 5:13 that is not to be found in more recent commentators. Here, he says, the prophet John is able to 'voice the purpose of universal Nature; he becomes conscious that it exists solely to glorify God and the Lamb'.[76] This theocentric and non-anthropocentric view of creation is even more apparent in the living creatures considered as the representatives of the animate creation. One of them has a human face, but the affinity of the others is with the other great categories of the animal creation. The human has no privilege or precedence here. The human-like creature is just one among the four, not even listed first. As creatures engaged in the worship of God, humans find themselves not set over but alongside other creatures, caught up with them in the common worship of their common Creator. We need this perspective to balance the exaggerated focus on the human dominion of Genesis 1:26 in the western Christian tradition of the modern period.

The second point is the eschatological aspect of this vision, its direction towards the renewal of all creation in the coming kingdom of God. This obliges us to recognize that the creation does not glorify God now as fully as it was created to do. We might have thought the theme of creation's praise of God in the Psalms puts the matter differently, but on closer inspection we may observe that all those passages in the Psalms are not statements but imperatives. They call on all the creatures to worship, just as they do on all people. In both cases a full response has not yet been forthcoming. Moreover, these psalms do not lack an eschatological perspective of their own. It is found in psalms that announce 'a new song' (Pss 96:1; 98:1), a term taken up in Revelation (5:9; 14:3), and it coheres closely with Revelation's expectation of the coming of God's judgment and kingdom (Pss 96:11–13;

---

[76] Swete, *Apocalypse*, p. 83.

98:7–9).[77] Nevertheless, there is a distinctive aspect to Revelation's treatment of this theme. It lies in the phrase to which I have already drawn attention: 'those who destroy the earth' (11:18). The coming of God's rule on earth will not only liberate people from evil, but will liberate the earth from those who are destroying it.[78] If the non-human creation fails to glorify God as fully as it might, this is not due to itself. Unlike humans, it glorifies God simply by being itself, as God made it to be. But powers of evil, superhuman and human, can despoil its glory and muffle its praise. Our human responsibility in this respect is not, as some argue, to voice creation's praise for it or to mediate its praise to God, but to let it be itself. Humans and other creatures are made to be partners in praise, like the four living creatures.

---

[77] For the important allusions to these psalms in Revelation, see Bauckham, *Climax*, pp. 286–9.

[78] See Bauckham, *Theology*, p. 51–3.

9.

Creation Mysticism in Matthew Fox and Francis of Assisi

In this chapter we shall study and compare two examples of 'creation mysticism' in the Christian tradition. The work of Matthew Fox provides probably the best-known contemporary example, while Francis of Assisi is without doubt the greatest nature mystic in the Christian tradition, and some would say the first.[1] I shall argue that Francis's form of creation mysticism is a more authentically Christian form than that of Fox, who moves away from elements central both to the Christian tradition in general and to Francis's spirituality in particular.

Matthew Fox

Matthew Fox, former Dominican friar, is well known as the proponent and exponent of what he calls 'creation-centered spirituality' (or, more briefly, 'creation spirituality' or, sometimes, 'creation mysticism'). We can appropriately call this a form of mysticism, partly because Fox's thought is deeply inspired by several of the medieval Christian mystics, especially Meister Eckhart, Hildegard of Bingen and Mechtild of Magdeburg, but also because he believes that 'creation spirituality liberates the mystic in us all'.[2] 'A basic teaching of all in the creation mystical tradition,' he claims, 'is this: everyone is a mystic'.[3] The mystical is the repressed

---

[1] Sorrell, *St. Francis*, ch. 4.
[2] Matthew Fox, *Creation Spirituality* (San Francisco: HarperSanFrancisco, 1991), p. 105.
[3] Matthew Fox, *The Coming of the Cosmic Christ* (San Francisco: Harper & Row, 1988), p. 48.

shadow side of the western personality, which only the recovery of a sense of belonging to a sacred cosmos can liberate. Thus Fox is not interested in a mysticism that is only attained by a spiritual elite, as the great mystics of the Catholic tradition have sometimes been seen, and certainly not in a mysticism which offers mystical experience only as the culmination of a long and arduous process of ascetical practice. Much as he looks to some of the great Christian mystics, those he sees as creation mystics, for inspiration, his concern is with a mysticism that can be experienced and lived by ordinary people in experience of the cosmos, in new and revitalized forms of meditation and ludic ritual, in all forms of artistic creativity and imagination, and which is inseparable from the practice of prophetic justice in relation to the earth and to the poor. When he speaks of his extensive experience that 'all kinds of persons are waking up to the mystic within them today',[4] we can easily recognize the cultural reality to which his understanding of mysticism corresponds.

Essential to mysticism as he sees it are awe and playful wonder and celebration in relation to a cosmos seen as sacred.[5] Also definitive of mysticism for him are the themes of unity and wholeness:

> Our mystical experiences are unitive experiences. They may occur on a dark night with the sparkling stars in the sky; at the ocean; in the mountains or fields; with friends or family; with ideas; in lovemaking; in play; with music and dance and art of all kinds; in work; in suffering and in letting go. What all mystical experiences share in common is this experience of nonseparation, of nondualism . . . [As] Julian of Norwich put it, 'Between God and the soul there is no between' . . . Here Julian is celebrating the end of the primary dualism – that between humans and divinity. The mystics promise that within each of us there is a capacity – the experience of the 'no between' – to be united and not separate. Mysticism announces the end of alienation and the beginning of communion, the end of either/or relationships (which form the essence of dualism) and the beginning of unity. Yet the unity that the mystics celebrate is not a loss of self or a dissolution of differences, but a unity of creativity, a coming together of different existences.[6]

This view of 'nondualism' is central to Fox's thought and we must return to it. Not unconnected is the definition of mysticism, borrowed

---

4   Fox, *Coming*, p. 42.
5   Fox, *Creation Spirituality*, pp. 29–30; cf. *Coming*, p. 51.
6   Fox, *Coming*, pp. 49–50.

from Josef Pieper, as 'an affirmation of the world as a whole'. This is 'to embrace a cosmology' which, in spite of human degradation of the world, affirms the goodness of the cosmos as a whole and therefore finds the cosmos a source of sustenance.[7]

Fox's creation spirituality can be situated both in its present cultural context and in relation to the Christian tradition of the past. While Fox writes deliberately within the Christian tradition, there are many features of his work which connect with that very diverse and characteristically post-modern religious phenomenon known as the New Age movement. There is the turn from anthropocentric thinking, focusing on the human apart from the rest of nature, to a focus on the cosmos and nature and the human in relation to nature. There is the turn from rationality to imagination, or at least an attempt to balance analytic and logical thinking with imaginative, intuitive, and mythic thinking. There is the turn from dualistic to holistic thinking, from compartmentalizing reality to appreciating the interdependence and connectedness of all things. There is the turn from divine transcendence beyond the world to divine immanence within the world, even to the divinity of the world. There is the attempt to see justice and peace in human society as equivalent to harmony in nature and harmony with nature. There is the appeal, against patriarchy, to the allegedly feminine principles of intuition and imagination, connectedness and relationality, bodiliness and fertility, embodied in images of the divine as female (the divine motherliness), the earth as female (Mother Earth), and the neologism 'birthing' as a constantly recurrent metaphor. Of course, many of these features are not confined to the New Age movement, but can be found in other contemporary trends of thought such as feminist theology and Green thinking. They express a certain kind of cultural (or perhaps one should say: countercultural) mood, into which Fox taps with something of the eclecticism of the New Age movement itself.

Finally, there is the common sense of the dawning of the new age itself. Fox calls this the birth of a global renaissance, or, using Christian mythical imagery, the coming of the cosmic Christ. This he envisages, much as New Age thinkers do, as an emerging paradigm shift in religious conceptuality, sensibility and world-view, a paradigm shift that is at the same time a return to forgotten, ancient wisdom. In Fox's case the ancient wisdom is the so-called creation-centred tradition of spirituality within Christianity, though he is quite

---

[7] Fox, *Coming*, pp. 51–2

prepared to draw on, for example, Native American traditions and to emphasize the spiritual wisdom of traditional peoples. The global renaissance will be a move beyond the alienation of religion, science and art, to a newly holistic outlook that Fox calls a living cosmology. In this will coalesce science (in the form of the new creation story which contemporary science tells, a universal cosmological story to replace the creation stories of the various religions); mysticism (in the form of a new awakening of the human psyche's potential for unitive cosmic imagination); and art (as the new form of meditative religious practice in which our awe at creation is expressed).

A particular understanding of the history of the Christian tradition, with a resulting discernment as to what can be retrieved and what we should discard, is integral to Fox's project. This is a process of 're-visioning' history in order to allow 'the best and most often forgotten and repressed elements of our tradition . . . to come to the fore'.[8] Fox presents the tradition of creation spirituality as the alternative to what he calls the fall/redemption tradition of Christian spirituality, which has been more dominant especially in the modern period. Christian theologians, mystics and spiritual writers in the western tradition from Augustine onwards he assigns to either one or the other of these two traditions, one of which, the fall/redemption tradition, has promoted a negative view of creation, while the other, the creation spirituality tradition, has maintained that positive view of creation which Fox sees himself reviving. In Fox's now notorious family tree of creation spiri-tuality[9] he lists a very diverse range of people he approves of and eval-uates them with stars, as though they were hotels. Only Jesus gets five stars, but three people get four stars. These are Fox's favourite medieval mystics: Hildegard of Bingen, Francis of Assisi and Meister Eckhart. The other tradition, the fall/redemption tradition, stems from Augustine of Hippo, whose vast influence over the western Christian tradition Fox seems to evaluate as indiscriminately regrettable.

Fox sometimes identifies the fundamental fault of the fall/redemp-tion tradition as dualistic thinking – a rather slippery term in his as in other people's usage. Dualistic thinking sets up oppositions between matter and spirit, between body and soul, between humans and the rest of creation, and (apparently the most pernicious of all) between God and creation. According to Fox, the various dualisms inherent in the fall/redemption tradition promote a kind of anthropocentrism in

---

[8] Fox, *Creation Spirituality*, p. 33.
[9] Fox, *Original Blessing*, Appendix A, pp. 307–15.

which human beings consider themselves apart from the rest of creation and seek God not in the cosmos but introspectively within their own souls. This disastrous tendency is further promoted by Augustine's doctrine of original sin, which, according to Fox, 'grew to become the starting-point for western religion's flight from nature, creation, and the God of creation'.[10] In place of the fundamental goodness of creation, human and non-human, the fall/redemption tradition is obsessed with the fallenness of human and non-human nature, and seeks liberation from sin and guilt in purely personal spiritual salvation, understood as redemption from this fallen, material world. A world-rejecting and body-hating asceticism is a prime characteristic of spirituality in this tradition. By contrast, the creation-centred tradition emphasizes 'original blessing', concerns itself with the people of God and the cosmos, is aesthetic rather than ascetic, emphasizes thanksgiving, praise and creativity rather than guilt, redemption and obedience.

Many critics have challenged this typology of the two traditions as a misleading view of history.[11] Of course, the western Christian tradition is such a complex historical phenomenon, subject at many points to very varied influences, spawning many different schools of thought and traditions of spirituality, that almost any contemporary Christian thinker will be able to find precedents with which he or she can closely identify, as well as examples of what he or she thinks the most aberrant or deleterious forms Christianity can take. But the fact is that most of the thinkers and mystics of whom Fox approves lived and worked within the same broad theological framework as those of whom he disapproves, that is, a framework in which creation, fall and redemption are closely related. (We shall see later how this is true of Francis of Assisi.) The variations occur within this common framework rather than constituting two opposed traditions.

In fact, even Fox's own work throws doubt on the way he polarizes the two traditions. It might seem as though Fox himself has no place for sin or salvation, but in fact he has his own definitions of sin, such as the damage humans do to creation, and of salvation, such as the

---

[10] Fox, *Original Blessing*, p 48.

[11] E.g. T.E. Clarke, 'Theological Trends: Creational Spirituality', *The Way* 29 (1989), p. 77; B. Newman, 'Romancing the Past: A Critical Look at Matthew Fox and the Medieval "Creation Mystics"', *Touchstone* 5 (1992), pp. 5–10 (I owe this reference to Lawrence Osborn); M. Goodall and John Reader, 'Why Matthew Fox Fails to Change the World' in *The Earth Beneath: A Critical Guide to Green Theology* (ed. Ian Ball, M. Goodall, Clare Palmer and John Reader; London: SPCK, 1992), pp. 115–16.

healing of creation in which we help to establish cosmic harmony. Indeed, he even has a substitute for the Augustinian understanding of original sin that he rejects: dualism, 'the dualism that human, sexual, racial, economic exploitations are all about', is 'the basis of all sin'.[12] Dualism 'is what the creation-centered tradition considers to be original sin or the sin behind sin'.[13] Another major flaw in Fox's historical typology is that he misses the extent to which the depreciation of the material world and the introspective turn to the spiritual within, real tendencies in much of the tradition of Christian spirituality, were due, not to the fall/redemption doctrine as such, but to the quite different influence of Platonism in the Christian tradition. Finally, he also leaves secularization and the loss of religious belief largely out of his account of what has gone wrong in modern western history. He joins in a popular contemporary game of blaming on the Christian tradition or part of it such things as the modern project of technological domination of the world that have in fact coincided with the progress of western rejection of the Christian tradition.

Rather as New Testament scholars in the first half of the twentieth century tended to use first-century Judaism as a foil to set off the virtues of early Christianity, attributing to Judaism precisely the faults which Christianity remedied, so Fox's account of the fall/redemption tradition is little more than a means of highlighting all the attractions of the creation-centred tradition by contrasting it with everything it was not. How else can we read, for example, Fox's exhortation 'to let the preoccupation with human sinfulness give way to attention to divine grace'?[14] – as though Augustine and the Reformers (among others), seriously as they took human sinfulness, did not give at least equal attention to divine grace! Fox's work is best read, not as the recovery of a lost tradition, but as his own eclectic creation, drawing on many sources in the tradition and the contemporary world.

Fox's work is too wide-ranging to be adequately summed up here. Instead, I shall pick out some features which seem to me of special interest for pursuing a comparison between Fox and Francis of Assisi, who is widely considered the first and the greatest 'creation mystic' in the Christian tradition. Are there aspects of Fox's thought which positively correspond, in a helpfully contemporary way, to aspects of Francis's spirituality? Are there aspects which seem more problematic

---

[12] Fox, *Original Blessing*, p. 296.
[13] Fox, *Original Blessing*, p. 210.
[14] Fox, *Original Blessing*, p. 26.

from the position centrally within the Christian mainstream that Francis, for all his remarkable exceptionality, certainly occupies, as we shall see? I shall briefly discuss two themes in each of these two categories.

Creation as well as Salvation

The Christian tradition has always understood salvation as the restoration and renewal, as well as completion, of God's good creation. When Fox insists that salvation loses its meaning if creation drops out of view,[15] he is representing, not a minority tradition of creation-centred spirituality, but the mainstream of the Christian tradition, which, incidentally, has never denied that the goodness of God's creation is more fundamental than the sin that has damaged and distorted it. It may well be the case that in the modern period, Christianity of several types has taken creation for granted just at the juncture of history when it could no longer be taken for granted, and focused too exclusively on human salvation, whether in an individualistic way or in terms of a social gospel of reforming society. In the long run, the loss of a sense of creation has undermined the meaningfulness of salvation, while the understanding of God as Saviour without an equally strong sense of God as Creator has unwittingly colluded with the general loss of a sense of God in our time. It is for the sake of God and the gospel, as well as for the sake of the earth and its non-human inhabitants, that Christian recognition of the world as God's good creation and ourselves as part of that creation is urgently needed. As Fox knows, such recognition is not a merely intellectual matter, but a deeply experiential way of relating to God and creation.

Gift and Gratitude

To such an experience, as Fox stresses, the themes of blessing, gift and gratitude are central: the blessing of creation in God's continuous and extravagant lavishing of goodness on it, the giftedness of creation, including ourselves, as given to us, and thankfulness and praise as the wellspring of life ('a thanks from the depths of the cosmos that we are for the cosmos in which we live').[16] Fox rightly identifies 'taking for

---

[15] Fox, *Original Blessing*, p. 108.
[16] Fox, *Original Blessing*, p. 115.

granted' as one of the peculiar afflictions of modern western human-ity and a prime source of its ills,[17] and one could add that a false esti-mation of achievement, rather than being given, as what matters, an unwillingness to recognize that every achievement is deeply indebted to what we are given, is a closely related failure. Though Fox does not say this, one way in which salvation is related to creation in experi-ence is in the sense of being given oneself and the world afresh in 'grace' (which means God's generous gift) – a redemption from 'taking for granted' such that all of life becomes experience of gratu-itousness. Once again, one does not have to polarize the Christian tra-dition in order to recover this: it runs through the whole tradition and has been lost through secularization rather than Augustinianism.

Theism, Panentheism and Dualism

One of the most important of the differences between the two tradi-tions as Fox constructs them is the difference between theism and panentheism. This is also, in terms of Fox's key category of dualism, a difference between a dualistic understanding of the relationship of God and the world and a non-dualistic understanding of that rela-tionship: 'The idea that God is "out there" is probably the ultimate dualism, divorcing as it does God and humanity'.[18] Fox makes the common mistake of supposing that theism posits God's transcen-dence as distance between God and the world, whereas the true meaning of transcendence is difference between God and the world. This is a mistake of very considerable significance for the way Fox thinks about God. For theism he substitutes panentheism, which cer-tainly does, as he claims, distinguish God from creation without sep-arating God from creation: 'everything is truly in God and God is truly in everything'.[19] But what gets lost in Fox's particular version of a move from theism to panentheism is a sense of God's personal oth-erness and a sense of God's surpassing God's creation. The former seems to be flatly denied in the statement that panentheism 'does not relate to God as subject or object'.[20] The latter is from time to time affirmed, but generally lacks relevance to experience.

---

[17] Fox, *Creation Spirituality*, pp. 92–3.
[18] Fox, *Original Blessing*, p. 89.
[19] Fox, *Original Blessing*, p. 90.
[20] Fox, *Original Blessing*, p. 90.

The more one reads Fox the more striking, by comparison with the whole Christian tradition, is the lack of inter-subjective relationship with God and the lack of an awareness of God in which God is distinguished from the creation. These things have been abandoned in the repudiation of dualism, but it is far from clear why they should have been. The passage quoted near the beginning of this chapter about mystical experience as unitive rather than dualistic[21] clearly states that lack of separation does not mean denying difference, that the opposite of dualism is not identity but communion. So why may a non-dualistic experience of God not be one of intensely intimate relationship to God as personal other? The statement that panentheism 'does not relate to God as subject or object'[22] seems to result, by a *non sequitur*, from the claim that all 'theisms are about subject/object relationships to God'.[23] Dualisms in Fox are about subject/object relationships, which are *ipso facto* oppressive.[24] But subject-to-subject communion of persons is not oppressive. This has been left out of the possibilities of relationship to God by sleight of hand, not argument.

The lack of inter-subjective relationship with God appears, for example, in what Fox does with such traditional elements of the spiritual life as faith and forgiveness. He, quite appropriately, translates faith as 'trust' and makes a great deal of this theme, but trust is almost always a matter of trusting the cosmos[25] or of trusting ourselves[26] or simply of trusting *tout court*,[27] almost never a matter of trusting God (the only instance I have found is at *Original Blessing*, p. 283, where it may well equate with trusting ourselves as God's image). This must be a deliberate avoidance of the traditional language. Similarly, forgiveness is a matter of 'letting go', of forgiving ourselves, and of forgiving others, not of being forgiven by God.[28] What is operative here and elsewhere is a fundamental assumption that relationship to God is nothing other than relationship to oneself and the cosmos. Because God is in all things and all things are in God, our relationships to all things certainly are relationship to God. Fox is neither an atheist nor a pantheist. But in his work there is no

---

[21] Fox, *Coming*, pp. 49–50.
[22] Fox, *Original Blessing*, p. 90.
[23] Fox, *Original Blessing*, p. 89.
[24] Cf. Fox, *Original Blessing*, p. 119.
[25] E.g. Fox, *Original Blessing*, p. 203; *Creation Spirituality*, p. 99; *Coming*, p. 53.
[26] Fox, *Original Blessing*, pp. 120, 259, 260; *Coming*, p. 49.
[27] E.g. Fox, *Original Blessing*, p. 164.
[28] Fox, *Original Blessing*, pp. 163, 171.

distinguishing of God from creation, such that to trust God amounts to anything more or other than to trust the cosmos. Relationship to God simply is the right kind of relationship (e.g. trusting rather than fearing) to the cosmos. A curious effect is that while personal language about God is sparse in Fox, he is not averse to personifying the cosmos.[29]

In fact, Fox is capable of saying an extraordinary amount about mysticism without mentioning God. At one point he justifies this: 'As one grows more deeply into a panentheistic awareness, one's need to invoke the actual name of God becomes less compelling'.[30] But in support for this statement he can only observe that the biblical books of Esther and the Song of Songs never name God, and that Francis of Assisi's *Canticle of the Creatures* does not mention Jesus Christ.[31] The latter point is entirely spurious, since although the canticle does not mention Jesus, it invokes God by name in every single stanza. In fact, the idea that mystical awareness of God in creation reduces the need to refer to God has no support from the Christian spiritual tradition at all, not even from Fox's own favourite mystics. Those who find God in creation feel the need to say so, because finding *God* in creation requires distinguishing God from creation. They recognize God in the creatures precisely as the creatures refer beyond themselves to the God who made them and surpasses them.

A section called, 'What is Creation?', in the first chapter of Fox's book *Creation Spirituality*, is instructive. From a traditional Christian perspective in which creation is distinguished (not separated!) from its Creator, in which creation is the gift and God the giver, in which creation reflects its Creator but in such a way as to distinguish itself as creation from its Creator, this section of Fox's work describes creation in terms some of which are appropriate to creation, some of which are appropriate only to the Creator. Thus, for example, on the one hand, the cosmos is 'sacred',[32] because it is God's creation, and the 'gift'[33] of the Creator, but also, on the other hand: 'Creation is the source, the matrix, and the goal of all things – the beginning and the end, the alpha and the omega. Creation is our common parent, where "our"

---

[29] Fox, *Creation Spirituality*, p. 10.

[30] Fox, *Original Blessing*, pp. 90–1.

[31] Oddly, Fox in his own, later exposition of the canticle, takes the 'Lord' and the 'Most High' to whom the canticle is addressed to be the Cosmic Christ (*Coming*, p. 112).

[32] Fox, *Creation Spirituality*, p. 9.

[33] Fox, *Creation Spirituality*, p. 11.

stands for all things. Creation is the mother of all beings and the father of all beings, the birther and the begetter.'[34]

The terms applied to 'creation' here are mostly scriptural terms which in Scripture and tradition refer precisely to the uniqueness of the one God who alone brought all things into being and who alone is the goal of all things (for 'the beginning and the end, the alpha and the omega' see Isa. 41:4; 44:6; 48:12; Rev 1:8,17; 21:6; 22:13). It is hard to see what Fox, who certainly knows their biblical usage, means by applying them to creation, since 'creation' is, by definition, the sum total of 'all things' created by God. What does it mean to call *creation* the creator of all things? That Fox can speak without apparent difficulty of 'creation' both as creator of 'all things' and as itself 'all things' that are created by God is significant. Despite a formal distinction between the Creator and the creation, what Fox is primarily concerned to express is the divinity of the cosmos, the cosmic whole, to which all particular creatures relate as those who owe their existence and their reverence to this cosmic whole. In thus relating to the cosmos, rather than in acknowledging the cosmos to which they belong to be the creation of the transcendent One who made it, they are relating to God. It is odd that Fox uses the term 'creation-centered spirituality' for a spirituality in which the *createdness* of the cosmos plays so negligible a role.

In such a theological context, is the 'gratitude' of which Fox so importantly speaks (see above) directed to God or to the cosmos? In the place Fox gives it[35] in his discussion of 'the new creation story' (i.e. the contemporary scientific account of the origins and development of the universe) God is unmentioned and gratitude to the cosmos seems the appropriate meaning.[36] The distinction is clearly not significant to Fox. Yet why should we feel the awe and gratitude of which Fox speaks simply from learning from this story 'how gratuitous our existence is'? Why should we not feel the absurdity of our existence as a meaningless accident in a cosmos without purpose or meaning? The scientific story of the universe, simply as a scientific account, is precisely *not* a 'new creation story', for it does not speak of a Creator. For us to respond to our 'gratuitousness' with gratitude there must be intentionality and love to thank. Gratitude must be directed either to the one Creator of all things, transcendent beyond his creation (as in the whole Christian tradition), or to the universe conceived mythologically as itself a

---

[34] Fox, *Creation Spirituality*, p. 10.
[35] Fox, *Creation Spirituality*, p. 28.
[36] Fox, *Creation Spirituality*, pp. 27–9.

purposive, intentional being. What Fox calls 'living cosmology' is really a cosmic myth of the latter kind, with occasional support from the biblical and Christian faith in the transcendent Creator.

Jesus and the Cosmic Christ

In *The Coming of the Cosmic Christ* Fox makes a notable attempt to repristinate the notion (and experience) of 'the cosmic Christ' found in the New Testament and the theological tradition, and to give it a key role in his creation-centred spirituality: 'The coming together of the historical Jesus and the Cosmic Christ will make Christianity whole at last.'[37] As this quotation suggests, Fox is aware that in the New Testament and the theologians and mystics who have spoken about the cosmic Christ, this Christ in whom all creation coheres should not be separated from Jesus of Nazareth, the figure whose human life is narrated in the Gospels. In arguing that the modern 'quest of the historical Jesus' now needs to be supplemented by a quest for the cosmic Christ, he acknowledges that a 'theology of the Cosmic Christ must be grounded in the historical Jesus, in his words, in his liberating deeds . . . in his life and orthopraxis', and speaks of a dialectic between the two: 'a dance between time (Jesus) and space (Christ); between the personal and the cosmic; between the prophetic and the mystical'.[38]

The relationship between the two is evidently that Jesus is one form of incarnation of the Cosmic Christ: 'Wisdom [a term for the cosmic Christ] has been made flesh not only in Jesus the Christ but in *all expressions of the Cosmic Christ*.'[39] This means that the divinity suffused throughout the cosmos (the cosmic Christ) imparts divinity to all creatures,[40] and especially comes to 'birth' in the lives of humans, who consciously mirror the divine qualities: 'A theology of the Cosmic Christ is not embarrassed by the deification of humans.'[41] One of the messages to us that Fox puts into the mouth of the cosmic Christ is: '"Be still and know that I am God" (Ps. 46:10). And you are too.'[42] In this sense, Fox's use of the idea of the cosmic Christ is another expression of his wish to avoid a 'dualism' of God and creation: 'divinity' is

---

[37] Fox, *Coming*, p. 7.
[38] Fox, *Coming*, p. 79.
[39] Fox, *Coming*, p. 147, italics original.
[40] Fox, *Coming*, p. 145.
[41] Fox, *Coming*, p. 109.
[42] Fox, *Coming*, p. 142.

really a quality of things, rather than a way of naming the One to whom all things owe their existence and their goodness. The purpose of the incarnation of the cosmic Christ in Jesus of Nazareth is therefore to reveal the immanence of the cosmic Christ 'in the sufferings and dignity of each creature of the earth'.[43] Quite remarkably Fox takes the Johannine Jesus' use of the 'I am' declaration, that in the biblical tradition indicates the mysterious uniqueness of the one God, as a 'challenge to name (or claim) our lives and beings in a similar fashion'.[44] Jesus claims the unique divinity of the one God in order to encourage us all to do the same.

But Fox's most original contribution to Christology is his proposal for 'naming the paschal mystery anew for the third millennium of Christianity'.[45] The paschal mystery is the Christian story of the passion, resurrection and ascension of Jesus Christ. Fox proposes that for our age of ecological destruction: 'the appropriate symbol of the Cosmic Christ who became incarnate in Jesus is that of Jesus as Mother Earth crucified and rising daily'.[46] As not infrequently, it is hard to pin down Fox's language to a precise statement. Having spoken of Mother Earth's 'crucifixion' as a 'symbol' of Jesus,[47] he goes on to speak of it as how we are to understand the paschal mystery. In his fullest summary of the new naming of the paschal mystery, he claims that:

> matricide, mysticism, and the Cosmic Christ name the Paschal story we have understood as the death, resurrection and second coming of Jesus the Christ. The death of Mother Earth (matricide) and the resurrection of the human psyche (mysticism) and the coming of the Cosmic Christ (a living cosmology) name the mystery of the divine cycle of death and rebirth and the sending of the Spirit in our time.[48]

This is how Fox conceives the 'resurrection' of Mother Earth as occurring through a worldwide renaissance of mysticism and 'living cosmology' (i.e. understanding and experience of the cosmos as sacred). It is not at all clear how this relates to the particular story of Jesus of Nazareth, other than as a more universal playing-out of the cosmic

---

[43] Fox, *Coming*, p. 155.
[44] Fox, *Coming*, p. 154.
[45] Fox, *Coming*, p. 162.
[46] Fox, *Coming*, p. 145.
[47] Fox, *Coming*, pp. 145, 149.
[48] Fox, *Coming*, pp. 162–3.

principle that was made known to us through its particular occurrence in Jesus' case.

Much as Fox wishes to retain a significant place for the human story
of Jesus of Nazareth, he treads a fine line between attributing universal significance to the particular historical man Jesus and his story (as
any Christology must) and dissolving that particularity of Jesus into a
universal divine presence. It is a line between a spirituality that focuses on Jesus in his relationship to the whole cosmos and a spirituality that focuses on the divinity of the cosmos. Perhaps there is room to
read Fox in both ways, but the overall trend of his thought pushes in
the latter direction.

With a view to ways in which we shall see that the mysticism of
Francis of Assisi differs significantly from Fox's creation-centred mysticism, we could summarize the last two sections by saying that there
is a strong tendency in Fox for the transcendence of God to be reduced
to the cosmos and for the particularity of Jesus to be dissolved in the
cosmos. While Fox does retain some qualifications from the Christian
tradition that mitigate these tendencies, on the whole the trend of his
thought is to a spirituality of cosmic divinity, to which neither the
transcendence of God as Creator nor the particularity of God's incarnation as Jesus are important.

Francis of Assisi

It has become commonplace to lament that Francis's attitude to the non-
human creation, remembered in some of the most attractive stories of
his relationships with animals, has been sentimentalized and thereby
trivialized in popular perceptions. The stories are important, because,
as with the Jesus of the Gospels, much of what we know of Francis is
found in the stories told about him, and it is primarily these that convey the irresistible attractiveness of Francis, a figure like few others in
the history of Christianity. We cannot understand Francis's 'nature mysticism' outside its context in the extraordinary intensity, self-giving and
joyousness with which Francis lived his whole life in his devotion to
God and his compassionate 'being-with' God's creatures, human and
others. Leonardo Boff lists 'his innocence, his enthusiasm for nature, his
gentleness with all beings, his capacity for compassion with the poor,
and of confraternalization with all the elements',[49] and considers his

---

[49] Boff, *Saint Francis*, p. 18.

'communion and confraternalization with all of reality such as has never been seen since'.[50] Though Francis was no theologian in the academic sense, his attitude and relationships with the non-human creation reflect a profoundly theological vision of the community of God's creation in relation to its Creator. They also belong to an integrated ideal of life and praxis, which included a particular vision of the ascetic life, including absolute poverty, radical humility and constant prayer. Humility and poverty were the radical alternatives to status, power, possession and domination, removing these from all of Francis's relationships with humans and other creatures. By not valuing them as objects of possession, power or gratification for himself, he was freed to treat them all 'fraternally'[51] as fellow-creatures with the value they have for God their Creator. With the poorest of the poor, such as the lepers he tended, and the lowliest of God's creatures, such as the worm and the cicada, Francis was able to be brotherly and compassionate only because of the rigorous asceticism through which he was freed from other desires. Of course, there was also the ecstatic joy in God and God's creation that has led to the view that he was the first true 'nature mystic' in the Christian tradition.[52]

---

[50] Boff, *Saint Francis*, p. 19.

[51] The word is unfortunately gender-specific (at least in its etymology) and has no feminine equivalent, but I use it to refer to the way in which Francis considered all creatures as sisters and brothers.

[52] In this section the abbreviations I use for Francis' works and the early biographical literature about him are those used in Regis J. Armstrong, J.A. Wayne Hellmann and William J. Short ed., *Francis of Assisi: Early Documents*, vo. 1: *The Saint* (New York: New City Press, 1999), p. 32. Quotations in the text are from this volume (AHW), for works it includes; otherwise from Marion A. Habig, *St. Francis of Assisi: Writings and Early Biographies: English Omnibus of the Sources for the life of St. Francis* (Chicago: Franciscan Herald Press, 1983((Habig).
The Abbreviations are as follows:

Adm	*The Admonitions*: AHW 128–137
AP	*The Anonymous of Perugia* (= *Legend of Perugia*): Habig 957–1101
1C	*The Life of Saint Francis by Thomas of Celano* (= *First Life*): AHW 171–297
2C	*The Remembrance of a Desire of a Soul* (= *Second Life by Thomas of Celano*): Habig 357–543
CtC	*The Canticle of the Creatures*: AHW 113–114
ER	*The Earlier Rule*: AHW 63–86
ExhP	*Exhortation to the Praise of God*: AHW 138
LFl	*The Little Flowers of Saint Francis*: Habig 1267–1530
LMj	*The Major Legend by Bonaventura*: Habig 627–787
2LtF	*The Second Letter to the Faithful*: AHW 45–51
LtOrd	*A Letter to the Entire Order*: AHW 116–121
OfP	*The Office of the Passion*: AHW 139–157

It is important, first, to recognize that Francis does not at all conform to Fox's 'two traditions' model of Christian history. Theologically, he stands unequivocally in the mainstream, with a balanced and integrated view of creation, fall, sin and redemption:

> You have created everything spiritual and corporal and, after making us in Your own image and likeness, You placed us in paradise. Through our own fault we fell. We thank you for [,] as through Your Son You created us, so through Your holy love with which You loved us You brought about his birth . . . and You willed to redeem us captives through His cross and blood and death (ER 23:1–11).

God, for Francis, is the Trinity, 'Father, Son and Holy Spirit, Creator of all, Savior of all who believe and hope in Him, and love Him' (ER 23:11). Creation and salvation belong together in God's relationship to the world. Francis's strong sense of human sinfulness ('by our own fault, we are disgusting, miserable and opposed to good, yet prompt and inclined to evil' (ER 17:7); 'nothing belongs to us except our vices and sins')[53] by no means impedes his delight in God's good creation.[54]

One aspect that holds creation and salvation together is Francis's strong sense of God as the Giver and all good things as God's gift:

> Let us refer all good to the Lord, God Almighty and Most High, acknowledge that every good is His, and thank Him, from whom all good comes, for everything (ER 17:17).

PrOF   *A Prayer Inspired by the Our Father*: AHW 158–169
PrsG   *The Praises of God*: AHW 109–111
SalV   *A Salutation of Virtues*: AHW 164–165

[53] Fox, in *Original Blessing*, p. 275, blames Bonaventure's *Life of Francis* for conforming him to the fall/redemption theological tradition, but the quotations from the above paragraph are all from Francis's own writing. Fox is here probably following Lynn White, 'Historical Roots', pp. 1203–7 (and subsequently reprinted in several edited collections). Against White's claim that Bonaventure suppressed Francis's views on creation, see Sorrell, *St. Francis*, p. 148.

[54] Waddell, *Beasts* is a collection of some of the best of the Latin stories in translation. Many of the stories about the desert fathers can be found in translation in Norman Russell and Ward, *Lives*. Some of the stories of the Celtic saints are retold in Van de Weyer, *Celtic Fire*. Studies of the stories include Bratton, 'Original Desert Solitaire'; Sorrell, *St. Francis*, pp. 19–27; and especially Short, *Saints* (I am grateful to Dr Short for providing me with a photocopy of this book, which is unobtainable in Britain).

[L]et us all love the Lord God who has given and gives to each one of us our whole body, our whole soul and our whole life, Who has created, redeemed and will save us by His mercy alone, Who did and does everything good for us (ER 23:8; and also 2LtF 61).

There is no ambiguity in Francis as to whether it is to God or the cosmos that we owe creation and ourselves. All creation is gift of the transcendent and only ultimate Creator, the only ultimate source of good (since he 'alone is good' (LtF 62; ER 23:9) in the sense that all other good is by derivation and gift from God). The Creator alone is therefore worthy of all thanks and praise. Francis finds God in all things, but he finds *God*, the Creator and Saviour of all, only by at the same time distinguishing God from all things, by finding all things the gift of the God who exceeds and surpasses them.

We should now begin to be able to see that Francis's spirituality is really neither creation-centred not anthropocentric, but *centred on God*. His own writings contain remarkable passages of praise and devotion which require the dedication of the whole person to God alone and that God should be the only goal of human desire(e.g. ER23:8–11; PrsG; PrOF 5; LtOrd 50). This does not demean the creatures, but gives them their true dignity and worth as precisely creatures of the one Creator. As such they are loved and honoured by those who love God. By thus ensuring that the devotion of the whole person is owed to the one who surpasses creation Francis rules out the idolatry that divinizes creation and expects of it therefore what it was never able to supply: a true object of total, all-encompassing trust and devotion. Instead, the creatures can be for Francis truly themselves, his creaturely brothers and sisters, forming a community of mutual dependence, assisting each other in their common praise of the Creator who made them all and values them all, each in its own distinctive reality.

Francis and the Non-Human Creation

The many stories of Francis's delight in the companionship of animals and his loving care for animals are not at all unprecedented. There was a long tradition of stories of saints and animals (doubtless some historical and others legendary) reaching back to the desert fathers and including especially the Celtic saints.[55] We do not know whether Francis

---

[55] Listed in Sorrell, *St. Francis*, p. 44.

knew any of them, but they have in common with Francis a context in the ascetic tradition of hermits who went to live (permanently or temporarily) apart from human society in order to devote themselves entirely to God. Because they deliberately sought out places remote from human habitation, these hermits lived amid wild nature, closer than most people to nature unmodified by human use. Alone with the non-human creatures they came to love them and to value them as fellow-creatures of God. So it was with Francis, who spent long periods alone or with a few of his friar brothers in places where they would have close experience of wild creatures. Since Francis and his friars did not *own* animals, even as pets, relationships of mutuality with wild creatures were the easier to form. Many of the stories show Francis's care for animals in ways that are relatively traditional, though not exactly paralleled in the stories of other solitary saints. Like other saints, Francis fed and protected his fellow-creatures. He wanted Christmas Day, a festival of special importance to Francis, to be honoured by the provision of abundant food for birds and more than the usual amount of food for domestic animals (2C 200). He saw to it that bees were provided with honey or wine lest they die of cold in the winter (1C 80). Several stories portray him saving animals from danger or harm, freeing animals that had been caught and brought to him, returning fish to the water, even removing worms from the road lest they be trampled.[56] Many of the stories stress the reciprocity of Francis's relationships with the creatures: they are tame and friendly as he is gentle and concerned.

A feature of many of the earlier stories of saints and animals that continues in those about Francis is the theme of the restitution of paradise. Because these saints are living closely with God their dealings with animals reflect the originally intended relationship of humans to the rest of creation. One aspect of this is that the friendly and non-violent harmony of paradise is restored. Another, closely connected, is that the saints exercise the human dominion over other creatures, given in creation, as it was originally intended. This introduces a hierarchical element into the relationship, but it is one in which the animals willingly serve and obey the saints, and in which the saints care for the animals. The hierarchy is one of mutual service and care. In the stories about Francis, he frequently acts with authority to command the animals.[57] The fierce wolf which was terrorizing the town of Gubbio was tamed and became friendly under Francis's influence

---

[56] Examples listed in Sorrell, *St. Francis*, p. 43.
[57] Sorrell, *St. Francis*, pp. 66, 127–8.

(LFl 1:21). Animals serve him, like the falcon, which during Francis's residence in his hermitage at La Verna used to wake him in time for matins, but showed such consideration for the saint that when Francis was tired or ill it would delay waking him until dawn (2C 168). Like many of the stories in the earlier tradition, this one emphasizes the affectionate friendship between the saint and the bird. The creatures respect Francis's authority, but they do so lovingly and willingly, as friends rather than slaves.

Francis is reported as saying that 'every creature says and proclaims: "God has created me for you, O man!"' Although this reflects the medieval theological commonplace that the rest of the material creation was made for humanity, the context should be noted. Francis was telling the brother gardener not to plant vegetables everywhere, but to reserve part of the garden for plants whose scent and flowers 'might invite all men who looked at them to praise God' (AP 51). Thus Francis refuses to limit the value of the rest of creation for humanity to its practical usefulness but sees it as consisting also in its assisting humanity's praise of God. But his principle (expressed most fully at the end of his life in the *Canticle of the Creatures*) was that because the 'creatures minister to our needs every day' and 'without them we could not live', therefore we should appreciate them and praise God for them (AP 43). Thus the theme of human dominion is understood theocentrically rather than anthropocentrically. The creatures' service of humanity is properly received only as cause for praise and thankfulness to God. Therefore the human dominion over the creatures becomes for Francis primarily a matter of dependence on the creatures, with whom humanity shares a common dependence on the Creator. The creatures on whose service we depend are not to be exploited, but to be treated with brotherly/sisterly respect and consideration.

This means that in Francis the sense in which humanity has been given a special place in creation is only to be understood in relationship to his overwhelming sense of the common creatureliness that makes all creatures his 'sisters' and 'brothers.'[58] This linguistic usage seems to be distinctive of Francis. The Celtic saints had called the animals who befriended them their brothers in the monastic sense. Francis regards all the creatures (not only animals, but also fire and water, sun and moon, and so on) as brothers and sisters, because they are fellow-creatures and fellow-members of the family of those who

---

[58] See Sorrell, *St. Francis*, pp. 69–75.

serve God. The terms denote affection and especially affinity. Thus, while there is a residual element of hierarchy in the relationship, this does not negate the common creatureliness of humans and other creatures. Francis was a man of the thirteenth century, not the twenty-first, and so the chivalric notion of 'courtesy', current in his time, was one idea that helped Francis to understand the relationship of humans and other creatures in terms not of domination but of mutuality.[59] Courtesy is the magnanimous, deferential, respectful attitude that enables love to be shown up and down the social hierarchy. In the community of creation, brothers and sisters on different levels of the hierarchy can interact with mutual respect and loving deference. With the chivalric notion of courtesy Francis fused the traditional monastic virtues of obedience and humility,[60] so that he can say that obedience 'is subject and submissive to everyone in the world, not only to people but to every beast and wild animal as well [,] that they may do whatever they want with it insofar as it has been given them from above by the Lord' (SalV 14).

Here the hierarchy is virtually subverted by mutuality: the obedience that the creatures owe to humanity is reciprocated by an obedience of humanity to the creatures. What Francis envisages, in the end, is a kind of mutual and humble deference in the common service of the creatures to their Creator. When Boff refers to Francis's view of the world as 'cosmic democracy',[61] the description is too modern to be entirely appropriate, and it does not distinguish a 'democracy' of political rights from one of mutual service, which would be more appropriate for Francis's view. But with all due qualifications it does suggest something of the direction in which Francis characteristically developed the Christian tradition.

---

[59] On the relationship of humility (and poverty) to Francis's confraternity with creatures, see Boff, *Saint Francis*, pp. 38–40.

[60] Boff, *Saint Francis*, p. 34.

[61] The *Benedicite* is the canticle that appears in the Greek version of the book of Daniel as Daniel 3:52–90. This makes it part of the canonical book of Daniel for the Orthodox and Roman Catholic churches, but, since it is absent from the Hebrew and Aramaic text of Daniel, the Protestant churches assigned it to the Apocrypha, where it occurs among the Additions to Daniel, as the Song of the Three. But White, 'Continuing the Conversation', who remarks that it 'contradicts the historically dominant Judeo-Christian anthropocentrism', is quite wrong in supposing that it shows the influence of hellenism or was ever thought in the least heretical. On the contrary, it merely develops at length the theme of nature's praise of God to be found in the Psalms (especially Ps. 148). See Chapter 7 in this volume.

All Creatures' Praise of God

Francis's exceptionally positive valuation of all his fellow-creatures did not derive simply from his encounters with them. It reflected his profound sense of God as Creator and therefore also of the creatures as each valued by God. He recognized God's generous giving in his provision for all of the animate creation, following Jesus' words about the birds in the Sermon on the Mount (Matt. 6:25). In relation to the birds, for example, he recognized God's special gifts to them ('noble among His creatures') as constituting their particular worth within the community of creation (1C 58). Another theme with strong biblical and traditional roots Francis made very much his own and fundamental for the way he related to his fellow-creatures and, with them, to God. This is the idea that all creatures praise their Creator and that human worship of God is participation in this worship of the whole creation.

In his own works Francis echoes the main biblical sources of this idea: the *Benedicite* (Daniel 3:52–90 in the Vulgate);[62] Psalms 69:34; 96:11–12; 103:22; 148;[77] Revelation 5:13.[63] These texts would have been very familiar to Francis, especially since the two most ample in their depiction of the praise of the creatures feature prominently in the daily offices he recited according to his breviary: Psalm 148 was to be said every morning, the *Benedicite* every Sunday and feast day morning.[64] Most revealing are Francis's own liturgical compositions, which often consist of a collage of texts carefully selected from Scripture, especially the Psalms. One of these (*The Praises to be Said at All the Hours*) was to be used by the friars before each hour of the office. This outpouring of praise to the Trinity is based largely on the heavenly liturgy depicted in Revelation 4 – 5, and like that liturgy it culminates in the praise of God by every creature in the cosmos. Calls to all the creatures to praise alternate with a refrain ('Let us praise and glorify

---

[62] For a valuable study of this theme in the Psalms, see Fretheim, 'Nature's Praise', pp. 16–30.

[63] The allusions are in Regis J. Armstrong, Hellmann and Short, *Francis of Assisi, Exhortation to the Praise of God*, p. 138 (Ps. 69:35; Dan. 3:78; Ps. 103:22; Dan. 3:80); *Francis of Assisi, Second Letter* (Rev. 5:13); *The Praises to be Said at All the Hours* (Dan. 3:57; Ps. 69:35; Rev. 5:13); *Francis of Assisi, The Office of the Passion*, pp. 139–57, 7:4 (Ps. 96:10–11); *Francis of Assisi, The Canticle of the Creatures*, pp. 113–14 (Ps. 148; *Benedicite*). On the relationship of *The Canticle of the Creatures* to Psalm 148 and the *Benedicite*, see Sorrell, *St. Francis*, pp. 99, 102–5.

[64] Sorrell, *St. Francis*, p. 99.

Him forever') based on that in the *Benedicite*. *The Exhortation to the Praise of God* calls on all the creatures, including both general references and specific references to rivers and birds, to praise God. In these liturgies of creation there is no hierarchy, not even an order of importance in calls to praise. Before God, as his creatures, humans stand alongside other creatures, and are united with all other creatures in a harmony formed by their common praise of the one Creator. Expressed here is not only a 'living cosmology' (Fox) in which humanity finds its place, but a wholly theocentric cosmology in which the transcendent Creator is distinguished from his creation in the praise that unites his creatures. The ideal harmony and interdependence of creation are most fully realized when humans join other creatures in praise of the Creator.

Characteristically and originally, Francis also translated this liturgical usage into an actual practice of addressing the creatures themselves.[65] This began with the famous sermon to the birds (1C 58; LFl 1:16), which initiated a regular practice: 'From that day on, he carefully exhorted all birds, all animals, all reptiles, and also insensible creatures, to praise and love their Creator, because daily, invoking the name of the Savior, he observed their obedience in his own experience' (1C 58; cf. 81).

The reference to 'the name of the Savior' is significant, because it relates creation and salvation in a way that is rarely explicit in the material about creation's praise of God (see also 1C 115, quoted below), but is surely often implicit. Since salvation entails the restoration of creation to its proper har-mony and order in relation to God, the praise of the creatures is directed to Christ as Saviour as well as to God as Creator. This is what occurs at the end of the great cosmic lit-urgy in Revelation 4 – 5, which Francis evidently knew well: when the slaughtered Lamb is enthroned in heaven, every creature in the cosmos joins in the doxology addressed to God and the Lamb. This eschatological goal of all worship Francis anticipated whenever he invoked the name of Jesus and called on creatures to praise their Creator.

We should also remember Francis's habit of singing along with cicadas or birds in what he understood as their praise of their Creator (2C 171; KNi 8:9).[66] In this way he translated the sentiments of the

---

[65] It is typical of Francis to put biblical passages into practice in a way that might seem naively literal, but really constituted a particularly potent expression of a biblical theme.

[66] See also (for the nightingale) Moorman, *A New Fioretti* 57, in Habig, *St. Francis of Assisi*, pp. 1881–2.

Benedicite into a real human solidarity with the rest of creation understood as a theocentric community existing for the praise and service
of God. There is no trace in Francis of the idea that the creatures need
humans to voice their praise of God for them. On the contrary, the
cicadas and the birds are already singing to God's glory; Francis joins
their song.

The Canticle of the Creatures

In the famous *Canticle of Brother Sun* or *Canticle of the Creatures*, written at the end of his life, Francis summed up much of his attitude to
creation. It is important to appreciate fully the opening two stanzas
that praise God before reference is made to the creatures:

> Most High, all-powerful, good Lord,
> Yours are the praises, the glory, and the honour, and all blessing,
> To You alone, Most High, do they belong,
> and no human is worthy to mention Your name.

That God surpasses the creatures in such a way as to be the only
praiseworthy one could not be clearer. So, when the next stanza continues: 'Praised be You, my Lord, with all Your creatures', the praising
of the creatures can only be a way of praising their Creator, from
whom their praiseworthy features derive. This praise of God *with the*
creatures (stanza 3–4) is a transition from the praise of God without
the creatures (stanzas 1–2) to the praises of God *for* the creatures,
which occupy stanzas 5–13. In these stanzas the various qualities of
the creatures are lovingly detailed, so that God may be praised for
them. Each of these stanzas begins (in Francis's Italian original):
'*Laudato si, mi Signore, per* . . .' followed by reference to one or more of
the creatures. There has been controversy over whether the meaning
is 'Be praised, my Lord, by . . .', 'Be praised, my Lord, through . . .' or
'Be praised, my Lord, for . . .' Divergent interpretations of the phrase
go back to soon after Francis's death,[67] and any would be consistent
with his thinking about the creation. But the latest detailed study by
Roger Sorrell argues very convincingly for the translation: 'Be
praised, my Lord, for . . .'[68] In that case the canticle does not call on

---

[67] Sorrell, *St. Francis*, pp. 116–17, 119.
[68] Sorrell, *St. Francis*, pp. 118–22.

Sister Moon, Brother Wind, Sister Water and the rest to praise God, even though Francis, as we have seen, could well have done this. Rather the canticle takes up Francis's conviction, which we have also noticed, that human beings should praise God for their fellow-creatures. The creatures are appreciated in three ways: for their practical usefulness in making human life possible and good, for their beauty, and for the way their distinctive qualities reflect the divine being (in particular 'Sir Brother Sun', in his beauty and radiance, resembles God). This is an appreciation of the God-given value of creation that goes far beyond a purely utilitarian, anthropocentric view. It celebrates the interdependent harmony of creation. The canticle is designed to teach people to think of creation with gratitude, appreciation and respect.[69]

Differently from Francis's earlier hymns of liturgical praise, the closing stanzas of the canticle,[70] praising God for 'those who give pardon for your love and bear infirmity and tribulation' and 'for Sister Bodily Death, from whom no one living can escape', make reference to negative aspects of the world and the painful reconciliation they require to make all good: forgiveness of injuries, endurance of suffering, acceptance of death. The canticle thus moves through the ideal harmony of the creatures, reflecting God's goodness in creation, through the painful healing of the negative, reflecting God's patient and forgiving love in salvation, to the final stanza which calls on its hearers to praise:

> Praise and bless my Lord and give Him thanks
> and serve Him with great humility.

In the light of Francis's earlier compositions and practice, this is surely addressed not only to humans but to all the creatures.

Murray Bodo's comment on the Canticle is apt:

> [T]he final poem of [Francis's] life reveals what happened to that man for whom the love of God was everything. And the surprise is that when God is everything, then everything else becomes more important and holy. The whole creature world is enhanced instead of being neglected and de-emphasized for some spirit world, as so often happens in pseudo-spirituality. For Francis, whatever demeans and devalues the creature demeans the Creator, so that reverence

---

[69] Sorrell, *St. Francis*, p. 124.
[70] These sections were added later, the one on Sister Death shortly before his death.

for and joy over every thing and every person becomes *the* sign of the love of God.[71]

Thus we see in Francis that the alternative to a spirituality that despises the created world does not have to be one that divinizes the created world (as Fox tends to imply). It can be one in which the created world is sacred and valued for love of its Creator who always surpasses it. Love of the Creator can include the creation without being reduced to love of the creation.

The whole canticle is a hymn to the Creator and Saviour of all, a theocentric celebration of creation, stemming both from Francis's own intense nature mysticism and also, in the closing stanzas, from his christological mysticism of identification with Jesus Christ, that climaxed in his receiving the stigmata. It is the only text from Francis himself in which these two aspects of his mystical awareness of God and creation clearly come together, no doubt because it was written during the painful and dark days of the last two years of his life. We turn to consider each briefly.

Creation Mysticism

We have considered various aspects of Francis's attitude to and relationships with the non-human creation, but we have still to register the intensity of delight in the creatures that frequently raised Francis to ecstatic rejoicing in their Creator. Some comments from his early biographers will illustrate this:

> He used to extol the artistry of [the bees'] work and their remarkable ingenuity, giving glory to the Lord. With such an outpouring, he often used up an entire day or more in praise of them and other creatures (1C 80).

> He had so much love and sympathy for [the creatures] that he was disturbed when they were treated without respect. He spoke to them with a great inner and exterior joy, as if they had been endowed by God with
>
> feeling, intelligence, and speech. Very often it was for him the occasion to become enraptured in God (AP 49).

---

[71] Bodo, *Way of St Francis*, p. 150.

[H]e caressed and contemplated [the creatures] with delight, so much so that his spirit seemed to live in heaven and not on earth (AP 51).

Christ Mysticism

Equal to the intensity of Francis's glorification of God the Creator with and for the creatures was the intensity of his identification with the human Jesus, the incarnate Son of God. Just as there is no loss of transcendence in Francis's adoration of the Creator of all things, so there is no loss of particularity in his devotion to the Saviour in his humanity. Francis was christocentric in his praxis, following as fully as possible the humility and poverty of Jesus and his confraternity with the poor and the marginalized. He was christocentric also in his communion with God through intense meditation on Jesus and identification with his passion.

Ewert Cousins calls this 'the mysticism of the historical event': 'In this type of consciousness, one recalls a significant event in the past, enters into its drama and draws from it spiritual energy, eventually moving beyond the event towards union with God.' The Christian form of this mysticism, which in Cousins' view began with Francis, consists in contemplation of the events of the story of Jesus.[72] It was to facilitate spiritual participation in such an event that Francis, famously, created the first Christmas crib (with live animals) (ie 84–86). (Christmas was his best-loved festival because it recalled the humility of Christ in undergoing birth as a human being and in poverty.) But Cousins' characterization of Francis's Christ mysticism perhaps misses the intensity of his devotion to the person of Jesus that accompanies his desire to participate in Jesus' story. Again we may rely on comments from the early biographers:

> [Of the period soon after his conversion:] Every day he meditated on the humility and example of the Son of God; he experienced much compassion and much sweetness from this, and in the end, what was bitter to his body,

> was changed into sweetness. The sufferings and bitterness which Christ endured for us were a constant subject of affliction to him and a cause for interior and exterior mortification; consequently, he was totally unconcerned with his own sufferings (AP 37).

---

[72] Cousins, 'Francis of Assisi', p. 166.

The brothers who lived with him know that daily, constantly, talk of Jesus was always on his lips, sweet and pleasant conversations about Him, kind words full of love . . . Often he sat down to dinner but on hearing or saying or even thinking 'Jesus' he forgot bodily food . . . Often as he walked along a road, thinking and singing of Jesus, he would forget his destination and start inviting all the elements to praise Jesus(1C 115).

Francis's desire to identify with his Saviour was granted finally when he received the stigmata.

The two different aspects of Francis's mysticism – his nature mysticism and his Christ mysticism – could be said to correspond to creation and redemption. This may be broadly true, but we have already noticed that it was not characteristic of Francis to hold creation and redemption apart. The last sentence just quoted (from 1C 115) illustrates how easily they could come together. Another example derives from the way Francis, following the medieval practice of seeing religious allegories in nature but as always making something characteristically his own out of it, used to be moved to praise or reflection by features of nature that recalled scriptural images of God, Christ or humanity. Especially he loved lambs, because they symbolized the humility of Jesus. In one story, Francis came upon a flock of goats:

There was one little sheep walking humbly and grazing calmly among these many goats. When blessed Francis saw it, he stopped in his tracks, and touched with sorrow in his heart, he groaned loudly, and said to the brother accompanying him: 'Do you see that sheep walking so meekly among those goats? I tell you, in the same way our Lord Jesus Christ, meek and humble, walked among the Pharisees and chief priests. So I ask you, my son, in your love for him to share my compassion for this little sheep. After we have paid for it, let us lead this little one from the midst of the goats' (1C 77).

Spontaneously compassionate though they were, incidents like this functioned as acted parables, conveying something of Francis's deepest apprehensions of God to his brothers.

Conclusion

There are aspects of Francis, such as this last example, which doubtless seem alien to our time and place. But there is much in Francis to
be appreciated and retrieved. His is a creation mysticism thoroughly
rooted in and coherent with the orthodox mainstream of Christian
belief and life. Essentially it was the biblical understanding of creation
that Francis lived more profoundly and intensely perhaps than any
other Christian has done.

10.

Biodiversity – a Biblical-Theological Perspective

Living in an Age of Mass Extinction

In a recent book Heather Rogers describes a scene in Indonesia (now the world's third largest emitter of carbon dioxide, after China and the USA):

> Imagine millions of acres of dense rain forest teeming with the world's most diverse flora and fauna. A crew armed with chain saws and bull-dozers forges a narrow path through the trees. The workers begin to rip away and flatten the forest, as wildlife, including endangered species such as orangutans, flee for their lives. A bulldozer shoves innumerable splintered trees into tangled piles that stretch for miles, and crews set them alight. Ferocious fires blast through what was once a dynamic web of life, leaving behind a carbon dioxide-filled haze and a silent, charred wasteland. After the forest has been erased it's almost impossi-ble to imagine what was done there.[1]

These huge clearances are to make way for oil palm plantations, which are grown partly to be used as vegetable oil in all sorts of processed food, but also to a considerable extent to produce biofuels, the allegedly green fuels that it was hoped would cut the level of car-bon dioxide emissions from cars. In fact, burning the forests releases massive amounts of CO_2 and the palm oil plantations themselves can-not absorb nearly as much CO_2 as the rain forests they replace.

---

[1] Heather Rogers, *Green Gone Wrong: How Our Economy is Undermining the Environmental Revolution* (London: Verso, 2010), p. 2.

Deforestation globally accounts for 20 per cent of the world's CO_2 emissions. Nevertheless, Indonesia aims, despite its formally strict environmental regulations, to expand the acreage it devotes to oil palm plantations from its current 16 million acres to almost 26 million by 2015.[2] (Brazil, on the other hand, has had some success in reducing the rate of deforestation in the Amazon.) The Indonesian story goes to show the complexity of the predicament the world is in. What seemed like a good way of slowing climate change without having to reduce automobile use in the USA (and other parts of the affluent West) turns out to exacerbate perhaps the most effective way in which human beings are currently destroying the world's biodiversity – and without even reducing CO_2 emissions.

In most people's environmental awareness the ongoing process of mass extinction of species has been overshadowed recently by climate change – or else simply absorbed into climate change. It is true that climate change will magnify the processes of extinction that are already underway, but those processes have a momentum of their own. There was, of course, a green movement and much public concern about the environment long before climate change entered our radar. There was already much to be concerned about, and while too many people are still sceptical about climate change, there is no denying the destruction of the rainforests or the worldwide decline of amphibians, the emptying of life from the over-fished areas of the oceans or the very worrying decline of bees. Understandable though a focus on climate change may be, the loss of biodiversity for other reasons merits our attention.

The statistics of biodiversity are staggering. About 1.8 million species have been described, classified and named. But the number of unknown species is undoubtedly much higher than that. Scientists can only make informed guesses, but the guesses range from ten million to a hundred million. A vast number of these are insects and micro-organisms – without which the rest of the community of living things would disintegrate. Globally there are biodiversity hotspots, many in the tropics or on islands, where the concentration of biodiversity is astonishing, but it is remarkable enough in many other places. Previously unknown species are turning up all the time, at the rate of more than three hundred a day. Many, of course, are the insects and micro-organisms, but there are plants and animals too, even large ones. In 2008 a massive palm tree, eighteen metres in height, one of

---

[2] Rogers, *Green Gone Wrong*, pp. 99–100.

the largest flowering plants on the planet, previously unknown to science, was discovered in Madagascar. More than four hundred new species of mammal have been described since 1993, and they include twenty-five new species of primate discovered as recently as the last decade. A single expedition to north Vietnam in 2002 discovered more than a hundred new plant species. New species still appear even in the United Kingdom. Increasingly, it seems, known species are being found actually to consist of two distinct species, as in the case of the British pipistrelle bat, which was recognized to comprise two species only in the 1990s. The ocean floors, 70 per cent of the surface of the planet, are undoubtedly rich in undiscovered species of astonishingly different kinds from anything we otherwise know.

Of course, a great many species are disappearing from the world before they have even been discovered. One small piece of tropical forest might contain thousands of species limited to that area. Who knows what industrial trawling of the ocean floors must have destroyed forever? One reaction to such considerations is to point out that extinction of species is a natural part of the history of life on earth. Species have always gone extinct and new species evolve. While this is true, the scale is incomparable. What the scientists call the background rate of extinction – the normal rate at which species go extinct outside abnormal periods of mass extinction – is one species per million per year. The current rate is estimated to be at least a thousand species per million a year. The current rate is at least a thousand times the normal. To replace those extinct species with new ones would take nature thousands, probably millions of years. As one source puts it, 'The extinction outputs far exceed the speciation inputs, and Earth is becoming biologically impoverished because of it.'[3]

We are living through an age of mass extinction, the sixth in the history of life on earth. The last such extinction, the fifth, occurred 65,000 years ago, when the dinosaurs, after dominating the earth for 150 million years, died out, mainly, it is now thought, through the effects of an asteroid hitting the earth. In the sixth mass extinction, humans are the asteroid.

This process of anthropogenic mass extinction is not of recent origin. It seems to have begun many thousands of years ago as humans spread across the earth. Before they arrived there were megafauna in

---

[3] P.R. Ehrlich and A.H. Ehrlich, 'The Value of Biodiversity', in *Biodiversity and Conservation*, vol. 1: *History, Background and Concepts* (ed. Richard J. Ladle; London: Routledge, 2009), pp. 609–89, here p. 683.

most places – the big animals (weighing ten kilograms or more), such as now survive only in Africa and tropical Asia. There were, for example, the big flightless birds (nine or ten feet tall) of New Zealand and Australia, the elephant birds of Madagascar, tortoises the size of cars, woolly mammoths, gigantic deer, giant ground sloths, twenty-three feet long lizards, and in the oceans the sea-cow – I mention only a few of those that are easily described or have names other than Latin ones. There were many more. Whether the megafauna went extinct mostly because humans hunted them is debated. There are at least three other suggested explanations (including the possibility that humans successfully competed with them for the same resources). But there is a common pattern: the megafauna of an area of the globe go extinct soon after humans first settle there. As one scholar puts it: 'Direct human responsibility for these ancient extinctions . . . has not been conclusively proved, but we have been repeatedly found at the scene of the crime holstering a smoking gun.'[4] These were animals with no natural predators until humans arrived, therefore easily hunted, and with a slow birth rate that made it hard for the species to recover from losses. In the case of New Zealand, the phenomenon happened as late as the thirteenth-fourteenth centuries, because the islands had no human inhabitants until the Maoris arrived, a few hundred settlers who soon butchered some 160,000 moas.

It is not perhaps appropriate to pass moral judgment on our ancestors, who lived, after all, before agriculture made hunting less vital to survival. But don't we feel the loss of the megafauna? Aren't we thrilled to hear about them, like the fabulous beasts in the medieval bestiaries? Medieval people thought they could find the griffons, the unicorns and the dragons if they travelled far enough; we know that the elephant birds, the giant koalas and the ground sloths are gone forever. Small children are fascinated by dinosaurs, but for most adults the age of the dinosaurs seems alien. We humans would not belong in it, but the megafauna lived in our world and we miss them. I like to imagine the scene in Genesis 2 where God brings the animals to Adam for him to give names to them, for him to recognize them as fellow-members of his world, and I see not just the familiar species, but also the ten-foot high moas, the giant kangaroos and the huge lumbering beasts whose proper names, given to them once by their human predators, we have forgotten.

---

[4] Jonathan Silvertown, *Fragile Web: What Next for Nature?* (London: Natural History Museum, 2010), p. 167.

Nostalgia for the megafauna has a more practical effect in the contemporary world. It is the surviving megafauna that most people most want to save from extinction. The flagship species, everybody's favourite endangered species, are mostly big ones: the giant panda, the mountain gorilla, the tiger, the bald eagle, the humpback whale, and others. We love them now that we have lost most of them.

The megafauna were not the only casualties of human colonization. Across the Pacific islands where the Polynesians settled, half the species of birds vanished, especially the flightless ones that didn't know they needed to fly until humans arrived. 'Homo sapiens, serial killer of the biosphere,' biologist Edward O. Wilson calls us.[5] Modern Europeans and Americans continued the process by bringing technology to bear. The invention of steam-powered trawlers in Victorian Britain began the deadly trawling of our seas that has turned habitats once teeming with life into oceanic deserts. But the engine of the mass extinction now occurring all around us is, of course, destruction or pollution of habitat.

> Humanity today is on a rampage of changing natural habitats dramatically: cutting them down, plowing them up, overgrazing them, paving them over, damming and diverting water, flooding or draining areas, spraying them with pesticides and acid rain, pouring oil into them, changing their climates, exposing them to increased ultraviolet radiation, and on and on.[6]

It is important to remember that living creatures belong to ecosystems, delicately balanced communities of life. If we wish to preserve biodiversity we shall not get far by saving individual species, even if some can be transplanted elsewhere, with unpredictable results as the history of invasive species shows. Preserving ecosystems has to be the priority, and it is at least moderately good news that the Nagoya protocol, agreed in October 2010 by 103 nations, sets targets of increasing protected land across the world from the present 12 per cent to 17 per cent and protected oceans from the present 1 per cent to 10 per cent.

---

[5] Edward O. Wilson, *The Future of Life* (London: Abacus, 2003), p. 94.
[6] Ehrlich and Ehrlich, 'The Value', p. 683.

Biodiversity and Conservation of Species in the Old Testament

The Old Testament recognizes biodiversity

The Old Testament writers were well aware of biodiversity. This is most obviously the case in the very first chapter of the Bible, the account of the creation of the world in six days (which I take to be a poetic, not a literal account of creation). It is a very formulaic account, with key phrases repeated over and over. One such phrase is: 'of every kind' or 'according to their kind'. We hear of fruit trees of every kind, seed-bearing plants of every kind, sea creatures of every kind, birds of every kind, wild animals of every kind, domestic animals of every kind, creeping things (i.e. reptiles and insects) of every kind. In all the phrase occurs ten times, scattered across the accounts of the third, the fifth and the sixth days of creation (Gen. 1:11,12,21,24,25). To say that this passage recognizes biodiversity is an understatement. It *celebrates* biodiversity. It paints a picture of a world teeming with many, many different forms of life. Another formula that occurs in the accounts of the fifth and sixth days is the statement that 'God blessed them' (1:22,28). God's blessing is his gift of fecundity. He enables the creatures to 'be fruitful and multiply'. Not only diversity but also abundance belongs to the Creator's will for his creation.

All the English translations of Genesis 1 seem to use the word 'kind' (creatures 'of every kind' or 'according to their kinds'), but we could justifiably translate the Hebrew word (*min*) as species. In the Hebrew Bible this word is only used for kinds of plants or animals, not for kinds of any other things. That is how we use the word species in English. In the story of Noah we can see that the writers did have the concept of species in at least rudimentary form. In the case of animals, at least, they knew that it takes a male and a female of a particular species to reproduce that species. For each species to survive, there have to be two of everything, one of each gender. Not all ancient people were quite so clear about that. This does not mean that ancient Israelites could distinguish species with the accuracy we can today, and they certainly had no idea of the vast numbers of species we now know to exist. But they did know that if you breed a horse and a donkey, you get a mule, which is infertile, and so they did not approve of mules. Cross-breeding of species seemed to violate the fundamental distinctions that made for diversity in God's creation and so was forbidden by the law of Moses (Lev. 19:19).

The sheer, abundant variety of the creatures is also celebrated in the great creation psalm, Psalm 104. When the psalmist has described some of the creatures of the land, he breaks into praise:

> O LORD, how manifold are your works!
> In wisdom you have made them all;
> the earth is full of your creatures. (v. 24)[7]

Then he moves on to the sea:

> Yonder is the sea, great and wide,
> creeping things innumerable are there,
> living things both small and great. (v. 25)

The Israelites were not very familiar with the sea. They were not a sea-faring people. They thought of the sea as a peculiarly dangerous place for humans. But they knew that it was teeming with living creatures, strange and wonderful, far more than they could count or catalogue. Most likely in those days the eastern Mediterranean was much more abundantly full of life than it is now. For the psalmist, this sheer diversity is part of what makes God's creation so admirable and amazing. The diversity of creation manifests the wisdom of the Creator. For the Old Testament writers it is natural to connect the two.

God delights in biodiversity

Another refrain that runs through the six-day creation story in Genesis 1 is: 'God saw that it was good.' At the end of his work of creation on each day, God looks at his work, is satisfied with it, admires it, pronounces it good. At the end of the sixth day, he 'saw . . . that . . . it was very good'. The whole is greater than the parts. It all belongs together and the finished whole is not just good, but very good. Still, every part of creation, just in itself, is good. It has value for God. We can enliven the language a bit. 'God saw that it was good' means: he was delighted with it. And among the things that delighted him must be, because it is such a prominent feature of the account, the sheer, abundant variety of creatures.

God's delight in the diverse reality of his creatures also appears in the book of Job. When God finally answers Job's complaints, what he

---

[7] Biblical quotations in this chapter are from the NRSV.

does is take Job on a panoramic tour of God's creation – not a physical tour, but a tour in the imagination, as the great poetry of these chapters evokes one after another the wonders of the natural world. The intention is to evoke Job's awe and to put Job in his place, as it were.

Having taken Job in imagination through the cosmos, God homes in on the animal creation and describes ten specific creatures – all animals or birds. They are the lion, the raven, the mountain goat, the deer, the wild ass, the wild ox, the sand grouse (usually translated as ostrich),[8] the warhorse, the hawk and the vulture. These particular ten are selected largely because of their magnificent wildness. They are to remind Job that the world does not revolve around him, that it is full of creatures with whom he has nothing to do and whom he could not dream of controlling. Yet God delights in them, and the poetry conveys his delight. Take, for example, the vulture. God says to Job:

> Is it at your command that the vulture mounts up
> > and makes her nest on high?
> She lives on the rock and makes her home
> > in the fastness of the rocky crag.
> From there she spies the prey;
> > her eyes see it from far away.
> Her young ones suck up blood;
> > and where the slain are, there she is. (Job 39:27–30)[9]

The vulture, with its blood-sucking chicks, is not perhaps a bird for whom most of us have instinctively warm feelings. But the poetry works rather like a David Attenborough wild-life documentary. We are moved by the wondrous otherness of the creatures. None of us would want to control such a creature. Its wildness delights us, and we can sense God's own delight in it. In all their wildness and diversity, God is proud of these creatures.

These ten animals and birds are among the jewels in the crown of creation. They are the sort of charismatic creatures few people would want to go extinct. It is easy to raise support for the conservation of creatures like these – like the panda, the tiger, the polar bear, or the

---

[8] I have been persuaded by Arthur Walker-Jones, 'The So-Called Ostrich in the God Speeches of the Book of Job (Job 39, 13–18)', *Bib* 86 (2005): pp. 494–510, that the reference is more probably to the sand grouse.

[9] This translation is adapted from the NRSV, substituting 'vulture' for 'eagle', and 'she' for 'it'.

great white shark. And with creatures like these, it is easy to appeal to something more than narrow utility to humans. People simply feel that it is good that such creatures exist, even if they never encounter them themselves. People have a gut-feeling sense of what a loss it would be to the creation if such magnificent creatures went extinct.

Of course, the vast majority of the millions of species that may be in danger of extinction do not have such an appeal. To most of us one species of beetle looks much like a hundred others. We have even less appreciation for molluscs, fungi, very small plants and micro-organisms, and to care about their preservation we need arguments that go beyond the cuddliness of the panda or the magnificence of the tiger. But all of these very humble members of the community of creation have some who appreciate them, some people who enthusiastically devote their lives to studying them. Entomologists, I imagine, really can sense something of God's delight in every single species of beetle.

All creatures live to glorify God

A biblical theme that I think has been undeservedly neglected by Christians in the modern period is the idea that the whole creation worships God.[10] This is, so to speak, the corollary of God's delight in his whole creation. He responds to them with delight and they respond to him with praise and celebration. Not that in most cases they have words to do so, or even the sort of consciousness that can intentionally focus on their Creator, but simply by being themselves, being and doing what God created them to be and do, they bring glory to God.

In that sense we should see the other creatures as fellow-worshippers with us of the Creator who made us all. Psalm 148 is far from the only, but it is the fullest biblical passage on this theme.[11] It calls on all the creatures, from the angels in heaven, through all the different categories of creatures, to praise the Lord. Long before people are mentioned, it gives us a picture of creation as a great choir engaged in singing God's praises, a choir we are then invited to join. By praising God through all they are and do, the other creatures help us to praise him too, not only with our lips but in our lives. We who so easily fail

---

[10] See Chapter 7 in this volume.

[11] I am excluding here the *Benedicite*, which belongs to the apocryphal Additions to Daniel, which are part of the canon of Scripture for the Roman Catholic and Eastern Orthodox churches.

to praise God, whether in words or in life, are helped and encouraged to do so by all the ceaseless worship of the rest of creation.

In the ancient world many people worshipped other creatures – heavenly bodies, trees, even animals. The Bible redirects that praise. All the creatures are creatures, created by God, not gods who should be worshipped. On the contrary, the creatures themselves worship God, and our proper response to them is to join in their praise of God. From divinities to be worshipped they become fellow-worshippers of the only true God.

Many Christians have been suspicious of green attitudes to the world because they fear some sort of pantheism. The Bible, they point out, has de-divinized the creation. True, but I would say it has not de-sacralized creation. As creatures who belong to God their creator, the non-human creatures are not divine but they are sacred to God. If we gave more attention to the creatures as our fellow-worshippers, we would not be so prone to instrumentalize them, to regard them as having value only if we can make use of them for our own needs and desires.

The various creatures have specific habitats

Psalm 104 is the equivalent within the book of Psalms to the first chapter of Genesis within the Pentateuch. It is the psalm of creation, and we might even call it the ecological psalm. I have already mentioned it because like Genesis 1 it celebrates the immense diversity of creation, and makes that a subject of praise to God. But there is another prominent feature of it. As it ranges over the various categories of living creatures – mentioning each time the general category, such as wild animals or birds of the air, but then giving specific examples of each – it depicts for each a specific habitat that God has provided for each species: fir trees for storks to nest in, rocks for the rock badgers, forests for the lions, and so forth. There is even an allocation of the hours of the day: the night for the wild animals of the forest to hunt, the daylight hours for humans to do their work. All the various creatures have their place in God's carefully designed whole, and humans have a place among others. In this observation of habitat there is also a recognition of interdependence. The psalmist does not mean that trees were created only for birds to nest in, but he does see that some creatures depend on others for life. There is here at least a first step in the direction of recognizing what are now called ecosystems. We cannot consider each species independently of others, because they are so often bound up together in a delicate web of interdependence. Preservation of species requires, as we now know, preservation of the ecosystems within which they live.

Human kinship with other creatures

All too often in the history of Christian thought and in the history of western thought humans have been elevated above the natural world as though we did not really belong to it. We have tried to relate to other creatures as demi-gods rather than as fellow-creatures, and the results have been in many cases catastrophic. But this is not a biblical view. Humans are *distinctive* among the creatures, but the creation narratives also make quite clear our *kinship* with other creatures. Genesis 1 makes the point by placing the creation of humans not on a separate day, but on the day devoted to the creation of land animals. Being land animals themselves, humans do not get a day to themselves.

Genesis 2 depicts our kinship with the other creatures of earth more vividly and emphatically. God creates Adam out of the dust of the earth. As so often in the Hebrew Bible an ontological relationship is signified by a play on words. Adam is not really a name, but an ordinary word for human being, and Genesis 2:7 says that God formed the human being ('*adam*) from the dust of the earth ('*adamah*), just as he then also formed every animal and bird from the earth (2:19). We are earthy creatures, we belong to the earth, and we belong with the other creatures of earth. True, Adam only lives because God takes his earthy form and breathes the breath of life into him, but this too is the breath of life we share with all other living creatures (cf. 6:17; 7:15,22).

Had we paid sufficient attention to this, we could not have come to regard the earth and its creatures as dispensable, as though we did not really belong to it. Once we recover the sense of our kinship to all other creatures, we cannot be indifferent to the fate of other creatures on earth.

Humans and other creatures are fellow-creatures in the community of the earth

Much that I have said already implies this, but the notion of a community of creation is worth highlighting as a useful model for thinking about our place in creation. The term itself does not come from Scripture, but, like many of the terms we use to talk about what the

Bible teaches, it encapsulates a way of thinking we do find in Scripture. Perhaps one of its most potent expressions in the Old Testament is in Genesis 9.

After the flood, in which Noah has preserved every species of land animal and bird, God makes a covenant with (as he puts it, speaking to Noah) 'you and your descendants after you, and with every living creature that is with you, the birds, the domestic animals, and every animal of the earth with you, as many as came out of the ark' (Gen 9:9–10). He later calls it a covenant between God and 'all flesh that is on the earth' (9:16). The other creatures are partners to the covenant, along with humans. In this respect this covenant is unique among the biblical covenants, but the content of the covenant explains why it is. In this covenant God promises all earth's creatures that he will never again destroy the earth and its creatures in a deluge. The covenant secures the earth as a reliable living space for all the creatures of earth. So all the creatures of the earth are interested parties. The earth is their common home. With them we form the community to which God has given the earth for our common home. We have no right to evict other members of the community from the home God has given us all to share.

Genesis has no illusions about this community. After the flood it remains a community within which conflict and violence constantly break out. These evils for which the flood was a judgment are not eradicated but they are restrained. A price is put on the lives of living creatures (9:2–6). All is not sweetness and light, but God nevertheless does not surrender the intention that his creatures should share the earth he has given them. The covenant is his first step towards the renewal and perfecting of the community of his earthly creatures.

Adam as the first taxonomist

In Genesis 1 the birds and the animals are created before humanity, but in Genesis 2 it is the other way around – a sure sign that these accounts are not to be read literally. In Genesis 2, as the story goes, God sees that Adam, still the only living creature in God's world, needs a partner. It is not good for him to be alone. So, first, God creates every species of animal and every species of bird and brings them to Adam for him to give them names. He does so, but none of them is found suitable to be Adam's partner (2:18–20). Then God takes one of Adam's ribs and out of it produces the woman, whom Adam also names. But this time he really has a partner: 'This at last is bone of my bones and flesh of my flesh' (2:23) – a partner of the same species.

Clearly the animals in the story function partly as a foil to Eve. Their unsuitability to be partners for Adam highlights the fact that only a creature corresponding as closely to him as Eve does can be a suitable partner. We need not, of course, suppose that God had to try out all the animals on Adam, before realizing that it would need another kind of act of creation to make a creature who would really meet the need. Nor should we suppose that the female human being was an afterthought, created only when it became clear that the male could not manage by himself. These are just features of the way the story makes its point.

While the animals can evidently be no substitute for the very special relationship of man and woman, we need not suppose that they cannot be companions of humans in any way at all. Clearly that is not the case. But what the story says positively about the animals is that Adam gives them names. This has sometimes been understood as an act of authority, an exercise of the dominion over other creatures that God gave to humans in Genesis 1:28. But the idea that in the Hebrew Bible naming expresses authority is actually not at all well evidenced,[12] and we should not miss the implication that if Adam's naming of the animals is an assertion of authority over them, so must be his naming of Eve.

Adam is not in this story ruling the animals; he is recognizing them as fellow-creatures and giving them a place in his mental construction of the world. We do not give names to other species so that we can exercise power over them, but in order to recognize their place in the natural world. Adam is the first taxonomist. He appreciates the diversity of the creatures. He recognizes their diversity and writes it into his vision of the world by giving each species its own name.

Solomon as naturalist

King Solomon is the Bible's pre-eminent example of wisdom. In the biblical narrative God gives Solomon his exceptional wisdom (1 Kgs. 3:3–14), and if Solomon's wisdom failed him when it came to ruling his subjects and assembling his harem, it was signally expressed in other ways that made him an international reputation and brought even the queen of Sheba from the proverbially wise East to test Solomon's wisdom and marvel at it (1 Kgs. 4:29–34; 10:1–13).

---

[12] See George W. Ramsey, 'Is Name-Giving an Act of Domination in Genesis 2:23 and Elsewhere?' *CBQ* 50 (1988): pp. 24–35.

The passage in 1 Kings that concerns us now is this:

> God gave Solomon very great wisdom, discernment, and breadth of
> understanding as vast as the sand on the seashore, so that Solomon's
> wisdom surpassed the wisdom of all the people of the east, and all the
> wisdom of Egypt. He was wiser than anyone else, wiser than Ethan the
> Ezrahite, and Heman, Calcol, and Darda, children of Mahol; his fame
> spread throughout all the surrounding nations. He composed three
> thousand proverbs, and his songs numbered a thousand and five. He
> would speak of trees, from the cedar that is in the Lebanon to the hys-
> sop that grows in the wall; he would speak of animals, and birds, and
> reptiles, and fish. People came from all the nations to hear the wisdom
> of Solomon; they came from all the kings of the earth who had heard of
> his wisdom. (1 Kgs. 4:29–34)

Evidently much of Solomon's wisdom concerned natural history. He
was interested in flora as well as fauna. In the Bible's capacious understanding of wisdom, these things evidently have a positive and
important place.

Humans to fill and to subdue the earth (land), but not at the expense of other creatures

I have deliberately left until this point any discussion of the famous
passage about the role of humans in creation in Genesis 1, where God
says to the newly created human pair: 'Be fruitful and multiply, and
fill the earth and subdue it; and have dominion over the fish of the sea
and over the birds of the air and over every living thing that moves
upon the earth' (Gen. 1:28). It is not often well enough noticed that
this command refers to two rather different matters. It refers first to
the relationship of humans to the earth, secondly to their relationship
to other living creatures. The latter is the dominion, and we will come
to it under the next heading. Having dominion over other living creatures is not the same thing as subduing the earth.

'Be fruitful and multiply, and fill the earth and subdue it.' Humans
are not alone in being told to be fruitful and to multiply and to fill. The
fish are to multiply and fill the sea, the birds are to multiply on earth
(1:22), and although the text is not explicit we must assume that the
creatures of the land are also to be fruitful and multiply. Only humans
are told to fill the earth and *to subdue* the earth – and in their case the
two activities go closely together. Only by means of agriculture were

humans able to fill the earth, to live in at least a large proportion of the available land space. To subdue the earth is to take possession and to work the soil in order to make it yield more food for humans than it would otherwise do.

But what about all the other land animals? Are humans to fill the earth at their expense? Are humans supposed to supplant them? God's words to the humans continue in this way:

> See, I have given you every plant yielding seed that is upon the face of all the earth, and every tree with seed in its fruit; you shall have them for food. And to every beast of the earth, and to every bird of the air, and to everything that creeps on the earth, everything that has the breath of life, I have given every green plant for food. (Gen. 1:29–30)

Why does God tell humans that he has given every plant for food for the other living creatures? Why doesn't he say this to the animals themselves? It is not because they cannot understand him, for in verse 22 he has already spoken to the sea creatures and the birds. Surely it is because humans need to know this. They need to know that the produce of the earth is not intended to feed them alone, but also all the living species of the earth. Humans are not to fill the earth and subdue it to the extent of leaving no room and no sustenance for the other creatures who share the earth with them. God has given them too the right to live from the soil. So the human right to make use of the earth, to live from it, is far from unlimited. It must respect the rights of other creatures. Once again, we come up against the biblical fact that we are one creature among others, and that that is how God intended it to be.

Humans have 'dominion' (caring responsibility) for other living creatures

The idea of dominion, an enormously influential idea historically and variously interpreted over the centuries, is what more than anything else has tempted people who knew the text to forget their own creatureliness, to set themselves over the rest of creation as though they did not belong to it but could do as they wished with it, even remake it to their own design. But this is only possible if we take it out of its biblical context – and this is why I have delayed discussion of it until this point in the argument, when we have learned a great many other things from the Bible about the relationship of humans to other creatures.

Dominion is a role within creation, not over it. Other creatures are first and foremost our fellow-creatures, and only when we appreciate them as such can we properly exercise the distinctive role that the Genesis creation narrative gives us in relation to other creatures. It is not the only way we relate to other creatures, but it is a distinctive one.

There is no need here to labour the point that the dominion should be understood as a role of caring responsibility, not exploitation, because this is now widely agreed. The point I do wish to labour is that it is a responsibility for *fellow-creatures*. Since Genesis depicts it as a kind of royal function, the rule of a king over others, it is worth recalling the only passage in the law of Moses that refers to the role of the king in Israel (Deut. 17:14–20). There it is emphasized that the king is one among his brothers and sisters, his fellow-Israelites, and should not forget it, should not accumulate wealth or arms or indulge in any of the ways kings usually exalt themselves above their subjects. Only if they remember their fundamental solidarity with their people will kings be able to rule truly for the benefit of their people. Similarly, only when humans remember their fundamental solidarity with their fellow-creatures will they be able to exercise their distinctive authority within creation for the benefit of other creatures.

Finally, in our present context it is very well worth pondering the fact that the most obvious example Genesis itself provides of the exercise of the dominion is Noah's preservation of all the species of earth in the ark.

Dominion begins from appreciating God's valuation of his creation

A significant aspect of the Genesis 1 six-day creation account is that before we humans read of our responsibility for other living creatures we are taken through a narrative of creation that stresses God's delight in each stage of his work. We are invited to share God's appreciation of his creation before we learn of our distinctive role within it. It follows, surely, that our approach to exercising dominion should be rooted in that fundamental appreciation of the created world as God has made it. We may then be less inclined to spoil it in our attempts to reshape it.

Dominion is to be exercised in letting be just as much as in intervention

Over the centuries people got used to thinking of the human dominion over other creatures as activity. It got to the point in the modern period where the human task came to be conceived as constant, ongoing activity to transform the world into one that would suit us much better than the natural world does. The result is that in fact there is little if any part of the planet that has not been to some extent affected by human activity, and we have all too slowly woken up to the fact that there is a lot we would really like to preserve as it is, because the natural world has value that does not require our constant interference to improve it.

In this situation it is vital that we re-conceive the Genesis dominion as a matter of letting creation be, at least as much as it is a matter of intervention. In fact, this aspect is really rather clear in Scripture itself if we consider those parts of the law of Moses that prescribe Israel's ways of relating to the land of Israel and its other living creatures. We should recall the sabbatical institutions – the weekly Sabbath, when no work was to be done, even by domestic animals, and the Sabbatical Year and the Jubilee, when the land was to be left fallow and not farmed. In the Sabbatical Year, fields, vineyards and orchards were to be left to rest, the produce not gathered, so that 'the poor of your people may eat; and what they leave the wild animals may eat' (Exod. 23:11; cf. Lev. 25:7). Even within the cultivated part of the land of Israel, wild animals are expected to be able to live. We could see this as a kind of symbol of respect for wild nature, reminding both ancient Israel and ourselves that dominion includes letting nature be itself.

Why Try to Preserve Biodiversity?

Environmentalists who advocate conservation, seeking to persuade others of its importance, tend to accumulate a variety of arguments, some of which may appeal to some people, others to others. This is a reasonable strategy in view of the fact that widespread support is necessary if the earth's biodiversity is to be preserved to any significant extent. But perhaps the impression is too often given that most people are only going to be convinced by appeals to self-interested pragmatism, whereas these environmentalists themselves owe their passion for preserving biodiversity to other kinds of consideration.

There are, of course, many reasons why much of the natural world is useful to us. There are also good arguments to the effect that there are probably many benefits to us of which we are as yet unaware. Since a third of prescription medicines have been produced from chemical compounds found in plants and fungi, especially those of the tropical forests, it is more than likely that many of the thousands of species unique to very small areas of habitat in the rainforests –

those that are disappearing daily before they can be discovered – will prove of pharmaceutical value in time, provided they survive.

However, the most recent trend in argument for conserving biodiversity is prompted by the recognition that it is economists who really run the world. One has the impression that for many environmentalists this is a sad recognition, born of disappointment. For some environmental scientists admitting that it is not scientists who rule the world is a bitter pill to swallow. Others are disillusioned idealists who have transformed themselves into hard-nosed players in the capitalist global marketplace. In any case, we hear increasingly the slogan that people only value what they can put a monetary value on. It has spawned the extraordinarily ambitious attempt to evaluate the benefits of the biosphere, in other words to put a market price on what are called ecosystem services.

Ecosystem services are the direct and indirect services provided by ecosystems. Take, for example, the humble dung beetle, whose services to humanity we probably do not often think about. Dung beetles are invaluable to cattle-farming. 'They prevent fouling of forage, promote dung decomposition into useful plant fertilizer, and reduce the populations of pests and flies.' According to my source the 'value of this service amounts to $US 380 million annually at 2006 prices'.[13] But in many cases it is not just the contribution of one species that counts, but the services of whole ecosystems. Forests soak up a lot of the CO_2 we emit. They remove pollutants from the atmosphere. Vegetation and soil biodiversity reduce flooding and release clean drinking water. Released in October 2010, the UN's report known as TEEB (The Economics of Ecosystems and Biodiversity) calculated that the real cost of damaging nature is at least ten times greater than the cost of maintaining the ecosystem as it is so that we can reap the associated benefits. For example, setting up and running a comprehensive network of protected areas across the world would cost US$45 billion a year globally, but the benefits of preservation within these zones would be worth US$4–5 trillion a year. This report trumps the Stern report which did the same thing for climate change. TEEB claims that the financial case for preserving biodiversity is even stronger than the financial case for tackling climate change.

There are problems with such calculations (even if we could really suppose that they are more than wild guesses). Although they seek to

---

[13] Ken Thompson, *Do We Need Pandas? The Uncomfortable Truth about Biodiversity* (Dartington, Devon: Green Books, 2010), p. 59.

play economists at their own game, for them to make any difference within the free market requires a revolution in the ways humans – not to say corporations – think about and do business. According to another report only two of the world's hundred biggest companies believe that declining biodiversity is a strategic threat to their businesses.[14] There is also a question about what kinds of biodiversity would benefit from taking these reckonings seriously as the basis for conservation. Consider the flagship endangered species, those that easily engage many people's concerns. Would it make any significant difference to the ecosystem services if the Yangtse river dolphin, the giant panda or the tiger disappeared? Even if one threw the profits of tourism into the calculations, would the monetary value of the ecosystem services be appreciably affected?

It is sometimes pointed out that these species, at least, have 'existence value' for many people. In other words, people just feel good about knowing such creatures exist, even if they never see them. What this really means is that people recognize intrinsic value in these creatures. They recognize that it is good that such creatures exist, much as the Genesis creation account does. But the prevalent discourse that requires everything to be put into terms of human benefit and interest states this in the form of a value for people – existence value. It is somehow good *for us* that such creatures exist. As an attempted appeal to self-interest this seriously distorts the fact that people are actually recognizing some objective good, something that is good in itself and for its own sake, whether any of us feel good about it or not. Here the believer has a big advantage, because the world of Genesis 1, for example, is not a human-centred world in which everything has to be justified as somehow in the interests of humans, but a God-centred world in which everything created has value for God. God's appreciation of the natural world and all its members as good bestows intrinsic value on his creatures. That is also where human worth comes from.

I do not mean that believing that God values other creatures leads us to recognize value that we would otherwise, if we did not believe that about God, not recognize at all. I think, on the contrary, that people do recognize intrinsic good in other creatures, especially when it so to speak overtakes us, jolts us out of our more familiar egocentric attitude to the world – when, for example, the beauty of a landscape strikes and absorbs us, when the majesty of a tiger enthralls us, even

---

[14] *Guardian* newspaper, 22 May 2010.

when the cuteness of a giant panda charms us, when we marvel at the intricate design of the smallest and ugliest of insects seen under a microscope. For whereas many of us most of the time are not particularly entranced by the majority of the members of ecosystems – the bugs and the microbes, the algae and the molluscs – they all have their admirers and inspire passionate interest in the scientists who specialize in them. What belief in God and God's valuing of all his creatures can do for us is to draw us out of the egocentric perspectives that so often prevent us from attending to the manifold worth of other creatures. Attending to God should enable us to attend more to his creatures and vice versa.

As creatures of God the creatures are literally priceless and we degrade them by setting a price on them. Compare how we think of other humans. In a commercial world we may set some sort of price on the services other people perform for us but we do not set a price on the existence of other people. The economic arguments for conserving biodiversity, even if we decide they are needed in a world controlled by economists, are nevertheless regrettable and misleading because they reinforce the human-centred illusion that everything else has value only if we think it has value for us and marginalize the real intuitions of intrinsic worth that all of us actually have. It would be better to foster such intuitions and to use them to challenge the world-view of the economists.

There is a more adequate way to think about the so-called ecosystem services. It is not just that the natural world does a lot of things for us, but that we ourselves belong to the natural world. We depend on the intricate web of planetary life just as other creatures do. Because we have spread ourselves so widely and developed such complex and demanding ways of life we are even more intimately interconnected with everything else than most creatures are. We are even more dependent on the health of the whole biosphere than many other creatures are. Destroying any more of the biosphere than we have done already will not just cost us a lot, as though it were just a matter of financial profit and loss. We shall impoverish human life in the process of impoverishing the planet.

Bibliography

Andersen, Francis I. '2 (Slavonic Apocalypse of) Enoch,' in *The Old Testament Pseudepigrapha*, vol. 1 (ed. James H. Charlesworth) London: Darton, Longman & Todd, 1983.

Anderson, Bernhard W. 'Creation and Ecology,' in *Creation in the Old Testament* (ed. Bernhard W. Anderson; London: SPCK/Philadelphia: Fortress, 1984), pp. 1–24.

Anderson, Bernhard W., ed. *Creation in the Old Testament*. London: SPCK/Philadelphia: Fortress, 1984.

Armstrong, Edward A. *Saint Francis: Nature Mystic*. Berkeley/Los Angeles/London: University of California Press, 1973.

Armstrong, Regis J., J.A. Wayne Hellmann and William J. Short eds. *Francis of Assisi: Early Documents*, vol. 1: The Saint. New York: New City Press, 1999.

Attfield, Robin. 'Christian Attitudes to Nature.' *JHI* 44 (1983): pp. 369–386.

Attfield, Robin. *The Ethics of Environmental Concern*. 2nd edition. Athens, Georgia/London: University of Georgia Press, 1991.

Aune, David E. *Revelation 1–5*. WBC 52A. Dallas: Word Books, 1997.

Bacon, Francis. *The Great Instauration and New Atlantis*. Ed. Jerry Weinberger. Arlington Heights, Illinois: AHM Publishing, 1980.

Bacon, Francis. *The Works of Francis Bacon*. Ed. James Spedding, Robert Leslie Ellis, Douglas Denon Heath. London: Longman, 1857–1858.

Ball, Ian, M. Goodall, Clare Palmer and John Reader. *The Earth Beneath: A Critical Guide to Green Theology*. London: SPCK, 1992.

Baranzke, H., and H. Lamberty-Zielinski. 'Lynn White und das dominium terrae (Gen 1,28b): Ein Beitrag zu einer doppelten Wirkungsgeschichte.' *Biblische Notizen* 76 (1995).

Barbour, Ian G., ed. *Western Man and Environmental Ethics*. Reading, Massachusetts/London/Ontario: Addison-Wesley, 1973.

Barr, James. 'Man and Nature: The Ecological Controversy and the Old Testament.' *Bulletin of the John Rylands Library* 55 (1972): pp. 9–32.

Bartholomew, Craig and Thorsten Moritz. *Christ and Consumerism: Critical reflections on the spirit of our age.* Carlisle: Paternoster, 2000.

Bartolomé, Juan José. 'Los Pájaros y los Lirios: Una Aproximación a la Cuestion Ecologica desde Mt 6,25-34.' *EstBíb* 49 (1991): pp. 165–190.

Bauckham, Richard. *Bible and Ecology: Rediscovering the Community of Creation.* London: Darton, Longman & Todd/ Waco, Texas: Baylor University Press, 2010.

Bauckham, Richard. 'First Steps to a Theology of Nature.' *Evangelical Quarterly* 58 (1986): pp. 229–231.

Bauckham, Richard. 'Jesus' Demonstration in the Temple,' in *Law and Religion* (ed. Barnabas Lindars) Cambridge: James Clarke, 1988.

Bauckham, Richard. *The Climax of Prophecy: Studies on the Book of Revelation.* Edinburgh: T.&T. Clark, 1993.

Bauckham, Richard. *The Theology of the Book of Revelation.* Cambridge: Cambridge University Press, 1993.

Beale, Gregory C. *The Book of Revelation.* NIGTC. Grand Rapids: Eerdmans/Carlisle: Paternoster, 1999.

Beckwith, Isbon T. *The Apocalypse of John.* Grand Rapids: Baker 1967 (reprint of 1919 edition).

Beckwith, Roger T. 'The Vegetarianism of the Therapeutae, and the Motives for Vegetarianism in Early Jewish and Christian Circles.' *Revue de Qumran* 13 (1988): pp. 407–410.

Bell, David N. *Wholly Animals: A Book of Beastly Tales.* Cistercian Studies 128. Kalamazoo: Cistercian Publications 1992.

Berry, R.J., ed. *Environmental Stewardship: Critical Perspectives – Past and Present.* London: T.&T. Clark (Continuum), 2006.

Berry, R.J., ed. *The Care of Creation.* Leicester: Inter-Varsity Press, 2000.

Bertrand, Daniel A. *La Vie Grecque d'Adam et d'Eve. Recherches Intertestamentaires* 1. Paris: Maisonneuve, 1987.

Best, Ernest. *Mark: The Gospel as Story.* Edinburgh: T.&T. CLark, 1983.

Best, Ernest. *The Temptation and the Passion: The Markan Soteriology.* SNTSMS 2. Cambridge: Cambridge University Press, 1965.

Betz, Hans Dieter, ed. *Plutarch's Theological Writings and Early Christian Literature.* SCHNT 3. Leiden: Brill, 1975.

Bishop, Eric F. F. *Jesus of Palestine.* London: Lutterworth, 1955.

Black, Matthew. *The Book of Enoch or 1 Enoch.* SVTP 7. Leiden: Brill, 1985.

Blackwell, Trevor and Jeremy Seabrook. *The Revolt Against Change.* London: Vintage, 1993.

Block, Daniel I. *The Book of Ezekiel Chapters 1–24*. NICOT. Grand Rapids: Eerdmans, 1997.

Bodenheimer, Friedrich Simon. *Animal and Man in Bible Lands*. Collection de Travaux de l'Academie Internationale d'Histoire des Sciences 10. Leiden: Brill, 1960.

Bodenheimer, Friedrich Simon. *Animal Life in Palestine*. Jerusalem: L. Mayer, 1935.

Bodo, Murray. *The Way of St Francis*. Glasgow: Collins, 1985.

Boehmer, Julius. *Neutestamentliche Parallelen und Verwandte aus altchristlicher Literatur*. Stuttgart: Greiner & Pfeiffer, 1903.

Boff, Leonardo. *Saint Francis: A Model for Human Liberation*. London: SCM Press, 1982.

Borgen, Peder. 'Man's Sovereignty over Animals and Nature According to Philo of Alexandria,' in *Texts and Contexts* (ed. Tord Fornberg and David Hellholm: Festschrift for Lars Hartman; Oslo: Scandinavian University Press, 1995), pp. 369–389.

Box, G.H. and J.I. Landsman. *The Apocalypse of Abraham*. London: SPCK, 1918.

Bratton, Susan P. 'Oaks, Wolves and Love: Celtic Monks and Northern Forests.' *Journal of Forest History* 33 (1989): pp. 4–20.

Bratton, Susan P. 'The Original Desert Solitaire: Early Christian Monasticism and Wilderness.' *Environmental Ethics* 10 (1988): pp. 31-53.

Brownlee, William H. *Ezekiel 1–19*. WBC 28. Waco: Word Books, 1986.

Buechner, Frederick. Godric. London: Chatto & Windus, 1981.

Caird, George B. *The Revelation of St John the Divine*. BNTC. London; A. & C. Black, 1966.

Cairns, David. *The Image of God in Man*. 2nd edition. London: Collins, 1973.

Cansdale, George. *Animals of Bible Lands*. Exeter: Paternoster, 1970.

Carcopino, Jérôme. *Virgile et le Mystère de la IVe Eglogue*. Paris: L'Artisan du Livre, 1930.

Charlesworth, James H. 'Folk Traditions in Jewish Apocalyptic Literature,' in *Mysteries and Revelations: Apocalyptic Studies since the Uppsala Colloquium* (ed. John J. Collins and James H. Charlesworth; JSPSup 9; Sheffield: Sheffield Academic Press, 1991), pp. 91-113.

Chilton, Bruce D. *Pure Kingdom: Jesus' Vision of God*. Grand Rapids: Eerdmans/ London: SPCK, 1996.

Clancy, Thomas Owen and Gilbert Márkus. *Iona: The Earliest Poetry of a Celtic Monastery*. Edinburgh: Edinburgh University Press, 1995.

Clark, Gillian. 'The Fathers and the Animals: the Rule of Reason?,' in *Animals on the Agenda* (ed. Andrew Linzey and Dorothy Yamamoto; London: SCM Press, 1998), pp. 67–79.

Clark, Stephen R.L. *How to Think about the Earth*. London: Mowbray, 1993.

Clarke, T. E. 'Theological Trends: Creational Spirituality.' *The Way* 29 (1989).

Cohen, Jeremy. *"Be Fertile and Increase, Fill the Earth and Master It": The Ancient and Medieval Career of a Biblical Text*. Ithaca/London: Cornell University Press, 1989.

Cohen, Jeremy. 'The Bible, Man, and Nature in the History of Western Thought: A Call for Reassessment.' *JR* 65 (1985): pp. 155–172.

Cohn-Sherbok, Dan, ed. *Using the Bible Today*. Bellew Publishing, 1991.

Collins, John J. 'Sibylline Oracles,' in *The Old Testament Pseudepigrapha*, vol. 1 (ed. James H. Charlesworth) London: Darton, Longman & Todd, 1983.

Collins, John J. and James H. Charlesworth eds. *Mysteries and Revelations: Apocalyptic Studies since the Uppsala Colloquium*. JSPSup 9. Sheffield: Sheffield Academic Press, 1991.

Colson, Francis Henry. *Philo*. Vol. 8. LCL. London: Heinemann/ Cambridge, Massachussetts: Harvard University Press, 1939.

Cooper, Tim. *Green Christianity*. London: Hodder & Stoughton, 1990.

Cousins, Ewert H. 'Francis of Assisi: Christian Mysticism at the Crossroads,' in *Mysticism and Religious Traditions* (ed. Stephen T. Katz) Oxford: Oxford University Press, 1983.

Croxall, T.H., trans. and ed. *Meditations from Kierkegaard*. London: James Nisbet, 1955.

Dalman, Gustaf. *Jesus-Joshua: Studies in the Gospels*. Trans. Paul P. Levertoff. SPCK, 1929.

Danby, Herbert. *The Mishnah*. Oxford: Clarendon Press, 1933.

Davies, William David and Dale C. Allison. *A Critical and Exegetical Commentary on the Gospel according to Saint Matthew*. Vol. 2. Edinburgh: T. & T. Clark, 1991.

Davies, William David and Dale C. Allison. *A Critical and Exegetical Commentary on the Gospel according to Saint Matthew*. Vol. 3. Edinburgh: T.&T. Clark, 1997.

Davila, James R. *Liturgical Works*. Eerdmans Commentaries on the Dead Sea Scrolls. Grand Rapids: Eerdmans, 2000.

Deissmann, Adolf. *Light from the Ancient East*. 4th edition. London: Hodder & Stoughton, 1927.

Diamond, Jared. *Collapse: How Societies Choose to Fail or Succeed*. London: Allen Lane, 2005.

Dodd, Charles Harold. *The Parables of the Kingdom*. Revised edition. Glasgow: Fontana (Collins), 1961.

Dubois, Jean-Daniel. 'Remarques sur le Fragment de Papias cité par Irénée.' *RHPR* 71 (1991): pp. 6–8.

Dubos, René. 'Franciscan Conservation versus Benedictine Stewardship,' in *Western Man* (ed. Ian G. Barbour), pp.114–136.

Eaton, John. *The Circle of Creation: Animals in the Light of the Bible*. London: SCM Press, 1995.

Echlin, Edward P. *Earth Spirituality: Jesus at the Centre*. New Alresford: Arthur James, 1999.

Echlin, Edward P. 'Let's re-enter God's creation now.' *Month* 252 (1991): pp. 359–364.

Ehrlich, P.R. and A.H. Ehrlich. 'The Value of Biodiversity,' in *Biodiversity and Conservation*, vol. 1: *History, Background and Concepts* (ed. Richard J. Ladle; London: Routledge, 2009), pp. 609–689.

Elliott, Allison Goddard. *Roads to Paradise: Reading the Lives of the Early Saints*. Hanover/London: University Press of New England, 1987.

Evans, Ernest, trans. and ed. *Tertullian's Tract on the Prayer*. London: SPCK, 1953.

Faricy, Robert. *Wind and Sea Obey Him*. London: SCM Press, 1982.

Farrer, Austin. *The Revelation of St. John the Divine*. Oxford: Clarendon, 1964.

Farrington, Benjamin. *The Philosophy of Francis Bacon: An Essay on its Development from 1603 to 1609 with New Translations of Fundamental Texts*. Liverpool: Liverpool University Press, 1964.

Fascher, E. 'Jesus und die Tiere.' *TLZ* 90 (1965): pp. 561–570.

Faulkner, Robert Kenneth. *Francis Bacon and the Project of Progress*. Lanham: Rowman & Littleford, 1993.

Fekkes, Jan. *Isaiah and Prophetic Traditions in the Book of Revelation*. JSNTSup 93. Sheffield: Sheffield Academic Press, 1994.

Feuillet, André. 'L'épisode de la Tentation d'après l'Evangile selon Saint Marc (I,12–13).' *EstBib* 19 (1960): pp. 49–73.

Fitzmyer, Joseph A. *The Gospel According to Luke (X–XXIV)*. AB 28A. New York: Doubleday, 1985.

Ford, Josephine Massyngberde. *Revelation*. AB38. New York: Doubleday 1975.

Fox, Matthew. *Creation Spirituality*. San Francisco: HarperSanFrancisco, 1991.

Fox, Matthew. *Original Blessing*. Santa Fe, New Mexico: Bear, 1983.

Fox, Matthew. *The Coming of the Cosmic Christ*. San Francisco: Harper & Row, 1988.

Freedman, Harry. *Midrash Rabbah: Genesis.* Vol. 2. London: Soncino Press, 1939.

Freedman, Harry. *The Babylonian Talmud: Kiddushin.* London: Soncino Press, 1936).

Fretheim, Terence E. 'Nature's Praise of God In The Psalms.' *Ex Auditu* 3 (1984): pp. 16–30.

Freyne, Sean. *Jesus, a Jewish Galilean: A New Reading of the Jesus-Story.* London: T.&T. Clark (Continuum), 2004.

Giblin, Charles Homer. *The Book of Revelation.* Good News Studies 34. Collegeville, Minnesota: Liturgical Press, 1991.

Glacken, Clarence J. *Traces on the Rhodian Shore: Nature and Culture in Western Thought from Ancient Times to the End of the Eighteenth Century.* Berkeley/Los Angeles: University of California Press, 1967.

Gnilka, Joachim. *Das Evangelium nach Markus.* Vol. 1. EKK 2/1. Zurich: Benziger/Neukirchen-Vluyn: Neukirchener, 1978.

Goodall, M. and John Reader. 'Why Matthew Fox Fails to Change the World,' in *The Earth Beneath: A Critical Guide to Green Theology* (ed. Ian Ball, M. Goodall, Clare Palmer and John Reader) London: SPCK, 1992.

Grässer, Erich. 'ΚΑΙ ΗΝ ΜΕΤΑ ΤΩΝ ΘΗΡΙΩΝ (Mk 1,13b): Ansätze einer theologischen Tierschutzethik,' in *Studien zum Text und zur Ethik des Neuen Testaments: Festschrift zum 80. Geburtstag von Heinrich Greeren* (ed. Wolfgang Schrage) Berlin/New York: de Gruyter, 1986.

Gruenwald, Ithamar. *Apocalyptic and Merkavah Mysticism.* AGAJU 14. Leiden: Brill, 1980.

Guelich, Robert A. *Mark 1–8:26.* WBC 34A. Dallas, Texas: Word, 1989.

Habel, Norman C. *The Earth Story in the Psalms and the Prophets.* The Earth Bible 4. Sheffield: Sheffield Academic Press/Cleveland: Pilgrim Press, 2001.

Habel, Norman C. and Vicky Balabanski ed. *The Earth Story in the New Testament.* Earth Bible 5. Sheffield: Sheffield Academic Press, 2002.

Habig, Marion A., ed. *St. Francis of Assisi: Writings and Early Biographies: English Omnibus of the Sources for the Life of St. Francis.* Chicago: Franciscan Herald Press, 1983.

Halkes, Catharina J.M. *New Creation: Christian Feminism and the Renewal of the Earth.* Trans. C. Romanik. London: SPCK, 1991.

Hall, Douglas John. *Imaging God: Dominion as Stewardship.* Grand Rapids: Eerdmans, 1987.

Hall, Robert G. 'Living Creatures in the Midst of the Throne: Another Look at Revelation 4.6.' *NTS* 36 (1990): pp. 609–613.

Halperin, David J. *The Faces of the Chariot: Early Jewish Responses to Ezekiel's Vision*. TSAJ 16. Tübingen: Mohr Siebeck, 1988.

Hardy, Daniel W. and David F. Ford. *Jubilate: Theology in Praise*. London: Darton, Longman & Todd, 1984.

Harper, William Rainey. *A critical and exegetical commentary on Amos and Hosea* ICC. Edinburgh: T.&T. Clark, 1905.

Hedrick, Charles W. *Parables as Poetic Fictions: The Creative Voice of Jesus*. Peabody, Massachusetts: Hendrickson, 1994.

Hendrikson, William. *More than Conquerors*. London: Inter-Varsity Press, 1962.

Herbert, George. T*he Country Parson, The Temple*. Ed. J. N. Wall. Classics of Western Spirituality. New York/Mahwah: Paulist, 1981.

Hiebert, Theodore. *The Yahwist's Landscape: Nature and Religion in Early Israel*. New York/Oxford: Oxford University Press, 1996.

Hiers, Richard H. 'Ecology, Biblical Theology, and Methodology: Biblical Perspectives on the Environment.' *Zygon* 19 (1984): pp. 43–59.

Himmelfarb, Martha. *Ascent to Heaven in Jewish and Christian Apocalypses*. New York: Oxford University Press, 1993.

Hirsch, Edward. *How to Read a Poem*. Durham, North Carolina: Duke University Center for Documentary Studies, 1999.

Hollander, H.W. and M. de Jonge. *The Testaments of the Twelve Patriarchs: A Commentary*. SVTP 8. Leiden: Brill, 1985.

Holmgren, Virginia C. *Bird Walk Through the Bible*. 2nd edition. New York: Dover, 1988.

Holzmeister, U. '"Jesus lebte mit den wilden Tieren": Mk 1,13,' in *Vom Wort des Lebens: Festschrift für Max Meinertz* (ed. Nikolaus Adler) Münster: Aschendorff, 1951.

Howard, G. 'The Gospel of the Ebionites,' in *Aufstieg und Niedergang der römischen Welt*, vol. 2/25/5 (ed. W. Haase; Berlin/New York: de Gruyter, 1988), pp. 4034–4053.

Howard-Brook, Wes and Anthony Gwyther. *Unveiling Empire: Reading Revelation Then and Now*. Bible and Liberation Series. Maryknoll, New York: Orbis, 1999.

Jeanmaire, Henri. *Le Messianisme de Vergil*. Paris: J. Vrin, 1930.

Katz, Stephen T. *Mysticism and Religious Traditions*. Oxford: Oxford University Press, 1983.

Kee, Howard C. 'Testaments of the Twelve Patriarchs,' in *The Old Testament Pseudepigrapha*, vol. 1 (ed. James H. Charlesworth) London: Darton, Longman & Todd, 1983.

Keel, Othmar. *Jahwe-Visionen und Siegelkunst: Eine neue Deutung der Majestätsschilderungen in Jes 6, Ez 1, und 10 und Sach 4.* SBS 84/85. Stuttgart: Katholisches Bibelwerk, 1977.

Keel, Othmar and Christoph Uehlinger. *Gods, Goddesses and Images of God in Ancient Israel.* Trans. Thomas H. Trapp. Minneapolis: Fortress, 1998.

Keener, Craig S. *A Commentary on the Gospel of Matthew.* Grand Rapids: Eerdmans, 1999.

Kingsbury, Jack D. *The Christology of Mark's Gospel.* Philadelphia: Fortress, 1983.

Klijn, Albertus Frederik Johannes. '2 (Syriac Apocalypse of) Baruch,' in *The Old Testament Pseudepigrapha*, vol. 1 (ed. James H. Charlesworth) London: Darton, Longman & Todd, 1983.

Kovacs, Judith and Christopher Rowland. *Revelation.* Blackwell's Bible Commentaries. Oxford: Blackwell, 2004.

Krolzik, Udo. *Umweltkrise-Folge des Christentums?* Stuttgart/Berlin: Kreuz Verlag, 1979.

Kulik, Alexander. *Retroverting Slavonic Pseudepigrapha: Toward the Original of the Apocalypse of Abraham.* SBL Text-Critical Studies 3. Atlanta: SBL, 2004.

Ladle, Richard J. *Biodiversity and Conservation*, vol. 1: History, Background and Concepts. London: Routledge, 2009.

Lang, David Marshall. *Lives and Legends of the Georgian Saints.* London: Allen & Unwin/New York: Macmillan, 1956.

Leclerc, Eloi. *Le Chant des Sources.* 3rd edition. Paris: Editions Franciscaines, 1975.

Leder, H.-G. 'Sünderfallerzählung und Versuchungsgeschichte: Zur Interpretation von Mc 1 12f.' *ZNW* 54 (1963): pp. 188–216.

Leiss, William. *The Domination of Nature.* New York: George Braziller, 1972.

Leloir, Louis. 'Anges et démons chez les Pères du Desert,' in *Anges et Démons: Actes du Colloque de Liège et de Louvain-La-Neuve 25-26 novembre 1987* (ed. Julian Ries and Henri Limet) Louvain-La-Neuve: Centre d'Histoire des Religions, 1989.

Levison, John R. *Portraits of Adam in Early Judaism: From Sirach to 2 Baruch.* JSPSup 1. Sheffield: JSOT Press, 1988.

Liedke, Gerhard. *Im Bauch des Fisches: Ökologische Theologie.* Stuttgart/Berlin: Kreuz Verlag, 1979.

Leske, Adrian M. 'Matthew 6.25–34: Human Anxiety and the Natural World,' in *The Earth Story in the New Testament* (ed. Norman C. Habel and Vicky Balabanski; *Earth Bible* 5; Sheffield: Sheffield Academic Press, 2002), pp. 15–43.

Lightfoot, Joseph Barber, John Reginald Harmer and Michael W. Holmes. *The Apostolic Fathers*. 2nd edition. Leicester: Apollos, 1990.

Linzey, Andrew. 'The Bible and Killing for Food,' in *Using the Bible Today* (ed. Dan Cohn-Sherbok) Bellew Publishing, 1991.

Linzey, Andrew and Dorothy Yamamoto ed. *Animals on the Agenda*. London: SCM Press, 1998.

William Loader, 'Good News – For the Earth? Reflections on Mark 1.1–15,' in *The Earth Story in the New Testament* (ed. Norman C. Habel and Vicky Balabanski), pp. 28–43.

Low, Mary. *Celtic Christianity and Nature*. Belfast: Blackstaff Press/ Edinburgh: Edinburgh University Press, 1996.

Luz, Ulrich. *Matthew 1–7: A Commentary*. Trans. Wilhelm C. Linss. Edinburgh: T.&T. Clark, 1990.

Macaskill, Grant. *Revealed Wisdom and Inaugurated Eschatology in Ancient Judaism and Early Christianity*. JSJSup 115. Leiden: Brill, 2007.

Macquarrie, John. 'Creation and Environment,' in *Ecology* (ed. David and Eileen Spring), pp. 32-47.

Malina, Bruce J. *One the Genre and Message of Revelation: Star Visions and Sky Journeys*. Peabody, Massachusetts: Hendrickson. 1995.

Marcus, Joel. *Mark 1–8*. AB 27. New York: Doubleday, 1999.

Marshall, E. 'Jesus and the Environment: How Green is Christianity?' *Modern Churchman* 33 (1992).

Marshall, I. Howard. *The Gospel of Luke*. NIGTC. Exeter: Paternoster Press, 1978.

Mauser, Ulrich. *Christ in the Wilderness: The Wilderness Theme in the Second Gospel and its Basis in the Biblical Tradition*. SBT. London: SCM Press, 1963.

Mayor, Joseph Bickersteth. 'Source of the Fourth Eclogue,' in Joseph Bickersteth Mayor, William Warde Fowler and Robert Seymour Conway, *Virgil's Messianic Eclogue: Its Meaning, Occasion, and Sources* (London: J. Murray, 1907), pp. 87–140.

Mayor, Joseph Bickersteth, William Warde Fowler and Robert Seymour Conway. *Virgil's Messianic Eclogue: Its Meaning, Occasion, and Sources*. London: J. Murray, 1907.

McDaniel, Jay B. *Of God and Pelicans: A Theology of Reverence for Life*. Louisville, Kentucky: Westminster/John Knox Press, 1989.

McKibben, Bill. *The Comforting Whirlwind: God, Job, and the Scale of Creation*. Grand Rapids: Eerdmans, 1994.

McKibben, Bill. *The End of Nature*. London: Penguin, 1990.

McNamara, Martin. *The New Testament and the Palestinian Targum to the Pentateuch*. AnBib 27. Rome: Pontifical Biblical Institute, 1966.

Maier, John P. *A Marginal Jew: Rethinking the Historical Jesus*, vol. 2: *Mentor, Message, and Miracles*. New York: Doubleday, 1994.

Mays, James Luther. *Amos*. OTL. London: SCM Press, 1969.

Moltmann, Jürgen. *God for a Secular Society*. Trans. Margaret Kohl. London: SCM Press, 1999.

Moltmann, Jürgen. *God in Creation*. Trans. Margaret Kohl. London: SCM Press, 1985.

Monbiot, George. *Heat: How to Stop the Planet Burning*. 2nd edition. London: Penguin, 2007.

Moncrief, L.W. 'The Cultural Basis of our Environmental Crisis,' in *Western Man* (ed. Ian G. Barbour), pp. 31–42.

Mora, Vincent. *La Symbolique de la Création dans l'Évangile de Matthieu*. Lectio Divina 144. Paris: Cerf, 1991.

Moritz, Thorsten. 'New Testament Voices for an Addicted Society,' in *Christ and Consumerism: Critical reflections on the spirit of our age* (ed. Craig Bartholomew and Thorsten Moritz; Carlisle: Paternoster, 2000), pp. 54–80.

Murray, Robert. *The Cosmic Covenant*. Heythrop Monographs 7. London: Sheed & Ward, 1992.

Nash, Roderick Frazier. *The Rights of Nature: A History of Environmental Ethics*. Madison, Wisconsin: University of Wisconsin Press, 1989.

Newman, B. 'Romancing the Past: A Critical Look at Matthew Fox and the Medieval 'Creation Mystics.'" *Touchstone* 5 (1992): pp. 5–10.

Newsom, Carol A. 'Merkabah Exegesis in the Qumran Sabbath Shirot.' *JJS* 38 (1987): pp. 11–30.

Newsom, Carol A. *Songs of the Sabbath Sacrifice? A Critical Edition*. Harvard Semitic Studies 27. Atlanta, Georgia: Scholars Press, 1985.

Nickelsburg, George W. E. and James C. VanderKam. *1 Enoch: A New Translation*. Minneapolis: Fortress, 2004.

Noble, David F. *The Religion of Technology: The Divinity of Man and the Spirit of Invention*. New York: Penguin, 1999.

Nolland, John. *The Gospel of Matthew*. NIGTC. Grand Rapids: Eerdmans/Bletchley: Paternoster, 2005.

Northcott, Michael S. *The Environment and Christian Ethics*. Cambridge: Cambridge University Press, 1996.

Northcott, Michael S. *A Moral Climate: The Ethics of Global Warming*. London: Darton, Longman & Todd, 2007.

Oelschlaeger, Max. *Caring for Creation: An Ecumenical Approach to the Environmental Crisis*. New Haven/London: Yale University Press, 1994.

Olsthoorn, M.F. *The Jewish Background and the Synoptic Setting of Mt 6,25-33 and Lk, 12,22–31.* Studium Biblicum Franciscanum Analecta 10. Jerusalem: Franciscan Printing House, 1975.

Olyan, Saul M. *A Thousand Thousands Served Him: Exegesis and the Naming of Angels in Ancient Judaism.* TSAJ 36. Tübingen: Mohr Siebeck, 1993.

Osborn, Lawrence. *Guardians of Creation: Nature in Theology and the Christian Life.* Leicester, Apollos, 1993.

Passmore, John. *Man's Responsibility for Nature: Ecological Problems and Western Traditions.* London: Duckworth, 1974.

Pedersen, Johannes. *Israel: Its Life and Culture.* Trans. A. Moller. London: Oxford University Press/Copenhagen: Pio/Povl Branner, 1926.

Pesch, Rudolf. *Das Markusevangelium.* Vol. 1. HTKNT 2/1. Freiburg/Basel/Vienna: Herder, 1976.

Pick, Bernhard. *Paralipomena: Remains of Gospels and Sayings of Christ.* Chicago: Open Court, 1908.

Preus, James Samuel. 'Religion and Bacon's New Learning: From Legitimation to Object,' in *Continuity and Discontinuity in Church History: Essays Presented to George Huntston Williams* (ed. F. Forrester Church and Timothy George} Leiden: Brill, 1979.

Rabbinowitz, Joseph. *Midrash Rabbah: Deuteronomy.* London: Soncino Press, 1939.

Ramsey, George W. 'Is Name-Giving an Act of Domination in Genesis 2:23 and Elsewhere?' *CBQ* 50 (1988): pp. 24–35.

Rankin, Dave Murray. 'The Inaugural Throne-Room Vision of the Book of Revelation: Its Background, Content and Context.' Ph. D. thesis (unpublished), University of St Andrews, Scotland, 2002.

Renan, Ernest. *Renan's Life of Jesus.* Trans. William G. Hutchinson. London: Walter Scott, 1905.

Richard, Pablo. *Apocalypse: A People's Commentary on the Book of Revelation.* Maryland, New York: Orbis, 1995.

Rissi, Mathias. *The Future of the World.* SBT 2/23. London: SCM Press, 1972.

Rogers, Heather. *Green Gone Wrong: How our Economy is Undermining the Environmental Revolution.* London: Verso, 2010.

Roloff, Jürgen. *The Revelation of John: A Continental Commentary.* Trans. John E. Alsup. Minneapolis: Fortress, 1993.

Rose, H.J. *The Eclogues of Vergil.* Berkeley/Los Angeles: University of California Press, 1942.

Rossi, Paolo. *Francis Bacon: From Magic to Science.* Trans. Sacha Rabinovitch. London: Routledge & Kegan Paul, 1968.

Rubinkiewicz, R. 'Apocalypse of Abraham,' in *The Old Testament Pseudepigrapha*, vol. 1 (ed. James H. Charlesworth; London: Darton, Longman & Todd, 1983), pp. 689–705.

Russell, Colin A. *The Earth, Humanity and God*. London: UCL Press, 1994.

Russell, Norman and Benedicta Ward. *The Lives of the Desert Fathers*. London/Oxford: Mowbray/Kalamazoo, Michigan: Cistercian Publications, 1981.

Sanders, Ed. P. *Jewish Law from Jesus to the Mishnah*. London: SCM Press/Philadelphia: Trinity Press International, 1990.

Sanders, Ed. P. *Judaism: Practice and Belief: 63 BCE – 66 CE*. London: SCM Press/Philadelphia: Trinity Press International, 1992,

Santmire, H. Paul. *The Travail of Nature: The Ambiguous Ecological Promise of Christian Theology*. Philadelphia: Fortress Press, 1985.

Schmidt, Thomas E. *Hostility to Wealth in the Synoptic Gospels*. JSNTSup 15. Sheffield: Sheffield Academic Press, 1987.

Schmithals, Walter. *Das Evangelium nach Markus*. Vol. 1. 2nd edition. Gütersloh: Mohn/ Würzburg: Echter, 1986.

Schochet, Elijah Judah. *Animal Life in Jewish Tradition*. New York: Ktav, 1984.

Schottroff, Luise and Wolfgang Stegemann. *Jesus and the Hope of the Poor*. Trans. Matthew J. O'Connell. Maryknoll, New York: Orbis, 1986.

Schultze, W.A. 'Der Heilige und die wilden Tiere: Zur Exegege von Mc 1 13b.' *ZNW* 46 (1955).

Segal, E. 'Justice, Mercy and a Bird's Nest.' *Journal of Jewish Studies* 42 (1991): pp. 176–195.

Sherrard, Philip. *The Rape of Man and Nature*. Ipswich: Golgonooza Press, 1987.

Shillington, V. George. 'Engaging with the Parables,' in *Jesus and His Parables: Interpreting the Parables of Jesus Today* (ed. V. George Shillington; Edinburgh: T.&T. Clark, 1997), pp. 1–20.

Shillington, V. George, ed. *Jesus and His Parables: Interpreting the Parables of Jesus Today*. Edinburgh: T.&T. Clark, 1997.

Short, William J. *Saints in the World of Nature: The Animal Story as Spiritual Parable in Medieval Hagiography (900–1200)*. Rome: Gregorian University, 1983.

Silvertown, Jonathan. *Fragile Web: What Next for Nature?* London: Natural History Museum, 2010.

Smalley, Stephen S. *The Revelation to John*. London: SPCK, 2005.

Smart, Christopher. *The Poetical Works of Christopher Smart*, vol. 1: *Jubilate Agno*. Ed. Karina Williamson. Oxford: Clarendon Press, 1980.

Smart, Christopher. *The Poetical Works of Christopher Smart*, vol. 2: *Religious Poetry 1763–1771*. Ed. Marcus Walsh and Karina Williamson. Oxford: Clarendon Press, 1983.

Smart, Christopher. *The Poetical Works of Christopher Smart*, vol. 3: *A Translation of the Psalms of David*. Ed. Marcus Walsh. Oxford: Clarendon Press, 1987.

Sorrell, Roger D. *St. Francis of Assisi and Nature*. New York/Oxford: Oxford University Press, 1988.

Spanner, Hugh. 'Tyrants, Stewards – or Just Kings?,' in *Animals on the Agenda* (ed. Andrew Linzey and Dorothy Yamamoto, 1998).

Spring, David and Eileen, ed. *Ecology and Religion in History*. New York: Harper, 1974.

Stevenson, Kenneth. 'Animal Rites: The Four Living Creatures in Patristic Exegesis and Liturgy,' in *Studia Patristica XXXIV* (ed. Maurice F. Wiles and Edward J. Yarnold; Leuven: Peeters, 2001), pp. 470–492.

Strack, Hermann Leberecht and Paul Billerbeck. *Kommentar zum Neuen Testament aus Talmud und Midrasch*. Vol. 1. Munich: Beck, 1922.

Sweet, John. *Revelation*. SCM Pelican Commentary. London: SCM Press, 1979.

Swete, Henry Barclay. *The Apocalypse of St John*. 2nd edition. London: Macmillan, 1907.

Tannehill, Robert C. *The Sword of his Mouth: Forceful and Imaginative Language in Synoptic Sayings*. Semeia Supplements1. Philadelphia: Fortress/ Missoula, Montana: SBL, 1975.

Terian, Abraham. *Philonis Alexandrini De Animalibus: The Armenian Text with an Introduction, Translation and Commentary*. Chico, California: Scholars Press, 1981.

Thackeray, Henry St. John. *Josephus*. Vol. 1. LCL. London: Heinemann/New York: Putnam, 1926.

Thomas, Keith. *Man and the Natural World: Changing Attitudes in England 1500–1800*. 2nd edition. London: Penguin, 1984.

Thompson, Ken. *Do We Need Pandas? The Uncomfortable Truth about Biodiversity*. Dartington, Devon: Green Books, 2010.

Toynbee, Arnold. 'The Religious Background of the Present Ecological Crisis,' in *Western Man* (ed. Ian G. Barbour), pp. 137–149; also in *Ecology and Religion in History* (ed. David and Eileen Spring; New York: Harper, 1974), pp. 137–149.

Trinkaus, Charles. *In Our Image and Likeness: Humanity and Divinity in Italian Humanist Thought*. London: Constable, 1970.

Tristram, Henry Baker. *The Natural History of the Bible*. London: SPCK, 1911.

Twelftree, Graham H. *Christ Triumphant: Exorcism Then and Now*. London: Hodder & Stoughton, 1985.

Urbach, Efraim Elimelech. *The Sages: Their Concepts and Beliefs*. Jerusalem: Magnes Press, 1975.

Van de Weyer, Robert. *Celtic Fire: An Anthology of Celtic Christian Literature*. London: Darton, Longman & Todd, 1990.

Van der Horst, Pieter W. *The Sentences of Pseudo-Phocylides*. Leiden: Brill, 1978.

Vargas-Machuca, Antonio. 'La tentación de Jesús según Mc. 1,12–13: Hecho real o relato de tipo haggádico?' *EstEcl* 48 (1973).

Vermes, Geza. *The Dead Sea Scrolls in English*. 3rd edition. London: Penguin, 1987.

Waddell, Helen. *Beasts and Saints*. London: Constable, 1934.

Walker-Jones, Arthur. 'The So-Called Ostrich in the God Speeches of the Book of Job (Job 39,13–18).' *Bib* 86 (2005): pp. 494–510.

Wallace, Howard N. 'Jubilate Deo omnis terra: God and Earth in Psalm 65,' in *The Earth Story in the Psalms and the Prophets* (ed. Norman C. Habel; *The Earth Bible* 4; Sheffield: Sheffield Academic Press/Cleveland: Pilgrim Press, 2001), pp. 51–64

Wallace-Hadrill, David Sutherland. *The Greek Patristic View of Nature*. Manchester: Manchester University Press/New York: Barnes & Noble, 1968.

Webb, James Francis. *Lives of the Saints*. Harmondsworth: Penguin, 1965.

Weinberger, Jerry. *Science, Faith, and Politics: Francis Bacon and the Utopian Roots of the Modern Age*. Ithaca/London: Cornell University Press, 1985.

Weinrich, William C., ed. *Revelation*. ACCS NT12. Downers Grove, Illinois: InterVarsity Press, 2005.

Westermann, Claus. *The Parables of Jesus in the Light of the Old Testament*. Edinburgh: T.&T. Clark, 1990.

White, Lynn. 'Continuing the Conversation,' in *Western Man and Environmental Ethics* (ed. Ian G. Barbour) Reading, Massachusetts/London/Ontario: Addison-Wesley, 1973.

White, Lynn. 'The Historical Roots of our Ecologic Crisis,' *Science* 155 (1967): pp. 1203–1207; reprinted in *Western Man and Environmental Ethics* (ed. Ian G. Barbour; Reading, Massachusetts/London/Ontario: Addison-Wesley, 1973), pp. 18–30; *The Care of Creation* (ed. R. J. Berry; Leicester: Inter-Varsity Press, 2000), pp. 31–42.

Whitney, E. 'Lynn White, Ecotheology and History.' *Environmental Ethics* 15 (1993): pp. 151–169.

Wilkinson, Loren, ed. *Earthkeeping in the Nineties: Stewardship of Creation*. Grand Rapids: Eerdmans, 1991.

Williams, George Hunston. *Wilderness and Paradise in Christian Thought*. New York: Harper, 1962.

Wilson, Edward O. *The Future of Life*. London: Abacus, 2003.

Witherington, Ben. *Revelation*. NCBC. Cambridge: Cambridge University Press, 2003.

Worster, Donald. *Nature's Economy: A History of Ecological Ideas*. 2nd edition. Cambridge: Cambridge University Press, 1994.

Worster, Donald. *The Wealth of Nature: Environmental History and Ecological Imagination*. New York/Oxford: Oxford University Press, 1993.

Wright, R.B. 'Psalms of Solomon,' in *The Old Testament Pseudepigrapha*, vol. 2 (ed. James H. Charlesworth; London: Darton, Longman & Todd, 1985), pp. 639–70.

Wright, Ronald. *A Short History of Progress*. Edinburgh: Canongate, 2005.

Wybrow, Cameron. *The Bible, Baconianism, and Mastery over Nature: The Old Testament and its Modern Misreading*. New York: Peter Lang, 1991.

Wybrow, Cameron. 'The Old Testament and the Conquest of Nature: A Fresh Examination.' *Epworth Review* 17 (1990): pp. 77–88.

Zizioulas, John D. 'Preserving God's Creation: Lecture 3.' *King's Theological Review* 13/1 (1990).

Index of Authors

Index of Ancient and Medieval Persons

Details of Previous Publication

Chapter 2 was previously published as chapter 7 ("Human Authority in Creation") in Richard Bauckham, *God and the Crisis of Freedom: Biblical and Contemporary Perspectives* (Louisville: Westminster John Knox Press, 2002), pp. 128–77.

Chapter 3 was previously published in *Ecological Hermeneutics: Biblical, Historical, and Theological Perspectives* (eds. David Horrell, Cherryl Hunt, Christopher Southgate and Francesca Stavrakopoulou; London: T&T Clark [Continuum], 2010), pp. 70–82.

Chapter 4 was previously published as chapter 4 ("Jesus and Animals I: What did he Teach?") and chapter 5 ("Jesus and Animals II: What did he Practise?") in *Animals on the Agenda: Questions about Animals for Theology and Ethics* (eds. Andrew Linzey and Dorothy Yamamoto; London: SCM Press, 1998), pp. 33–60.

Chapter 5 was previously published as "Jesus and the Wild Animals (Mark 1:13): A Christological Image for an Ecological Age" in *Jesus of Nazareth: Lord and Christ: Essays on the Historical Jesus and New Testament Christology* (eds. Joel B. Green and Max Turner; Festschrift for I. Howard Marshall; Grand Rapids: Eerdmans, 1994), pp. 3–21.

Chapter 6 was previously published in *Studies in Christian Ethics* 22 (2009): pp. 76–88.

Chapter 7 was previously published in *Ecotheology* 7 (2002): pp. 45–59.

Chapter 8 was previously published, in a shorter form, in *Biblical Theology Bulletin* 38 (2008): pp. 55–63.

Chapter 9 was previously published in *Mysticism East and West: Studies in Mystical Experience* (eds. Christopher Partridge and T. Gabriel; Carlisle: Paternoster Press, 2003), pp. 182–208.

Chapters 1 and 10 have not been previously published.